CHURCH AND FAMILY CONFLICTS

How to Settle Conflicts Peacefully in the House

MICHAEL W. DEWAR, SR.

Published in the United States by:
Dwelling Place Cleansing
PO Box 360196
Brooklyn, New York 11236

ISBN: 978-17334377-9-0

Dedicated to my grandson Jordan and granddaughter Megan; may they grow up to be peacemakers and peacekeepers in a world already fraught with conflict.

CONTENTS

Preface..V

Introduction: Need for A Peace Plan................................9

Chapter 1 Your Peace Theology......................................23

Chapter 2 Peace A Christian Duty...................................46

Chapter 3 Why Local Churches Need to Manage
Conflict effectively...78

Chapter 4 A Strategic Peacemaking Plan.........................97

Chapter 5 Church Dispute Resolution Plan:
A Biblical Precedence (OT)...............................122

Chapter 6 Settle It in The House:
A Biblical Precedence (NT)...............................151

Chapter 7 Church Conflict: Patristic and
Reformation Years..179

Chapter 8 Understanding the Nature of Conflict...........198

Chapter 9 Causes and Sources of Conflict......................219

Chapter 10 General Peacemaking Tools........................264
Chapter 11 Christian Peacemaking Tools.......................292

Chapter 12 Church Conflict and Social Media...............342

Chapter 13 Establishing A Resident Counsel.................352

Appendix A...376

Appendix B...382

Referrences..384

PREFACE

Fundamentally, this book is a resource guide to help pastors and lay leaders of local churches, ministries and faith-based organizations resolve situations of conflict before they become destructive and consume their life's work. It is a solutions book, intended to stem the culture of conflict in any church where conflict prevails and to help others prevent it. Bluntly stated, this book is a roadmap on how to establish a dedicated peacemaking and peacekeeping ministry in every local church that has none.

That peace ministry is herein referred to as a *Resident Counsel* (RC) on conflict management and resolution. Note that the word *counsel* is used interchangeably with the word *council;* counsel is author's preferred word in reference to the *RC*.

The RC is to educate church members, ministry staff and leaders in their Christian duties of peacemaking and peacekeeping, to resolve situations of conflict that arise in the church, to preserve the unity of the church from destructive conflict and safeguard the integrity of its mission and message to the community and the world (this is one recurring thesis throughout the book). For these reasons this book comes with the *Agent of Peace-Managers of Conflicts* curriculum (sold separately); there are two version: Instructor's version and the Student's Manual version.

This book draws upon over forty years of pastoral experience with conflicted churches and from my doctoral dissertation research in church conflict done for Regent University, School of Divinity (2016). This work is a response to the culture of conflict that prevails at many local churches; conflict has caused pastors to suffer burnout and has driven more than a few from the ministry. I intend this work to be a useful tool in the ministry practice of pastors, carried in their toolkit for immediate implementation.

The church is regarded as the family of God in scripture; therefore, church conflict is a family fight. At times, it is nothing short of a dirty family fight. Nonetheless, the Lord of the church wants it settled in the context of the family. That's the reason for the cover title. It is not written from a marriage and family perspective, but it will be beneficial to believers resolving conflicts in many walks of life: at church, home, school, the workplace and in the marketplaces of this world. The end goal is to have local churches, ministries, and faith-based organizations adopt the conflict resolution approach offered in this work with its accompanying curriculum (sold separately) to establish their own peace ministry.

My hope is that no church or ministry organization will operate without a strategic conflict management and resolution plan in place after reading this work. My pastoral experience and research tell me destructive conflict will strike at some point, and woe be the church and ministry leaders who are caught unprepared. Being prepared is a thousand times better than sifting through the ruins after the firestorm of destructive conflict burns through years of hard work. Adopting a peacemaking conflict resolution plan for your church or ministry is an act of responsible stewardship.

A research project such as this is like a symphony and orchestra with many players. I want to thank Dr. James Flynn and Dr. Mara Crabtree of Regent University, School of Divinity that help to guide my initial research as a doctoral student there, otherwise this book might not be. But let me hasten to say, any defects or short falls in this finished product are all my own and cannot be attributed to them in any shape or form.

Additionally, I owe a debt of gratitude to the officers and members of the New York Congregational Baptist Church who accorded me the honor of being their pastor for more than two decades now. You have stood with me and supported the ministry through calm and turbulent times and was gracious to be the subject of study and testing ground for my dissertation work and consequently this book.

I am also most thankful to those who have read the manuscript and provided helpful feedback. I know you share in my vision for this work and I pray such vision will come to fruition and bless many local churches and their leaders.

INTRODUCTION

NEED FOR A PEACE PLAN

Conflict sticks to churches as bees to honey, but unlike bees, most local churches have no strategic plan to deal with conflicts effectively. Yet, effective ministering and the survival of the organization demand a proactive conflict management and resolution plan. There has to be an intentional strategy to prevent destructive conflict from running its course and trashing the church. There has to be a proven way to manage and resolve conflict when it strikes.

The alternative to a conflict resolution plan, is often a panic reaction to conflict crisis; that approach does not work. Conflict has no mercy; like fire, it will serve you well under control but destroy everything in its wake when out of control. Most local churches have chosen to ignore the problem and that has resulted in the state crisis that now exist in many local churches. This work stands in the gap to help church leaders build up the hedges.

This book is not only an emergency trumpet call to action, it provides the resources to urgently put a workable peace plan in place at your church. Leaders of secular enterprises, institutions and organizations of significance, have long established inhouse dispute resolution mechanism to protect the integrity of their names and prevent destructive conflicts from disrupting business operations. Additionally, they have developed a massive collection of literature and best practices that now guide the secular discipline of dispute resolution.

Leaders of churches and other faith-based organizations are finding it exceedingly challenging to navigate the troubled waters of twenty-first century ministry work without a dispute resolution plan in their toolkit, one that is already deployed in practice. That is very troubling, because new areas of conflicts, including sexual harassment have emerged and are emerging from the shadows each day to scandal and topple powerful leaders. Ministry effectiveness could stand or fall with one such scandal.

These scandals or disputes find expression in the public square through social media, the legal profession and the Me-Too Movement. As a result, the mighty are falling from their seats and millions of dollars are being paid out for legal fees, victims' compensation and in some cases hush money. No professional title is exempted from these scandals and no organization, including the church, has immunity from such conflicts. This work is a clarion call to the faith community to be prepared to navigate the troubled waters of interpersonal and organizational conflicts of the twenty-first century. Churches are very fragile organizations with limited resources to defend themselves, so they are most at risk and more so when caught without a conflict resolution plan in place.

The late 1980s to the new millennium have witnessed a proliferation of peace training and conflict resolution programs not only in secular higher education, but in Christian colleges and universities, seminaries and divinity schools across the country. The secular programs are directed to three broad consumer audiences: 1) institutions of government, 2) national and multinational business corporations, and 3) domestic dispute resolutions. Institutions and business corporations in all three categories have deemed it a matter of survival and good business sense to adopt some form of dispute resolution program or plan as an integral part of their day to day corporate operation. This is preferred to expensive litigation.

In the first category, government institutions' personnel are trained to negotiate peace, better relationships, and win-win trade deals between nation states around the world. The consumers of this training are largely diplomats, military leaders, state department personnel, including United Nations' personnel. They learn how to negotiate peace, form policies, and keep the peace around the world. What's the ideal practice outcome for this group? Peaceful co-existence among nation states and cooperation in win-win trade deals.

Training in the second category is directed to leaders of business corporations whose job it is to negotiate business deals for their individual corporation and stakeholders. The Harvard Business School, the Harvard Negotiation Project, the Warton School of Negotiation are few of the many institutions of higher learning that are on the cutting edge of negotiation and dispute resolutions (Fisher, Ury and Patton,1981, xii-xiv). What is the ideal outcome for this group? Secure market for products, and close win or win-win multi-million-dollar deals.

Training in the third category is directed to personnel on the domestic front; these are leaders who deal with workplace disputes, family disputes, disputes with neighbors, as well as disputes in educational institutions (Dana 2001). What is the ideal outcome sought for this group? Harmony among individuals and groups, smooth enterprise operation, increased production, and protection from costly million-dollar lawsuits.

In as much as the Church is in existence over two millennia, she is relatively a latecomer to the discipline of conflict management and resolution as we know it today. Yet, the Church has had a conflicted internal and external history for two thousand and more years. Internal conflicts, for good or evil, have resulted in the current diversification called, denominations or faith traditions. The track record of the church on settling internal conflicts peacefully, is not one to be proud of. From medieval times, the church has fallen short of her own standard of peace and has not completely returned to New Testament (NT) standards since.

It is no exaggeration to say that the conflicted personality of the Church has hardly abated with the passage of time. For this reason, among others, Christian Schools have developed their own body of literature and training programs in dispute management and resolution to address the culture of conflict within the local church. This work is a small contribution to that body of literature.

Furthermore, church leaders and educators have discovered that while secular dispute resolution programs provide good foundation knowledge that all managers of conflicts and dispute resolution workers should know—they have also come to realize that secular programs are not exclusively the right-fit for local churches. Why? Secular programs are driven by a different set of values that are not necessarily Christian or rooted in Scripture.

Literature and experienced observation reveal that despite the valiant effort of Christian higher education to meet the needs of a conflicted church with their dispute resolution and peace training programs, a culture a conflict still prevails at the local church. In my Regent University, doctoral dissertation (2016), I cited five reasons this culture of conflict continues to bedevil local churches, one general and four specifics.

(1) The general and obvious reason the culture of conflict continues to prevail at the local church, is the fact that the higher education dispute resolution and peace training have not sufficiently filtered down to the local church to make a significant difference. There is a gap in the training that needs to be bridged. The next four reasons tell us why this gap exist.

(2) Conflict or dispute resolution training is most often directed to the professional leadership of the church at the graduate levels: masters and doctorate. Who are the primary beneficiaries of such training? They are divinity students entering the ministry and pastors already in the practice of ministry that have the time and money to do advanced studies.

Furthermore, unless there is a specialization track at both levels of studies, graduates will only have an introductory course or two in dispute resolution. In other words, it should not be assumed that because one is entering ministry with a master's degree from a seminary or divinity school or has gone back for a doctorate that he or she has training in conflict management and resolution. When it comes to dispute resolution and peacemaking, the academic funnel is small at the top and smaller and narrow at the bottom, little in and less out. The gap remains unabridged.

(3) "Peace education is not generally a stated ministry priority at most local churches, and therefore, not given budgetary consideration" (Dewar 2016). It is true, people will put their money and give their support to what is of greatest importance to them.

(4) Most peace education programs are not lay membership friendly, because they are most often given at the graduate level and require a baccalaureate or master's degree to access. Time and money are added hurdles to overcome. Progress is being made in providing distant learning via the Internet, making the time factor less problematic, but we are not quit there as yet in our effort to bridge the gap, a new paradigm is needed.

(5) The literature reveals that non-baccalaureate certificate programs and private consultant training are perhaps

effective. Some training programs at this level do not require a first degree to access, but they are few and far apart. One pioneer program is the now defunct Alban Institute. Foremost among this level of training now, is Peacemakers Institute; it also provides consultation for local churches.

Reports from the field show that private consultants have been effective in helping some churches resolve situations of conflict, but there are two strong negatives that come with this approach. First, while church consultants in the area of conflict management are effective, they are not enough to go around to significantly impact the nationwide church conflict situation. Second, churches generally engage consultants during or after a crisis, when the damage is already done. This strongly suggest that local churches need an inhouse conflict management and resolution system. I mean a dedicated, resident ministry of trained lay leaders, trained in dispute resolution from a Christian perspective. This book offers that alternative under many names, but the most preferred name is a *Resident Counsel* (RC). The reason for this name will become self-evident throughout this work.

It is important to note that the preceding five reasons do not tell us why conflict exists at the local church. They merely identify its existence and that there is a gap between higher education dispute training programs and the local church. This suggest that higher education training has not sufficiently filtered down to the local church to make a significant difference in the prevailing culture of conflict.

Again, this is the gap that this book seeks to bride. Churches, ministries and faith-based organizations that do not have a conflict management and resolution plan in place should be concerned. Consider this book an urgent call to make such plan a ministry priority, because destructive conflict can destroy a lifetime of work in a few short weeks. This destructiveness includes churches, pastors and their families.

Without a system to manage and resolve conflicts before they become destructive, churches and other faith-based organizations are most vulnerable and at risk; it is like a building without sprinklers, smoke alarm, fire extinguishers, and no direct connection to the fire station. By the time they realize that they are in the heart of a conflict crisis, it is already too late. The consuming flames are already out of control and the damage is already done. Some conflicts are scandals; they taint the name of the church and its leaders for a long time to come.

Destructive conflict is tearing up congregations all over the county, but very few leaders heed the warning with prior preparation. Conflict is one of those things we leaders don't want to think about, until we are in the middle of a crisis. Did we pack lifeboats? Is a question that should be asked before you put out to sea, not when the ship is in a crisis going down. The consuming fire of conflict comes upon us in our unguarded hour. But why? Because, we often believe the myth, that our nice, Spirit filled people will never destroy what they worked so hard to build, but the literature on church conflict has proven otherwise.

Like the fall of the Roman empire, churches generally implode; they fall from within. Those nice people turn upon each other and upon their leaders like they never heard of Jesus. Like Judas and Peter, we become betrayers and deniers of each other and our Lord. Unless there in an inhouse smoke detector to alert you before the flames start, the watchman wakes but in vain (Psalm 127:1).

A curriculum for training members at the local church accompanies this book (sold separately). The curriculum manual shows you how to establish your own lay-ministry peace plan at your local church, or for your ministry or faith-based organization. After training, you can setup what I refer to as a *Resident Counsel* (RC). The RC is a group of five to seven people, depending on the size of your congregation, trained in the principles of conflict management and resolution from a Christian perspective. This group is dedicated to the ministry of conflict management and resolution for the church. It educates members in their Christian duties of peacemaking and peacekeeping; it resolves situations of conflicts that arise in the church, and it safeguards the integrity of the local church and its mission to the community and the world.

Chapter Designations

This work is consisted of thirteen chapters, each building upon the other to unveil the heart and mind of Jesus Christ concerning the peaceful resolution of conflict among His people. This is done in a way that each member of the local church can participate to the glory of God. This Christian approach to dispute resolution draws upon both social sciences and biblical sources.

Chapter 1 shows that wittingly or unwittingly, each follower of Jesus Christ has a preferred way of dealing with conflict, but most often, it is not according to biblical standard. We humans approach conflict according to our unique personality and ways we were socialized. But Jesus Christ and the spiritual life beckon us to a higher standard of conflict resolution and peace, such standard is set forth in the New Testament (NT). Chapter 1, therefore, invites each believer to build a personal peace theology based upon the directives of Jesus Christ given in the NT.

Chapter 2 establishes the biblical reality that peacemaking and peacekeeping are Christian duties from which no believer or member of Christ's Church is exempted. The local church is tasked with the responsibility of training its members to live out this reality toward each other and mirror the same to world as the alternative culture to violence and war.

Peacemaking at the local church has to be an intentional, dedicated ministry, a system in place to manage conflicts and bring them to resolution, thus preventing conflicts from becoming destructive. This is the focus of Chapters 3 and 4. They zero in on a conflict management system (CMS) that is most fitting for the local church, the people of God.

The question of precedence is addressed in Chapters 5, 6 and 7. Human curiosity and caution like to ask, has this ever been done before, is it scriptural? What they are asking for is precedence, so these three chapters focus on the issue of precedence. The consistent nature and character of God give rise to a progressive revelation of Himself.

In other words, the present self-disclosure of God builds upon His past self-revelation. For this reason, chapter 5 looks at how God settled conflict in the Old Covenant; chapter 6, how Jesus, the apostles and the early church settled conflict under the New Covenant, and chapter 7, how the church handled conflict in the postapostolic eras (i.e. during the patristic, medieval and Reformation decades).

These periods through which the saints have trod, do they provide precedence that the contemporary church can draw upon to manage and resolve conflicts among the people of God in the twenty-first century? This question is explored in these three chapters (i.e. 5, 6 and 7).

Chapters 8 and 9 are diagnostic in nature and contents, they examine the nature, causes and sources of conflicts as they usually manifest in the local church. If destructive conflict is a disease, these two chapters try to understand its anatomy, etiology, mutation and symptomatology to arrive at the most effective prevention methodology and tools to manage and bring it to resolution in the context of the local church.

Destructive conflict is not unique to faith-based organizations; it does not only terrorize the people of God and bring down churches. Every people group, organization and institution must contend with conflict. For this reason, secular disciplines have developed effective tools to manage and resolve conflicts. Chapters 10 and 11 explores two sets of peacemaking or conflict resolution tools: the humanistic tools and the Christian or biblical tools. Both disciplines draw from each other to serve their unique audiences, but contents, process and outcome are not the same.

Chapter 12 is parenthetical and almost didn't make it in the book. It looks at church conflict in the context of social media, how to implement proper policy to safeguard the reputation of the church in the digital age from scandal and defamation. The church has a stewardship responsibility to protect its name, brand, contents and images from exploitation and improper use.

Chapter 13 pulls it all together in a unique *Resident Counsel* approach specific to the local church. The chapter shows how each local church can establish its own dedicated peace ministry in keeping with the peace theology of Jesus for His church. This approach takes some of the burden off the pastor because it takes him or her out of the hearth of conflict, to focus on the ministry of the word and other weighty matters. This approach educates church members in their Christian duties of peacemaking and peacekeeping so that conflict does not run wild and destroy what took years to build.

Finally, the *Agents of Peace-Managers of Conflict* curriculum for instructors and the *Student Manual* version come with this book (each sold separately) to assist the local church in the training of lay leaders for the launch of their peace ministry, generally referred to as a *Resident Counsel;* this is the author's preferred name for the approach set forth in this work. It is an approach that should bring vitality to any local church for it conforms more closely to the image of Christ and the peace theology of Jesus.

CHAPTER 1

YOUR PEACE THEOLOGY

If Jesus Christ is the prince of peace and His message the gospel of peace, it is logical to assume that His followers, churches, ministry entities and Christian faith-based organizations that represent Him, would want to operate under His theology of peace. While Jesus is authentically whom He is said to be, everything after that has fallen short of His standard of peace. This book is a roadmap; it guides believers and churches back to their Christian duties of peacemaking and peacekeeping advanced in the word of God. Jesus identifies His people as agents of peace, "Blessed are the peacemakers for they shall be called, children of God" (Matt.5:9).

Let me put it directly to you another way, do you have a peace theology that guides your life? If your answer is no, I hope by the time you are through reading this book, you will be opened to formulating or adopting your own peace theology. It will transform your life. What is a theology of peace or peace theology? It is an *intentional* guiding principle, anchored in Scripture that governs your attitude toward human conflict, violence and war. It is the standard that Jesus set for His people and His Church in the New Testament (NT). Jesus the Prince of peace is God's supreme peace model for His people.

The word, "intentional" is italicized in the preceding definition, because whether you are conscious of it or not, we all have a preferred way of dealing with conflict to which we invariably pivot every time we are faced with one. It's our usual way of responding. The scorpion, the snake, the skunk, all animals have a way to respond when threatened; we humans do the same.

Some of us have a *confrontational* personality; we love to argue, debate and fight. We will be up and in your face at the drop of the proverbial hat. You don't cross a confrontational person without getting a piece of his or her mind and more. This natural tendency to confront, is a window into our conscious and subconscious psyche as to how we are wired to respond to conflicted situations.

Of course, being confrontational is neither good nor bad. What is important is whether it works for you or not. If confrontation is your style of dealing with disagreements or conflicts, it is important to be aware of it. It is equally important to know that other styles of dealing with conflicts are available to you. Confrontation does not have to be a one-size-fits-all solution; for most assuredly, some conflicts will not respond to a confrontational templet. What do you do then?

There are individuals that are not the confrontational type. They are more *accommodating* when faced with conflicts; they are quick to say, "I am sorry!" They quickly become submissive and will go at length to stay clear from a fight and it works for them. But again, accommodation is neither good or bad and it will not resolve every conflict. Now and then you are going to come upon a situation that this approach does not work for you; it is just not the right fit.

On the same floor further down the hall, you will find another people group that is very *rationalistic* about conflict. These people say, let's reason about that. They present a good analytic argument with convincing rules of logic why things should be done a certain way. There is a type of rationalists that operates like the street-smart con, like Eddy Murphy in *Trading Places* and in *Hollywood Cops.* These are exceptions from the rule. The usual rationalist's approach is kind of noble and civilize. But as wonderful as that may sound, this approach will not work for every conflicted situation. You need other choices in your toolkit because some nuts call for a special kind of wrench. If you are a one-wrench practitioner, you will have serious problems frequently.

Further down the conflict settlement plaza, you will come upon the *bargain* hunter, every conflict for him is like buying something, so he wants to *bargain* or *negotiate* a deal. As popular and noble as this approach is, it is not the right fit for some situations. You will be left stranded in the middle of nowhere if negotiation is the only conflict resolution tool you have in your toolkit.

A manager of a department store unit may find it more beneficial to *collaborate* with managers of other divisions of the store to keep the enterprise smoothly running, so they can all look good in the eyes of the CEO. They sit-down and bring new ideas to the table to arrive at a solution rather than working against each other. Some practitioners laud collaboration as the golden approach. But again, no one approach is ideal for all problems. Collaboration may work well for the department store managers, the unit directors in a hospital, teachers in a school and ministry directors in the same church but it may fall flat in another context.

There are still others that will quickly deploy the *avoidance* approach to conflict settlement. These people are always on the run; they procrastinate. Sometimes, they fail to admit that a conflict exists. Or, they are so sweet and nice, they avoid the slightest disagreement. Some just can't tolerate not being cuddled by everyone. They avoid dealing with the problem. But again, this is not a good or bad style to conflict resolution; it just will not work, if applied to every conflicted situation. A dispute resolution practitioner, like a mechanic, needs a diversified toolkit.

Another way we human beings settle conflict is by force. John's neighbor is an ex-police officer turned attorney. He is aggressive as if he is still a police officer. He gravitates to the use of force at all times to settle disputes. He intimidates with arrest and lawsuits. We see this approach most vividly with law enforcement and the military enterprise. Force can be divided into three categories: persuasion, submission, and lethal. Persuasion is the mild use of force. An officer shows up at the scene of a conflict, and he or she will first attempt to use verbal persuasion in an attempt reason and defuse the conflict. He may want someone to leave the scene or come with him peacefully. If that fails, he apprehends and bring to submission. If the assailant refused to submit and fights back, then the conflict moves into the arena for lethal force. The military is the embodiment of force; they are not called in to negotiate.

In actuality, all levels of society use some form of force but most often in its milder form. Parents use persuasion with their children, and sometimes persuasion gets out of hand to become abusive. Spousal conflicts are sometimes abusive and violent. The employee that gave twenty-nine years to the company and was dismissed before his retirement a few months away, may resort to violence when persuasive argument fails. Force has a high potential to be destructive or even lethal. The employee returns to the workplace with a firearm to settle what he considers injustice toward him.

Persuasion, though listed at times as a mild form of force, is considered by some practitioners as a separate approach to dispute resolution because in our society only special entities are legally allowed to use force outside the context of self-defense. Threatening lawsuits, using the courts, court orders, order of protection, subpoenas are all persuasion instruments designed to restrain or settle a conflict.

Whatever way you now deal with conflict, that is the approach you are comfortable with, whether it gets you clubbed every time or secures for you a bag of delightful goodies. The important thing to know is the fact that the resolution of conflict has various styles and approaches and you need not lock yourself into one approach. A single approach may be the wrong wench for some nuts. Your toolkit needs several wrenches from which to choose to match any situation you are faced with. The training this book espoused will help you examine your natural tendencies to conflict and help you to use them intentionally and effectively. We will also help you to develop new ways in resolving conflicts, so that you have your own toolkit of proven skills to draw upon.

Have you ever come across a short-tempered man, aggressive, arrogant and foul mouth? That's the way he is. He did not become that overnight; it took years of socialization to shape the cussing, arrogant personality he has become. He is the type that provoked a gentleman like Moses to strike the rock and said things he would not normally say, things that got him in trouble with God. There are people that will appeal to your worst angels; they will pull you into conflict with them unless you have that special wrench in your toolkit to fit their situation. These people are everywhere: your workplace, marketplace, and even church you will find a close type.

The fact is, we were all socialized to deal with conflict one way or another, which is kind of instinctive and not necessarily Christian. We are also biologically programed to fight or flight in the face of danger; that is our built-in survival instinct endowed by our Creator. These natural gifts can be trained and channeled to deal with dispute resolution more effectively. As followers of Jesus Christ, we must bring our socialized behavior, our predisposed tendencies and our instinctive biological proclivities under intentional scrutiny and under the Lordship of Jesus Christ.

Behaviors that are not restrained by our personal moral code, divine or civil law, lead to anarchy on the one hand and bondage on the other, a fact most prisoners know all too well. It is in this context that each of us needs to formulate a peace theology anchored in the word of God, or at least, subscribe to one so rooted. If it is not rooted in the word of God, it is not a theology, it is a philosophy.

The Peace Theology of Jesus

A peace theology is not just a theorical construct; it is a practicing principle rooted in the word of God that governs our behavior in the face of conflict, violence and war. Since all true believers seek to please the Lord Jesus, we should first uncover His peace theology, then build our individual and corporate peace theology on His peace theology as the basis for our dispute resolution, a solid foundation to stand on.

The peace theology of Jesus Christ is evident not only in His Sermon on the Mount (Matt.5-7) but in His entire ministry practice. For one, Jesus sets a higher standard of righteousness than that practiced under the Mosaic Law. Jesus informs His followers that "unless your righteousness surpasses that of the Pharisees and the teachers of the law, you will certainly not enter the kingdom of heaven" (5:20). Every time Jesus said, "It was said but I say," He enforces the new standard which is based upon love and mercy. Before we examine this higher standard, we must ask where did it come from?

First, this new standard of love and righteousness that leads to the peaceful resolution of conflicts is not so much new as it is higher; it did not evolve out of thin air but finds its root in the Old Covenant. It is built upon the revealed character and ideals of Yahweh for His people as recorded in the Hebrew

Scripture. The commands issued by God through Moses, were ideally based upon love for God and love for neighbor as reflected in these words: "Hear, O Israel: The LORD our God, the LORD is one. Love the LORD your God with all your heart and with all your soul and with all your strength" (Deut.6:4-5).

When Jesus was asked to prioritize the importance of the commandments, He tagged the preceding Deuteronomic quote as the greatest (Mark 12:28-29). Second to that command is to love your neighbor as yourself (v.30), a quote from Leviticus (19:18). So then, love for God and love for neighbor were required among God's people under the Old Covenant; they are not New Testament (NT) inventions.

How is it then that Jesus said to his disciples? "A new command I give to you: Love one another. As I have loved you, so you must love one another" (John 13:34-35). The likely answer is this: In as much as the Mosaic Law (the Torah) was ideally based on love for God and love for neighbor, it was enforced on the basis of observable personal obedience. But love is a thing of the heart; it can only be correctly observed and read by God Himself who see the driving motives of the inner sanctum (1Sam.16:7).

People obey, not necessarily out of love, but out of fear of punishment; and since Israel's God was to be feared above all other gods, one cannot rule out that obedience to Him by some was out of fear. Perhaps, that is why the New Covenant is written inwardly upon a transformed heart (Jer.31:31-34; Heb.8:8-12). Additionally, the indwelling Holy Spirit is required to actualize it (Rom.8:3-9).

Second, obedience motivated by love is stronger and more desirable than obedience out of fear of punishment. When the threat of punishment wears off, people return to their native habits like an elastic band returning to its usual size when the stress is off. The golden calf debacle and the book of Judges show Israel's propensity to return to idolatry as soon as the threat of punishment subsided. One may well ask, was Israel obeying God out of sincere love from the heart or out of fear of His immediate wrath? If they were serving out of an obedient heart, motivated by love, perhaps they would not have had such obsession with idolatry. Or perhaps, they just lacked the internal firepower to live up to God's standard of righteousness. Like a highway signpost, the Law points but it could not take anyone there.

Third, obedience out of love requires a spiritual change of heart. Jeremiah reminds us that the human heart is "deceitful above all things and desperately wicked," and only God who searches the heart can truly understands it (Jer.17:9-10 KJV). The Law of God, given by Moses, despite its enjoined consequences, did not have the power to change the hearts of people that they could love God and serve Him out of obedient love. The apostle Paul tells us that the law was inherently weak, that it could not effect the inner spiritual transformation necessary to love God obediently (Rom.8:4-5, 12:1-3). The law was good, but it was *fatally flawed* precluding people obediently living by it in love (Heb.8:7-13).

Fourth, this explains why God forged a new and better covenant with laws written on changed hearts, so that people could love God and neighbor (Heb.10:16-17). Furthermore, Jesus broadens the concept of neighbor to mean all humankind bearing the imago Dei (image of God): family, friends, enemies, strangers, even those who abuse us. He sets the example in ministry, in living, and in dying. He forgave a thief while He was dying and prayed for the forgiveness of those who were murdering Him (Luke 23:32-34, 39-43). The cross is the demonstration of God's love (John 3:16). One poet expresses it this way: "When I got a glimpse of true love it was hanging from an old rugged cross."

Because of all these added requirements attached to love, Jesus labels His standard of love, *a new commandment*. One that summons us to a higher standard of righteousness. No more eye for an eye and tooth for a tooth, no more hating and cursing your enemies. Instead, you bless and curse not, and pray for them that despitefully use you, persecute and falsely accuse you (Matt.5: 38-48).

Fifth, the incarnation is God's supreme model of what unconditional, sacrificial love looks like. In a culture where gods were detached from human compassion and kings ruled with authoritarian brutally, how does one model to a group of former slaves the virtues of loving God and loving neighbor as you love yourself? Only one untainted by sin could be that perfect model. For this among other reasons, God pitched His tent among us in the person of Jesus Christ, the perfect model (John 1:1-4, 14). In this context, the command of Jesus makes perfect sense: "A new command I give to you: Love one another. As I have loved you, so you must love one another" (John 13:34-35).

The religion of the Scribe and Pharisees was lacking self-giving love, justice and mercy; this lack is illustrated in the story of the Good Samaritan. If this is lacking in the practice of one's religion, can it be said that he truly loves God? The apostle John answers the question with a question. How can one love God that he cannot see and hates his brother that he can see? John is making it clear that both God and neighbor are needed to complete God's love equation. Micah preached and penned these words decades before John wrote his epistle: "He has showed you, O man, what is good. And what does the LORD require of you? To act justly and to love mercy and walk humbly with your God" (Micah 6:8). Ideally, Micah certainly express what God wants in human relationships.

Much has been said about the peace theology of Jesus; here is the sum. From the beginning of human history, God's ideal for humans was for us to love Him and love our neighbors. The two requirements are extricable bound together. But perhaps, it was not received or understood the way God intended it. For Cain came along and in cold blood, murder his brother with no sense of remorse, because in his heart, he was not his brother's keeper. God proved him wrong and held him accountable and personally administer justice on behalf of his dead brother. God had the right and the authority to administer equal justice and take Cain's life for the life of his brother. But God did not. Why?

It appears that God was setting a precedence that He would adjust later. The precedence is that *God's justice is administered in the context of love and mercy.* In this case, love for Abel and mercy for Cain. It could be stated another way. God's justice is restrained by love and mercy. Later, God made it clear to Noah after the great flood, that He will require the life of any human being that takes the life of another, or any animal that takes the life of a human being (Gen.9:1-7). Still later, this oral law of God became the written law under Moses—you shall do no murder (Exod.20:13). God established the institution of the Priesthood and charged them with rendering due process, not vigilante justice.

The institution for due process distinguishes murder from manslaughter; one was premediated and intentional, the other was accidental with no premeditation (Deut.19:1-12).

Note well, God's preferred way for the administration of justice is that it must be carried out in the context of love and mercy, not revenge. This was not fully practiced under the Mosaic Law.

Enemies that were not brothers to the Israelites were treated differently even though they too were the image bearers of God. Jesus changed all that in the Sermon on the Mount. He built His new law of love upon the ideals that correspond with the true nature of God and was present in the Torah and the Prophets but was never fully achieved to the satisfaction of God. Every time Jesus said, "It was said but I say," He is calling attention to His new standard of righteousness.

Jesus is called the Prince of peace because His incarnation was not only a search and rescue mission to seek and to save the lost but a peace mission of reconciliation. His work of redemption was a bilateral peace assignment, designed to bring peace between God and humankind and peace in human relationships. Redemption is relational and it is one of God's ideals. The angels' anthem at the Lord's birth was, "Glory to God in the highest, and on earth peace to men on whom his favor rest" (Luke 2:8-14). But this redemption of peace was long coming because the peace theology of Jesus builds upon His Father's work of peace under the Old Covenant.

The incarnation phase of this redemptive wok is so radical, it sets a higher relational standard of righteousness based upon love (Matt.5:20). This standard of love is called a new commandment and it includes loving your enemies (5:44-45, John 13:34-35).

The Apostles and the Early Church

The apostles were not militant revolutionaries, nor was the church movement they headed. They closely followed the teachings and examples of Jesus Christ. He was to then the embodiment and advocate of peace, one who refused participation in the violent overthrow of the Roman government to relieve Israel of foreign occupation and oppression to restore the Davidic dynasty. Jesus made it clear that His kingdom was not of this world and it is one of peace, justice and mercy (Isa.9:6-7; John16:13).

For these reasons and more, the apostle and the early church did not constitute a Barabbas type resistant movement. They followed the examples of Jesus, who in the face of unjust incarceration, manufactured evidence, false trials and wrongful sentence of death, refused to call legions of angels to put down an unjust judiciary and a hostile crowd in His defense. Instead, He was led as a lamb to the slaughter and silent as a sheep before its shearers, so He opened not His mouth (Isa.53:7; Matt.27:11-13 NKJV).

The apostles and the early church aligned themselves with the teachings of the One who taught them, “Blessed are the peacemakers for they will be called children of God”

(Matt.5:9). They learned from what Jesus said to Peter about the use of violence. The night Jesus was arrested, Peter violently came to His defense wielding a sword to inflict bodily injury on Malchus (John 18 10-11). Jesus ordered him to put away his sword and cautioned him and his companions that, they that use the sword will be perish by the sword (Matt.26:52).

Violence is indeed the father of violence and war—they got the message, violence begets violence. Non-violence is better taught in practice than in theory alone; the leader must be the living example of what he teaches. Perhaps, that is why Jesus, the apostles, Mahatma Gandhi and Martin Luther King, Jr. were such transformative personalities of history.

The apostles and the early church practiced the teaching of Jesus and were guided by His example; despite the violence levied against them, they never once responded in kind. Yet, neither Jesus nor the apostles were pacifists. The gospel message preached by Jesus, the apostles and the early church, was confrontational and uncompromising. It often got them a good beaten, thrown into prison, stoned, run out of town and even murdered, but they were a peaceful bunch despite the message evoked a violent response from those not willing to change. The apostle built their theology on the foundation of peace laid by Jesus Himself. They practiced the peace theology of Jesus.

The apostles and the early church were up against the most brutal empire the world had ever seen up to that time. Rome was no friend of the church. Its rulers brutally executed the apostles they could get their hands on and martyred numerous defenseless Christians. But when Rome finally fell, the church took the reins of power and became more brutal than secular Rome was under the Caesars. Papal Rome departed from the peace theology of Jesus and the apostles. The Papacy introduced the Crusades and the Inquisitions which were violent institutions of a militant church. Thousands of innocent Christians that disagreed with the church were not only branded as heretics, they were brutally executed. The church, not only, wielded the sword for Christ, but against many followers of Christ who sought to serve Him more perfectly.

The Reformed Church

The Protestant Reformation did not end the brutality of the Roman church toward its members and nonmembers. In fact, rather that reflecting on those things Martin Luther brought to its attention and change, the church double-down on its absolute authority over all of life and set about to put down Luther and all who disagreed with it. The Papal throne not only ignored the New Testament and the teachings of Christ, it usurped the authority of Christ.

The churches of the Reformation, though bearing no comparison of abuse with Papal Rome, cannot be said to follow the peace theology of Jesus. They were also heavy handed and authoritarian but closer to the apostolic Church than the church under the papacy. The Papal Church has a far bloodier history, corruption and brutality. This history is well documented.

The Protestant arm of the church continued to have doctrinal and personality conflicts that led to its fragmentation to the various denominations we have today. From the writings of Augustine, the Church adopted the just war theory; it is an approach to conflict that goes counter to the Sermon on the Mount. The most important thing to bear in mind is this—Jesus gave the power of the sword to the secular State and the power of the keys to the Church (Matt.16:16-19; Rom.13:1-7). The sword is given to maintain an orderly society and the keys given to transact the business of the kingdom for Christ.

But the fall of secular Rome was a paradigm shift for the church, the church became the sole authority over human life and it greatly abused that authority. The Church made Cesar's throne the Papal throne and assumed the exercise of both the powers of the sword and the authority of the keys. On the one hand, the sword gives the right to wage war and take human life. On the other hand, the keys give the authority to selectively admit people to heaven or send them to hell. Or, even to create an intermediate place to punish people and extract them for a reasonable fee. They name this intermediate place Purgatory. By doing all this and more, the church departed from the peace theology of Jesus and the apostles and the entire New Testament.

Bear in mind that Jesus gave His Church a conflict management and resolution model that is frequently referred to as the peace theology of Jesus in this book. Since, the drastic departure of the church from this peace theology in medieval times, the church has not fully recaptured it. This is the larger context accounting for the culture of conflict prevailing in local churches today.

The Contemporary Church

Perhaps, the most effective weapon Satan has deployed against the Church of Jesus Christ is destructive conflict; it continues to rage like wildfire through the contemporary local churches. It divides them, turning members against each other and against leadership and vice versa. It downsizes congregations, assaults the integrity of worship and corrupts the witness of the church to the community and the world. Is there a way to deal with conflict and keep the peace at the local church?

The rest on this book addresses this question, but we must first conclude this chapter by answering the question asked in the opening lines of the first paragraph. Do you have a peace theology? (also called, a theology of peace). In other words, does your belief in God together with your relationship with Jesus Christ shape your attitude toward people you disagree with? Is your attitude about peace, violence and war biblically grounded? If it's not, this book challenges you to make that an area of spiritual growth to focus on. It will be nothing less than transformative.

Your Theology of Peace

This section summarizes the discussion of this chapter and brings it to a conclusion, so pay close attention. Earlier, I defined a theology of peace as adhering to "an *intentional* guiding principle, anchored in Scripture that governs our attitude toward conflict, violence and war." It is living out our Christian duties of peacemaking and peacekeeping in a Christlike manner.

Jesus informs us that in this world we will be faced with conflicts, tribulations, violence and war (Matt.5:10-12,43-48 24:3-44). Unregenerate humanity will continue to be conflicted and at war. But the people of God should stand as the counterculture of God's kingdom, mirroring to the world the culture and lifestyle of heaven, and what is possible when persons are in relationship with the God of peace through Jesus Christ. The community of faith stands as that well lighted city on a hill for all to see.

But if conflict, violence and war continue to divide us, the people of God, in our homes and churches, how are we different from the unsaved world about us? For the sake of the witness of the gospel, each member of the local church is called upon to adopt and internalize a theology of peace rooted in the word of God. This personal theology of peace not only transforms; it moves us to embrace a new lifestyle. It regulates our behavior in conflicted situations and equips us to stand as Christ's agents of peace wherever we are: home, work, church or the marketplaces of this world.

We observed earlier, how Jesus built His peace theology upon the character of His Father as revealed in the Old Covenant. In the Hebrew Bible, God is revealed as the God of peace, love, justice and mercy. He wants conflicts among humans to be settled in the context of love, justice and mercy in keeping with His nature. God wants us to love him and love neighbor as we love ourselves (Deut.6:4-5).

In our dealings with others (neighbors) God wants us to do justly and love mercy (Micah 6:8). When we love mercy, we are not quick to get even or take revenge. Again, Jesus built His peace theology upon the foundation laid down by His Father in the Old Covenant; it can be characterized in one word, *Shalom.* But God's ideal in the Old Covenant was not fully realized because of disobedience and unbelief. Yet, the Old Covenant was good and righteous, but it was given to a flawed people who were unable to have it actualized in them to God's satisfaction.

The Old Covenant also allowed for some principles that were not sustainable. For example, hating one's enemies (Matt.5:43-44). This reference to hate your enemies hardly appears in the Old Testament. Perhaps, neighbor was narrowly defined in the Old Covenant just to include the people of the covenant. For these and other reasons a new covenant was enacted (Jer.31:31-34; Heb.8:8-12). In the New Covenant Jesus changed several fundamental principles of the Old in His famous Sermon on the Mount (Matt.5-7) including extending neighbor to include all humankind, even one's enemies.

Jesus made it clear that under the New Covenant it is not enough to love your family and friends and hate your enemies, so he broadens the definition of neighbor to include all our fellow human beings. They are all bearers of the divine image and for whom Jesus came to provide salvation (John 3:16). We must love them and show mercy to them. So, Jesus affirms the Deuteronomic law of love for God and neighbor (Deut.6:4-5 with Mark 12:28-30). And He relaunches it as a new commandment with a higher standard (compare Matt.5:43-48 and John 13:14-15).

The apostles and the early Church adopted the peace theology of Jesus Christ and made it their own. The Church is built upon the foundation of the apostles and prophets with Jesus as the Chief cornerstone (Eph.2:19-22). We then, as believers, are called upon to build our own peace theology rooted in the Scriptures. Since we are a follower of Jesus Christ and cannot improve upon His word, like the apostles and the early church, we must adopt the peace theology of Jesus and make it our own. We must live by it in our homes, churches, and the marketplaces of this world. In the next chapter, we will look more closely at why we need to do this.

CHAPTER 2

PEACE A CHRISTIAN DUTY

In the previous chapter we looked at the peace theology of Jesus, the apostles and the early church and found that they were one and the same. In other words, the peace theology of Jesus became the practicing peace theology of the apostles and the early Church. They preached a gospel of peace and conquered the then know world with it. After the apostolic and patristic eras, Papal Rome became the governing religious and political authority and the Church departed from the gospel of peace to adopt a militant posture. The Protestant Reformation moved it back a little to the center but not equal to that of the apostles and the early Church. The church doesn't normally shed the blood of other believers today, but destructive conflict continues to retard its mission.

Jesus is still the Prince of Peace calling ever believer, local church and ministry entity back to practice the theology of peace He gave us in the New Testament. The Lord of the church made peace a Christian duty when he said, "Blessed are the peacemakers for they will be called the children of God" (Matt.5:9). Or, "love your enemies, bless those who curse you, do good to those who hate you, and pray for those who spitefully use you and persecute you..." (5: 44). Every true disciple of Christ is obligated to subscribe to this theology of peace given by Jesus Christ; it is our Christian duty and trademark in the context of the new command of love and mercy. But many believers are not yet so identified.

For whatever reason, some people label the music division of some churches as the war department. That might be an unfair characterization, for many churches have wonderful music ministry and they are at peace with the rest of the church. There are members that assigned the war label to the board of deacons, while others give it to the board of trustees or even to the pastoral office.

The subtext suggests that conflict reigns in our churches. That reality is supported by experience and in the research literature. It is self-evident that a church beset by destructive conflict cannot optimally fulfills its mission to itself, the community and the world to the glory of God. This chapter explores several important issues that the Christian duties of peacemaking and peacekeeping cover. But first, I must clarify the concept of church membership and second, define what is meant by Christian duty.

Church Membership Significance

For many churches, the current state of church membership needs to be rethought and redefined. Who or what is a church member anyway? The designation has lost its true meaning and significance. Since I serve in the Baptist tradition, I will use this tradition to illustrate. Of course, Baptist is a broad and diverse religious tradition, so the illustration may not be true of every local church in the tradition.

In the Baptist tradition, we generally think of a church member as a born again baptized person who comes into covenant relationship with the church, pledges to be faithful to Jesus Christ, exemplary in conduct, supports that local church, strives for its advancement, and hold it in one's affection above all organizations of human origin. That's how it is expressed in the Church Covenant *in The* New *National Baptist Hymnal* (1977). The covenant captures the essence of most churches' understanding of membership. Christ calls us to a particular lifestyle and responsibility; church membership gives us the opportunity to practice love and model Christ to the world.

The Baptist church covenant is a through document. If taken seriously and put into practice, the local Baptist churches would be regarded as a phenomenal and transformative gathering and some are; people would flock to them as they did the early church in the shadow of the Pentecost outpouring of the Holy Spirit (Acts 2). The disturbing fact is, most people do not understand church membership or take it seriously. Others take it so seriously that they do untold damage to the church. In both extremes there is a lack of understanding, perhaps due to another fact—the church covenant is not taught line upon line and held-up before the people as critically important, nor is it enforced and practiced.

In some Baptist churches, the covenant is read once a month at the communion service and that's about it. It is a forgotten document. It is just assumed that ones you are given the right hand of fellowship as an official member, you automatically know what your membership responsibilities are. As a result, the churches end up with a high percentage of pew-sitters, absentees and inactive names carried on the church roster. With the advent of nondenominational mega-churches and Christian centers attracting members away from traditional churches, headcount has become more important than spiritual formation, loyalty and responsibility; membership significance has become less sacrosanct. It is the count that matters.

With this limited understanding of its significance, church membership is unwittingly reduced to little more than a religious social club. Sometimes they behave less than the cultured social club members. When conflicts arise, they raise hell, cause chaos, then unrepentantly and unapologetically move to the church across town to take up membership there. Most often, no serious inquiry is made of their former church affiliation. Cross Town church is more concerned about numbers, so just about anybody meets their low membership qualification standard. The practice of conferring with the applicant's former church is almost nonexistent today. As a result of this error in the practice of ministry, some people are carried on the membership roster of two, three and more churches as members.

This unrepentant flight to Cross Town church in the face of conflict, is connected to two other issues: discipline and accountability. Jesus exercises the authority of discipline over those who are his disciples and such authority to discipline is exercised through the local church (John 15:1-5). The Bible teaches that believers who refused to be accountable to those who are over them in the Lord and refused to submit to the authority of the church are to be disfellowshipped or even handed over to Satan for discipline (Matt.18:15-18; 1Cor.5:1-5).

Today, if the church dear to discipline some members, the flight to Cross Town church is even swifter. Some leaders become intimidated by this behavioral trend, and as a result, discipline and accountability are laxed, and even nonexistent in some churches. Where there is no discipline, there is disorder and chaos and that is fertile ground for conflict.

The current social and spiritual climate of the local church urgently calls for a rethinking of church membership. Jonathan Leeman (2012), in his little book, *Church Membership*, gives us a compelling vision of the church and its membership. He asserts that "the local church is the authority on earth that Jesus has instituted to officially affirm and give shape...to Christian life." God gave the keys of authority to the church. The church is where God establish and exercise His "supreme rule" over His people who are citizens of His kingdom.

The local church is like an embassy that represents the interests of a nation within another nation—it is a satellite of the country it represents. Just as an embassy is not the country; it merely represents a country, so the local church is not the kingdom of God; it represents the kingdom. It is an outpost of the kingdom of God (Leeman 2012, 24-27).

For example, an American citizen in difficulty in a foreign country can walk into the American embassy in that country for help. The embassy does not make him a citizen but will check his credentials to verify he is indeed a citizen of the United States. Once verified, he is entitled to all the rights accorded to an American citizen. In like manner, the local church is God's embassy with the keys of authority to check the spiritual credentials of those who walk in claiming to be citizens of Christ's kingdom (Leeman 2012). One way to check is to contact the former church of anyone that walks in seeking membership, to learn what kind of member this applicant was in his former church. Is she truly a born-again follower of Jesus Christ or a church hopping troublemaker?

Leeman further asserts that "the local church guards the reputation of Christ by sorting out true [professions of faith] from the false." He clinches the point by declaring that "Jesus instituted the local church with authority over us, we don't just join one like we join clubs...; we submit to them as we do governments" (Leeman 2012, 28-30). This membership vision is a clarion call to the under-shepherds of Christ church to provide better membership oversight without lording it over God's heritage. Because right now, it is like there is no porter at the entrance of the local sheepfold, just about anyone can get membership without clear evidence of repentance.

Jesus is the one that instituted the church and handed the keys of authority and administration to His followers and the blessed Holy Spirit (Matt.16:16-19, 28:19-20; Acts 2:4,37-47). Paul uses the marriage metaphor to illustrate how in love we should submit to one another in the church (Eph.5:21-33). The naked individualistic egotism that prevails in many churches today, steadfastly resist submission to each other in love.

Church members now a days, if slightly offended, would rather joint the flight to Cross Town church than repent and change their ways. They ignore the exhortation to the Christlike humility that says: "In your relationship with one another have the same mindset as Christ Jesus: Who being in very nature God, did not consider equality with God something to be used to his advantage; rather, he made himself nothing by taking the very nature of a servant..." (Phil.2:5-7).

Again, the emulation of this selflessness is greatly ignored by many in Christian practice. If our submission to the Lordship of Christ is flawed, the same is true in our submission to each other. That is the message of Ephesian 5:21-33. Destructive conflict is always traceable to this lack of submission to Christ and each other in the fear of God. I think we have sufficiently clarified the issue of church membership; we will now turn our attention to the question of Christian duty.

Christian Duty Toward Peace

What do I mean by Christian duty? The first definition given by most secular dictionaries on the word duty is, "a moral or legal obligation; a responsibility." The United States English Thesaurus list the synonyms as: "responsibility, obligation, onus, burden, calling, liability, tax, payment, levy, toll." For our purpose, a moral or legal obligation or responsibility will do. The first thing to observe about duty—it is a legal or moral standard imposed by a higher authority. That authority could be human or divine.

The institution of family is the first and basic institutional authority and structure of society. Here spouses have duties to each other that are both moral and legal. For the Christian, God is the legal and moral arbiter that ordained and ordered the family, and this institution is first responsible to Him (Gen.1:27-28, 2:18-24). Children have a duty to parents and parents to children; this is a mix of legal and moral responsibilities (Eph.6:1-4). An employer has a duty to his employees and vice versa, and that duty is both legal and moral (Mal.3:5). A citizen has a duty to his or her country which includes recognizing the rights of fellow citizens; here again, duty is both legal and moral (Rom.13:1-5). Even duty (tax) imposed on a product is done by a higher authority; in this case, a government entity. One has a responsibility or obligation to pay taxes (vv.6-8). If you don't, consequences will be administered. God gives the state the power of the sword (v.4). The state can take away or abridge your freedom.

Now, the Christian is citizen in a kingdom under the authority of King Jesus. This kingdom has its legal and moral code captured in both Old and New Testaments. Jesus said, "A new commandment I give to you, that you love one another; as I have loved you, that you also love one another. By this all will know that you are my disciples, if you have love for one another" (John 13:34-35). Here Jesus is emphasizing the higher standard of righteousness announced much earlier in the Sermon on the Mount.

So then, the acceptable standard of behavior under this new commandment for those in the church is to love each other as Christ loves us. But it goes beyond that—it is to love your neighbor as you love yourself. Neighbor refers to all your fellow human beings, not just those people next door to your house or belong to your church. In fact, neighbor includes loving your enemies, praying for those who spitefully use you and persecute you (Matt.5:44).

The new command to love is an order, not a suggestion. Kings don't make suggestions as policy; they issue binding orders. This command is a moral standard and law He has established. Jesus expects the citizens of His kingdom to abide by His command; it is their duty, obligation and responsibility. Jesus is the head of the church; we are members of His body and we submit to His headship or Lordship. Peacemaking and peacekeeping in the local church are Christian duties to obey and practice.

Peacemaking Every Member's Business

Peacemaking then as a Christian duty, is the business of every member of the local church. It is the responsibility of the under-shepherd to ensure that the principles of this duty are taught to each member, so that members can practice them as part of their spiritual life. It is the duty and responsibility of every church member as keeping the laws of the state is the duty of every citizen.

For several years, I was a healthcare professional (Social Worker) in a major medical center and hospital. "Safety first" was the official policy of this institution and it was strictly enforced because the reputation of the facility rides on safety to this day. Administration made it clear at every inhouse training that safety was the responsibility of every employee. You may not be employed in housekeeping, but if you see water on the floor, you cannot just walk away and say, it is not my job! Or, if you see a broken chair that may collapse with the next person, or an electrical appliance with a frayed cord that can cause fire, you have a duty to do something and you must. If you don't, you are negligent in your duty and you become a liability to the institution and put your own employment at risk.

The water on the floor, the broken chair, the damaged electrical appliance, all pose a risk to the entire operation of this huge medical center and hospital. These defects are like destructive conflict to the local church. Conflict poses a risk to the entire operation of the local church; one member can drop the spark that ignites a forest fire. But if that church member is trained by the organization as an agent of peace to manage conflict—he or she will be looking for peacemaking opportunities, because the obligation of peace is now placed squarely on his or her shoulders. It becomes a personal duty.

When fire breaks out, all hospital employees know what to do because they have been trained to respond appropriately to save lives and protect the institution. They know to close all windows and doors; they also know how to use the fire extinguishers. In like manner, church members should be trained how to respond before the fire of destructive conflict breaks out. They should not be the arsonist or the cause of the fire. But sadly, this is where most churches and pastors have fallen down on the job; we have not trained our members to manage conflict or how to be peacemakers and peacekeepers. Because of these and other reasons, churches get destroyed from within by their own members, they implode.

Peacemaking is a primary Christian duty; it comes with a blessing and an identity attached. Here it is: "Blessed are the peacemakers for they shall be called children of God" (Matt.5:9). Destructive conflict, violence and warmongering come from a dark place. Jesus reminds us that the thief (Satan) comes to "steal," "kill and destroy" (John 10:10a). He steals not only personal peace, health and wellness but corporate peace, health and wellness, then he moves in for the kill.

Destructive conflict is most often Satan's point of entry into a congregation. He pits one member against the other, then people line up on their preferred side, before you know it, you have a major schism on your hand with people dug in for war. That's how Satan divides and conquer. If destructive conflict is often Satan's point of entry and it is not closed, we must at least have trained, Spirit filled agents of peace as managers of conflict on guard. Because like fire, most conflicts don't start off as destructive, but as disagreements and dissatisfactions or unmet needs. They go unaddressed and feelings of anger developed and explode overtime. If a country has no meteorologists to watch for storms and issue storm warnings, citizens are most at risk for being caught unprepared for devastating floods and hurricanes.

It is important to note that conflicts are not all bad. Periodic conflicts are good for an organization. In fact, the total absence of conflict in an organization is perhaps a symptom of lack of growth and the onset of death and dying. If leaders have only yes people around them and no opposing views, no counterintelligence, that is not healthy for any organization. A healthy, growing church will have vigorous debates and discussions around important issues and there will be disagreements. But healthy disagreements don't develop into destructive conflicts.

After vigorous discussion, the minority position should give way to the majority. The Baptist church covenant published in the National Baptist Hymnal previously referenced, gives us these words: "In case of difference of opinion in the church, we will strive to avoid a contentious spirit, and if we cannot unanimously agree, we will cheerfully recognize the right of the majority to govern." Baptist churches have a congregational polity (governance); the power resides in the body of believers. Pastors, bishops, deacons and elders are under-shepherds and overseers of God's flock and are not to lord it over God's heritage (Acts 20:28; 1Peter 5:1-4).

The Christian duty of peacemaking, among other things, involves three seminal ideas: the commitment to put away the sword, the commitment to seek peace and pursue it, and the commitment to seek the interest of others. As church members, we are called upon do all three to the glory of God. But let's briefly expound on these three uniquely Christian ideals.

First, *the commitment to put away the sword.* Once we accept the call to follow Jesus, that means the abandonment of some things. Collectively, it is the old way of life for the new lifestyle of the kingdom. What was Peter and his companion first called away from? The fishing business of course. They abandoned boats with all their fishing gears. For Matthew, it was his tax collecting booth, table, records and more. For Bartimaeus, it was his blind paraphernalia, including his panhandling cup.

Later in his walk, Jesus commanded Peter to put away his sword. The command of sword abandonment is for all disciples of Christ. This new lifestyle is a call to peace. You will no longer settle conflict with the sword. The church is not a mafia organization with its cloak and dagger, ready for revenge. Jesus wants us to know, the eye for an eye, tooth for a tooth, hate your enemy ways of relating to those who disagree or oppose us are over. A righteousness beyond pharisaic religion is the new standard. Self-centered pietism must be left behind.

We are called to live by a new rule, a new code of conduct. It is the love thy neighbor as thyself, love thy enemy code (Matt.5:38-48). Under this new code of conduct, vengeance is no longer yours to pay, God our Father has taken over the administration of vengeance in the context of justice (Deut.32: 35; Rom.12:19-21; Heb.10:30-31). He has given the sword to another group of ministers, they are the ministers of the secular state, they do not carry the sword for nothing (Rom.13:4). A sizable part of the church has not read this memo from Jesus that the war is over, put away the sword of your former life. You are engaged in a new fight with new equipment (Eph.6:10-18). “For the weapons of our warfare are not carnal, but mighty through God to the pulling down of strongholds” (2Cor.10:4 KJV).

Second, *the commitment to seek peace and pursue it* (1Peter 3:11). To seek is to search for it diligently; to pursue, to go after with determination, intentionality and purpose. Disciples of Jesus Christ do not have the luxury of setting preconditions for peace. Peace is work or the work of peace is never easy. Peter's exhortation to seek peace and pursue peace is based upon the teachings of Jesus to love our neighbor as we love ourselves; this includes our enemies. The exhortation is addressed to the body of believers in the local church.

Peter's exhortation has to be viewed, at least, within the immediate context which begins at verse eight (1Peter 3:8 NKJV): "Finally, all of you be of one mind, having compassion for one another; love as brothers, be tenderhearted, be courteous; not returning evil for evil or reviling for reviling, but on the contrary blessing, knowing that you were called to this, that you may inherit a blessing."

In this one verse, the apostle calls for unity, love and compassion in the local church in personal, relational and behavioral terms. Behaviors are attitudes that can be observed and measured for what they are. This is how people in the community of faith supposed to behave toward each other. But the apostle did not stop there; he goes on to give three exhortations necessary for peace and personal blessing, each one begins with the word, "let." These are exhortations to control specific behaviors. "For he who would love life, and see good days, let him refrain his tongue from evil, and his lips from speaking deceit. Let him turn away from evil and do good; let him seek peace and pursue it" (1Peter 3:10-11 NKJV).

Note well that exhortation one (1) is to control your tongue (lips, speech). The apostle James (3:1-12) tells us the damage the tongue can do. It is the cause for most conflict in the church and home, a reckless tongue out of control. The Prophet Isaiah gives us this intelligence report, "The Sovereign LORD has given me a well-instructed tongue, to know the word that sustains the weary" (Isa.50:4). The prophet's speaking apparatus (tongue, mouth and lips) must have gone through a *cleansing process* because he confessed earlier that he was a dirty mouth man (Isa.6:5-6). But now his mouth is sanctified and disciplined, so now what is spoken can *sustain the weary.* The word sustain here means to nourish, to build up or edify, not tear down and destroy. Being destructive of the good is Satan's work (John 10:10 a). Jesus came that we might have life to the full (10:10b). Peacemakers build up the body of Christ.

Exhortation two (2) is to turn away from evil and do good. This is repenting for the evils of the tongue in number one, as well as the doings of other members of the body that we have made instruments of unrighteousness. Exhortation three (3) is to seek peace and pursue it. Go after the things that make for peace. Jesus was never petty; He never kept grudges. He even forgave those who were murdering Him (Luke 23:34).

The apostle Peter goes on to give us an additional reason to yield to these exhortations: "For the eyes of the LORD are on the righteous, and His ears are open to their prayers; but the face of the Lord is against those who do evil" (1Peter 3:12). On those who cause discord among brethren, the mercy and judgment of God are reflected in these verses we just expounded on. Let's hear them again: "For he who would love life, and see good days, let him refrain his tongue from evil, and his lips from speaking deceit. Let him turn away from evil and do good; let him seek peace and pursue it" (1Peter 3:10-11).

Third, *the commitment to seek the interest of others* (Philip.2:3-4). Destructive conflict is almost always powered by selfishness and pride. Somebody is always demanding their pound of flesh at the expense of another. The lyrics of this selfish song is: "Me, Myself and I, we three and no one else." But there can be no peace between individuals, family members, local church members or between nations, if one does not consider the interests of the other. For the people of God in the local church, Jesus is the model. Paul exhorts us, "Do nothing out of selfish ambition or vain conceit. Rather, in humility value others above yourselves, not looking to your own interest but each of you to the interest of others" (Philip.2:3-4).

In other words, to be true agents of peace and managers of conflicts, the local church must conform to this indispensable biblical principle of *looking to the interests of others.* Even secular organizations and institutions have now come around to acknowledge and use this two-thousand-year-old biblical principle.

The principle is divine and was originated in heaven itself and is reflected in the incarnation (Philip.2:3-4). The apostle Paul goes on to say, "In your relationships with one another, have the same mindset as Christ Jesus: who, being in very nature God, did not consider equality with God something to be used to his own advantage...." Instead, he stepped away from that lofty position, and made himself nothing. He took on the position of a servant and became one of us and humbled himself to the death of the cross (vv.5-8). In other words, as Jesus Christ put aside self-interest and humbled himself to bring peace between God and the human family (Rom.5:1-2), peace in the local church between brothers and sisters must follow the same unselfish path, considering the interest of others.

The Christian Duty of Peacekeeping

Winning the peace is different from keeping the peace. You can win the battle and lose the war. The United Nations know this very well; that is why they have a peacekeeping force that goes into countries sometime after a ceasefire while the two sides negotiate a lasting peace. Peacekeeping is not simple or easy, because grievances, past injustices, needs, long held grudges must be addressed to the satisfaction of both sides. Such work of negotiation can take years.

I take the position that every member in a congregation has a peacemaking and peacekeeping duty and should be trained how to live out this duty to the glory of God. Beyond that there should be a highly trained Resident Council (RC) of five to seven people (depending on the size of the church) trained as agents of peace-managers of conflicts. The assignment of the RC is to manage conflict and bring them to resolution. The RC is both a peacemaking and peacekeeping force serving that local congregation. I referred earlier to my healthcare work in a major medical center and hospital, where the official policy was "safety first." They implemented that policy by making safety the business of every employee.

Employees are trained to know what to do when they see, hear or smell an unsafe situation. But in addition to that, the institution has several levels of safety mechanism in place. One of them is a resident security force that patrols the entire facility within and without. They monitor a bank of close circuit TV units connected to surveillance cameras posted throughout the entire facility. The security force is a rapid response force that can be deployed through the facility at a moment's notice; they are also connected to the external Police Station and fire department. The resident security force is equivalent to what I call a Resident Council (RC) on conflict management and resolution. The RC is a dedicated lay ministry in each local church (more on the RC later).

Three Big Ideas in The Duty of Peace

The duties of peacemaking and peacekeeping involve many important issues; they will be discussed throughout this work.

But I wish to highlight the three most important ones for the rest of this chapter. They are forgiveness, justice and restitution, and reconciliation.

First, working for forgiveness. Most Christians know the teachings of Jesus on forgiveness and are trying to live it out in their daily lives. The world was shocked when on June 16th, 2015 a young white man walked into a Bible study in a Black AME church in South Carolina and was well received, but in this their unguarded hour he pulled out a gun and killed nine of them including the pastor, Rev. Pinckney who was also a state senator. They have been referred to as the Emanuel Nine. One of the first things that the biological and church families said was, "We forgive him," the shooter.

Non-Christian marveled at that promptness to forgive and remarked, "how could they!" But most Christians know that is exactly what Jesus would have done. In fact, from the cross Jesus prayed this prayer for those who were murdering Him: "Father, forgive them, for they do not know what they do" (Luke 23:34). He taught us to forgive, and not to carry grudges to the grave with us. Jesus even connect God's forgiveness of us, to our willingness to forgive others (Matt.6:12, 14-15).

But not all Christians are quick and willing to forgive. There are those that know of forgiveness in theory but not in practice. For them, there is a great divide between what they believe and what they practice. That is perhaps one of the many reasons conflict thrive so well in many local churches. Some members may experience a slight bruise of their ego or they are not recognized to their satisfaction and that is reason enough to destroy the church fellowship and flee to the church across town to assume membership there without repenting. Nothing speaks to them that they have caused hurt to others, and they assume position at *Cross Town* church until offended, they cuss them out and move on to Uptown church. This is happening right now and there are no guardrails in place preventing this from happening.

In practice, some church members do not know what biblical forgiveness is. Yet for years they have been singing about it, listening to sermons on it, and praying *forgives us of our trespasses as we forgive those who trespass against us.* But when faced with the real practice of this set of beliefs—they behave as if they never heard of Jesus before or of His teachings on forgiveness.

Biblical forgiveness involves three actions: 1) acknowledging the hurt we cause others. It is otherwise called, repentance; especially, if God is one of the offending parties. This calls for Christian conscience, self-awareness, and a soft heart before God. 2) Forgiveness includes confession. Confession is more than acknowledging the wrong done and the hurt we caused others. It means to come clean, tell it all as it was, unburden your soul with sincerity and with a resolve not to repeat the hurt. 3) Forgiveness includes your decision to ask for forgiveness or to grant forgiveness. If you are the offender, you ask for forgiveness (that includes God). But, if someone offended you, you grant forgiveness.

It is important to note that if a person is deeply hurt and has suffered great loss, forgiveness will not come easy. Sometimes, the person might not be ready to forgive. The exercise of patience is necessary in this case to work through emotional issues. One should bear in mind that forgiveness does not mean to erase from memory or from your emotions the hurt that was done to you. That could take a long time to forget some memories. Forgiveness is a decision you make to bury the hatchet even though memory is still vivid or fresh and you are still hurting. You speak the word of forgiveness face to face (if possible); this is the starting point of your healing.

If you postpone granting forgiveness until you hurt no more, that could take years, and perhaps you never get around to it. So, you grant forgiveness to the offender not just for the offender's sake but for your sake as well, for this is the point where healing begins for you. The offender holds you hostage as long as you refuse to grant forgiveness, and this could precipitate the development of disease in your body or affect your mental health and your spiritual well-being as well.

Sometimes, focusing on a time you offended God and He forgave you when you repented, confessed and asked him, makes it easier to forgive those who offend you. Furthermore, the fact that God forgives you based on your willingness to forgive others is a good motivator to prod you and me to forgive from a sincere heart. There can be no peace without genuine forgiveness.

Second, the next big idea in the duty of peace is working for justice and restitution. These are two critical issues to consider in our duties of peacemaking and peacekeeping; they are connected here because restitution is dealt with in the context of justice. But bear in mind that God's justice is always restrained by mercy. Jesus says it this way, "Blessed are the merciful: for they shall obtain mercy" (Matt.5:7 KJV).

From the Old Covenant God wants his people to do "justly and love mercy" (Micah 6:8). When you are the one offended and suffered loss, your need for full and ungarnished justice could go too far, even to the point of being offensive to God. This point is illustrated in one of the parables of Jesus in which he likens the kingdom of heaven to a certain king who balancing his books found the account of one servant who owed ten thousand bags of gold. Since he was not able to pay, his lord commanded that he, his wife and children to be sold to pay off his debt. The man fell to his knees and pleaded for more time to pay the debt. The merchant was moved with compassion and cancelled his debt in full (10 thousand bags of gold).

But the same man went out and found one of his companions that owed him one hundred silver coins, and he grabbed and began to choke him. Pay back what you owe me! He demanded. His fellow servant fell to his knees and begged him, "Be patient with me and I will pay you back." But he refused, he had him thrown into debtor's prison. Someone saw this and reported it to the king that just forgave him. The king called him and throw him in debtor's prison until he paid the full debt. The king was disappointed that he forgave him that huge debt and he could not forgive a small debt. Jesus said, "This is how my heavenly Father will treat each of you unless you forgive your brother or sister from your heart" (Matt.18:21-35).

When the trespass is fraud and involves money or real property, perhaps the civil courts may be involved, and some situations will definitely warrant the courts' involvement. But even in such cases, as a Christian, you can petition the courts on behalf of your offending Christian brother or sister, so the court can render justice in keeping with your Christian conviction of mercy. Because the court wants to render justice reflecting the positions of both sides, in keeping with the law, the hurt party's input is weighty and is often considered. Don't forget that God wants justice restrained my mercy.

Additionally, if the offending party is a church brother or sister, efforts ought to be made to settle the matter among wise and informed counsel, short of going to court. It will help to preserve your Christian relationship, your testimony and the message of your church. In this context, an arrangement of restitution in keeping with justice and mercy can be made. When the chief tax collector, Zacchaeus met Jesus, of his own accord, Zacchaeus promised restitution to those he defrauded. Upon that sincere promise Jesus announced, "Today salvation has come to this house, because this man, too, is a son of Abraham. For the Son of Man came to seek and to save the lost" (Luke 19:1-10).

The New Testament teaches that the Lord of the church would prefer members of His church settle their disputes among themselves, in the spirit of Christ, rather than dragging each other to the civil court to settle their differences before the unbelievers (1Cor.6:1-11). Paul is not abrogating the role of the civil courts. He is more appealing to the conscience of believers and their role to set Christian examples. Things can get really ugly in a civil court; you may walk away with justice rendered, but at the loss of the relationships of Christian brothers and sisters. This brings us to the next important big idea or issue in the process of peacemaking, reconciliation.

Third, working for reconciliation. Reconciliation is the major objective to consider in peacemaking and peacekeeping in a local church or family; it is the ideal goal you want to achieve. Jesus Christ died not only to reconcile us to God, but to reconcile us humans to each other. The work of the ministry, therefore, is a two-directional work of reconciliation; we reconcile people to God and to each other (2 Cor.4:17-21). The church is where we mirror to the world of unbelievers what being reconciled to Christ looks like. As the community of faith, we live out this new reality as salt and light before an unbelieving world, showing them the alternative culture of the kingdom of God.

If indeed, we follow the Prince of peace, we should be able to settle our disputes among ourselves. This is not an anticourt statement; it a biblical statement. Furthermore, the Bible is not against courts. But if we fight as the unregenerate world does and drag each other before the law courts to settle our differences before unbelievers, how are we different from them? Church members fighting from the church house to the parking lot and into the public square, damage the witness of the church to the community and to the world. For the Christian, the work of peacemaking is not fully achieved if reconciliation of relationship is loss in the process.

There is an even more critical question to ask—when church brothers and sisters fight like cats and dogs, how do they authentically celebrate in peace at the Lord's table with each other? Where is the transformative grace to deal lovingly with one another? Such behaviors do not reflect the identification (ID) code of the people God. What is that ID? It is "love for one another" and peacemaking (Matt.5:9; John 13:34-35). Jesus counsels us to take the initiative and push for reconciliation, even when we might not be in the wrong. Even at the crucial point of "offering your gift at the altar and there [you] remember that your brother or sister has a grudge against you, leave your gift in front of the altar. First go and be reconciled to them; then come and offer your gift" (Matt.5:23-26). What are the implications here? I see four.

Implication one—if you have knowledge of the ill feelings against you, you should not wait for the brother or sister that holds the grudge against you to come to you. The matter is too urgent to wait. The Lord is impressing on us that immediate action is warranted, for something greater is at stake here; that is your relationship with Him. If you truly value your relationship with the Lord, make things right.

Implication two—your relationship with your church brother or sister takes precedence over your material offering to God. It is worship from a sincere heart that God wants. That is the fundamental reason Cain's offering was not accepted. It is not because his offering was not appropriate as some would have us believe. Cain had a murderous heart and he was given prior warning about his sinful heart, but he did not heed the warning (Gen.4:1-15).

Implication three—God will not accept your gift or worship, if there are misgivings between you and another worshipper. You must be first reconciled to each other. If this is ignored, worship is a display of hypocrisy and not acceptable to God (Rom.12:1-3).

Implication four—disputes that are not settled quickly God's way and to His glory, will likely fester to a larger dispute settled in the civil court (Matt.5:25-26). *Make every effort to live in peace with all people*, and especially those who are of the household of faith.

In all honesty, I must concede that there are cases that reconciliation of relationships may not be possible. For example, in the case of serious bodily harm, sexual assault and other situations of abuse where people must make a clean break and go their separate ways. A church must be very careful of holier-than thou attitude here, not to push the letter of the law over the spirit of the law.

There are cases of irreconcilable challenges and the Bible should never be held over anyone to force them to stay in bondage. Jesus came to set people free not to keep them in bondage. Perhaps, these are the cases the apostle Paul had in mind when these words were penned: "If it is possible, as far as it depends on you, live in peace with everyone" (Rom.12:18). Jesus never intended for you to be the punching bag of abuse in any relationship. Again, some cases, after forgiveness is granted, reconciliation of relationship is not possible, a clean break and a fresh start is necessary. This is the exception not the general rule. This is where a spiritual leader must be very cautious, less you damage fragile lives.

Summation

By now you have come to realize that the Christian duty of peacemaking is no simple matter; there is much at stake here. Being a peacemaker elevates your membership in Christ's church, as well as your citizenry in His kingdom to the bright lights for all to see. Christian peacemaking revolves around three seminal practice commitments: 1) the commitment to put away the sword, 2) the commitment to seek peace and pursue it, and 3) the commitment to seek the interest of others. You cannot do peace right if you eliminate any of the three.

We also come to realize that the duty of peacemaking involves the duty of peacekeeping. The two are interrelated but are not exactly the same; they are almost the two sides of the same coin. We discussed three core ideas of peacemaking and peacekeeping. One is forgiveness which includes addressing the hurt we cause the other party. Forgiveness happens within the context of repentance, confession, asking for forgiveness and giving forgiveness, and the resolve not to hurt the person in that way ever again.

The second is justice and restitution. Here we show that biblical justice is always restrained my mercy, that we should always try to settle our disputes in the Christian community, so that we can preserve the integrity of our Christian witness. Restitution should be done in the context of Christian love and understanding. The Christian is not anticourt; some situation may require the courts, especially untangling contracts and real property settlements. But even in such case, the Christian can let the court knows his or her desire for justice restrained by mercy in keeping with your Christian conscience and the word.

The third is to work for reconciliation. Reconciliation is the gold standard of Christian peacemaking and peacekeeping, though in some cases it is not achievable. In view of our fellowship at the Lord's Table, acceptable worship, having heaven hearing and answering our prayers, we strive to be reconciled with each other to the glory of God. But this does not mean returning to an unsafe situation; the Lord would not want that for you. Jesus wants you to live and full and free life to His glory (John 10:10b).

CHAPTER 3

WHY LOCAL CHURCHES NEED TO MANAGE CONFLICT EFFECTIVELY

This chapter answers the question, why the local church needs to learn how to manage and resolve conflicts effectively? This is a question of rationale, why we need to do this? Stated another way, does the local church really need a *conflict management system* (CMS) in place?

Perhaps, the simple answer is, yes! Because church folks like to fight and they "often fight dirty," asserts Hugh F. Halverstadt (1991, 1). As a pastor for over thirty-five years, I can affirm that church folks indeed fight. In fact, it is the fights that I witnessed and experienced that compelled the doctoral level research that gave birth to this book. I have seen my share of dirty fighting, but the broader answer to the question has several levels of complexities. I hope to flesh them out in this chapter.

In a sense, Chapter 2 answers the question on the individual level, showing that it is our Christian duty to be peacemakers and peacekeepers at home, work, the marketplaces and most certainly at church. But now, we take a closer look at the corporate body, the church, to see why a conflict management system (CMS) to practice the art of peacemaking and peacekeeping is necessary. This discussion is organized under three pivotal headings: *1) the nature of the* church demands it (i.e. CMS), 2) the mission of the church warrants it, and 3) the work of the church compels it. Remember, the "It" is referring to a conflict management system (CMS).

CMS is used interchangeably with *dispute resolution system* (DRS) or conflict management and resolution (CMR) throughout this work. It is critical for the church to have a thoughtful, proactive, formal conflict management system in place. I will show why this is necessary in this chapter.

The Unique Nature of the Church Demands A CMS

The church is unparallel to all other enterprises; it is fundamentally different in structure, polity and governance. It is a unique, voluntary organization or institution of divine origin. Jesus said to Peter and the other disciples, "Upon this Rock I will build my church, and the gates of Hades will not overcome it" (Matt.16:18-19). The word "build" in the quote means, to establish. Jesus Christ established His church as a doxological institution (i.e. for His glory). On the Day of Pentecost, the blessed Holy Spirit became its Chief Administrator on earth and Jesus the Chief Administrator in heaven (Acts 2; 1Peter 5:4).

Yet for all that, the ascended exalted Christ and the descended Holy Spirit work in conjunction with humans because the general operation of the church is under human leadership (1Cor.3:9). God has placed this divine institution in the hands of humans to do the work of the ministry and have the *oversigh*t of His people. Again, God has entered into partnership with us (Matt.28:19-20). First in creation and now in redemption, and the latter cost more to bring about than the former (creation was not a costly, painful process, redemption is).

This concept of redeemed humans having *oversight* of God's church is beautifully captured in Paul's farewell speech to the Ephesians elders: "Keep watch over yourselves and all the flock of which the Holy Spirit has made you overseer. Be shepherds of the church of God, which he bought with his own blood" (Acts 20:28). The apostle Peter gives a similar charge to the elders, "Be shepherds of God's flock that is under your care, watching over them..." (1Pet.5:1-2). The church as God's flock, needs a caring shepherd. As a flock bought with His own precious blood, that sets the church apart with a uniqueness and unparallel to any other institution on earth. That the responsibility of care is entrusted on us mere mortals is frightening, because we are not all that dependable, but God put a lot of confidence in us. We are God's flock! Of course, sheep are not very smart animals.

But the church is not made up of sheep; it is made up of people who are not yet perfect from human perspectives; we are still in the state of becoming. For that reason, there will be fights. Conflict is going to be inevitable in its ranks. But conflict is not always bad; at times, it serves for the growth and development of an organization. But if conflict is not managed, it will become destructive and destroy everything in its path. For that reason, therefore, the church like other people groups in institutions needs a resident conflict management system (RCMS) to resolve conflict before it destroys.

All organizations, Christian and non-Christian, need harmony to function orderly, productively and optimally. None has a mission in keeping with or as loft as the church. How much more then, the church needs to be an institution of peace! Peace cannot be left to chance; human nature will not allow it. Peace has to be intentionally sought after. Like fire, conflict can serve us well, but it is too risky a phenomenon not to watch and manage. As fire is a good servant but a bad master, so is conflict.

The Mission of the Church Warrants A CMS

The mission of the church warrants a conflict management system, so that members can learn to deal with conflict effectively. The church is tasked with local and global evangelization, that includes getting the gospel out, making disciples of all nations, guiding them into Christian maturity and enlisting them to productive Christian service (Matt.28:19-20). Believers were never intended to be barren pew-sitters but fruit bearing branches on the true vine (John 15:1-8).

Gary L. McIntosh sums up the mission of the church in a tri-level action of evangelism involving *presence, proclamation,* and *persuasion* (McIntosh 2016, 60-62). The church must be located somewhere; that means, it has presence in a real community. The church is given a message to tell; that is proclamation. That message must be told in a way to solicit a positive response; that is persuasion. It seems simple and ordinary, but it is everything but that.

Each member of the body of Christ has this treasure in fragile, earthen vessel (literally, jars of clay) but empowered by the blessed Holy Spirit to get the job done. Together then, the church is God's enterprise or business on earth; the product is the gospel. The prize is the souls of all humankind. This is an unparallel, massive and complex operation; no other enterprise is tasked with such a mission. But conflict can easily fracture its unity and paralyze its mission.

Speaking of complexity, the church is more than an organization or institution; the Bible designates it, a living organism, comparative to the human body (Rom.12:4-5;

1Cor.12:12-27). If the members of the human body do not function in harmony, confusion and chaos will result. The same is true of the church, the Body of Christ. Paul reminds us that "God is not the author of confusion, but of peace" (1Cor.14:33 NKJV). Confusion or chaos is from another place and does not bring glory to God.

Destructive conflict then is, perhaps, Satan's most effective weapon deployed against the church of Jesus Christ. Satan's strategy is to divide and conquer. He sought to divide heaven between himself and God but lost that fight but is hell-bent on winning the war (Rev.12:7-9). Satan's war with God goes on with his attack on the church (vv.13-17). Being thrown down to earth, Satan is on mission for his own glory, dividing humankind from his God. There are five challenges to its mission, the church faces.

First, the mission of the church stands or falls on the quality of its unity. The church cannot effectively execute its global mission with the absence of unity or with fractured unity. If Jesus feared anything for the church; it would have been fractured unity. He made it clear that no kingdom divided against itself can stand, not even Satan's kingdom (Matt.11:17-18). With that understanding, Jesus frequently emphasized to His disciples the importance of their love for each other and unity among them. Competition among them concerning personal greatness was discouraged because it leads to fractured unity (Matt.18:1-4; Luke 9:33-35). Jesus wanted the love and unity that binds His people together to be strong and of the highest quality in the universe. The best and only example Jesus could find is that bond of unity between the persons of the blessed Holy Trinity, and He prayed for that.

In His highly priestly prayer (John17), that quality of love and unity is liken to that which binds the persons of the blessed Holy Trinity as one. Note the repetitive expression, "that they might be one as we are one" (vv.20, 21). He wants believers to have "complete unity" among them (v.23). Jesus wants the unity of the church to be a witness to the world that they are the people of God, so He climaxed His prayer on believers' unity with these words, "Then the world will know that you sent and have loved them as you have loved me" (v.23b). This prayer reflects the heart of Christ for His Church.

Therefore, when church folks fight among themselves that from the church house it spills out into the streets, police cars gathered, neighborhood residents run out of their houses to behold the spectacle, and church fights become the talk of the town in shopping malls, barbershops, beauty salons and social media—that church has damaged its witness to the community and perhaps to the world.

Church fights are a disgrace to any local church, but unity exalts the message of Christ to the community. A building with a cross on it means nothing, if the people that gather together don't reflect a righteous, peaceful, godly lifestyle. That does not come by chance; it has to be taught and learned; it has to be cultivated. A conflict management system is needed to educate church members in their duty of peacemaking and peacekeeping and prevent the public disgrace just described.

Satan rejoices when church disputes divides a congregation to the point of making a public spectacle of themselves; it serves his purpose well. Satan is not afraid to penetrate any church group. He needs only one willing member to disrupt harmony and fracture unity. He tried it with Jesus' little group, and he found willing Judas and reluctant Peter. The betrayal of Judas and the denial of Peter were Satan's attempts to fracture the unity of Jesus' little group. Jesus forewarned Peter that *Satan has desired* to have him (Luke 22:31-34; John 13:2). Peter was a little too sure of himself and he failed publicly and miserably. After His resurrection, Jesus reinstated Peter to the ministry (John 21:15-22). Perhaps, Judas would have been reinstated had he not killed himself. He was replaced by Matthias to complete the fractured circle (Acts 1:15-26). Other competing differences among the disciples were settled by the arrival of the Holy Spirit on the Day of Pentecost, for on that day, "they were all in one place with one accord" (Acts 2:1 KJV).

Since Pentecost, the church has been through conflicts within and without, waves after waves, and only those local churches that were prepared for it have been able to make it unscathed. The number of them is at best few. A church is more likely to have conflict than not, therefore, it should never lower its guard against the influences of destructive conflict. Churches that succumb to destructive conflict almost always suffer loss of membership, loss of leadership, split to form other congregations, and some churches die. The apostles kept encouraging the churches to be of one heart and of one mind from its earliest days because they knew Satan divides and conquer (Acts 2:46,4:32).

Unity is strength; it has the power of agreement. Paul exhorts the churches of the Ephesians to walk worthy of the calling they received, "endeavoring to keep the unity of the Spirit in the bond of peace (Eph.4:1-3). The implication of the verse is that unity does not come automatically, you must exercise the effort to secure it and keep it. That means you should have the skills and abilities to manage conflict and bring it to resolution. This must be intentionally done with a system in place. A flight to the store to buy fire extinguisher after a fire has broken out is perhaps too late.

Second, malicious discord in a local church prevents the Holy Spirit from doing any great work in that church until the people are united in one spirit. I used to ask, why it took ten days from the ascension to the coming of the Holy Spirit. Did it take Jesus ten days to complete the journey? I don't think so. In that new resurrection body, He no doubt moves faster than the speed of light. Did Jesus have to get some rest and relaxation, refreshment and debriefing before appearing at an Executive Triune conference to send the Holy Spirit? I don't think so.

For a long time, I treated the matter lightly, convincing myself it was not all that important. But at a prayer and study hour one Ascension Day night, someone divine touched me on the shoulder and said, "The ten days is how long it took for the Upper Room gathering to be of one heart and one mind." I was a little ashamed, because it is right there in the biblical text: "And when the day of Pentecost was fully come, they were all with one accord in one place" (Acts 2:1 KJV). There was no more talk about who is going to be the greatest among us. Peter knew that without Jesus, he wasn't all that much; his failings had cut him down to size, but since Jesus reinstated him the matter was settled.

That the Holy Spirit came when they were in one accord is significant. For me, it suggests that this gentle dove of the Godhead is not ready to work with us until we put away our sword, get control of our egocentric, self-interest talk, and be at peace and unity among ourselves. He will help us to get there, but we must get there before anything big happens. That Upper Room prayer meeting did it.

It is commonly understood that the work of the church is not accomplished through secular intellectual genius, but through the anointing and enabling of the Holy Spirit (Zech.4:6;

Acts1:8). This does not mean we should check our intellect at the church door; Jesus said, "Come and learn of me" (Matt.11:28). The Holy Spirit is indispensable to the two-great works of the church: *worship and disciple making*. Apart from these them, the church has no reason for being, and this twin assignment cannot be accomplished in the context of strife.

Worship is doxological; it is done to the glory of God. Worship is the most exalted of human activities; it has no equal on earth or anywhere else. John MacArthur refers to worship as the church's "supreme duty for time and eternity" (MacArthur 2012, 3). He asserts that, "The decline of worship in evangelical churches is a troubling sign. It reflects a depreciation of God and a sinful apathy toward His truth among the people of God" (p.*12*). MacArthur sternly rebukes the charismatic segment of the evangelical community for substituting "strange fire" in worship for the Holy Spirit, a behavior reminiscent to that of Nadab and Abihu, the sons of Aaron (Exod.24:11). They were killed for their reckless disregard for the holy (MacArthur 2013, 179-97).

There are several things in a local church impacting worship negatively, but conflict is chief among them. Worship that God accepts cannot be generated in a conflicted church environment; it must come from a people of sincere hearts and driven by the blessed Holy Spirit (John 4:21-24). A conflict management system at the local church helps to guard the integrity of worship, so worship can keep its doxological character.

Disciple making, is the second great work of the church for which the Holy Spirit is indispensable. Human efforts alone cannot truly grow the church. It is the Lord who adds to the church those that are being saved (Acts 2:44-47). Preachers and members are mere instruments that God works through to build His church. Paul was acutely aware of this fact when he said that he and his companion Apollos were simply ministers through whom God works to bring people to into His kingdom. He planted, and Apollos watered, but it is God who causes thing to grow, increase and produce (1Cor.3:5-8). Making disciples is more than counting the number of heads gathered in a building. Saved people have entered God's kingdom through a new birth experience and must be nurtured to Christian maturity. This new birth comes from above through the agency of the blessed Holy Spirit, Jesus Himself informs us (John 3:1-16). A child can have a good birth but socialized in a dysfunctional environment; a conflicted church can retard spiritual development. It is not enough to bring new sheep into the fold; efforts must be made to make the sheepfold a healthy, nurturing place.

The Great Commission further informs us that disciple making is at the very heart of the church's mission and it includes: preaching, soul winning, baptism, and training (Matt.28:19-20). Winning people may get them through the front door of the local church, but without teaching, maturing and enlisting them for service, we lose them right through the back door, and nothing drives them away faster than an unloving, conflicted congregation. Bill Hull gives us this intelligence, "Disciple making takes more faith than any other task of the church. Since it is top priority for God, it is top priority for Satan. No work of God's servant draws more resistance than disciple making" (Hull 2007, 39).

Third, deficient practice of love. The practice of love goes beyond just the talk of love. The lack of the practice of love is at the root of all conflicted congregations. The apostle Paul informs us: "Love is patient, love is kind. It does not boast; it is not proud. It is does not dishonor others, it is not self-seeking, it is not easily angered, it keeps no record of wrongs. Love does not delight in evil but rejoices with the truth..." (1 Cor.13:4-6). At the heart of conflict is a deficit of these Christlike graces. Our sinful nature takes over and rules. The apostle James rhetorically ask, "What causes fights and quarrels among you?" He gives the answer in a second question, "Don't they come from your desire that battle within you? You desire but do not have, so you kill. You covet but you cannot get what you want, so you quarrel and fight. You do not have because you do not ask God" (James 4:1-2).

Even the secular therapists have long acknowledged the therapeutic power of love. Stephen Gilligan writes from the perspective of psychology and psychotherapy, asserts that "love as a skill and force...can heal and invigorate, reconnect and guide, calm and encourage" (Gilligan 1997, 11-13). If love is a skill, it can be learned, developed and put into practice. The church is a good place to start. Psychologist Eric Fromm considers love as an art, and as such, it "requires knowledge and effort" (Fromm 2013, 8). It is a fruit of the Spirit, but it can be cultivated (Gal.5:22-23). The community of faith has the textbook on love, and it is a great place to learn and practice love. The *greates*t of all spiritual gifts is love (1Cor.13:13). "Through the lives of its members, the local church defines love for the world," asserts Leeman (2012,131).

Fourth, destructive conflict endangers both the leadership and congregational health, and shortens pastoral tenure. A sick church with sick leadership cannot fulfill its mission responsibility to itself and to the word. Healthy leadership with a reasonable pastoral tenure is critical to a church fulfilling its mission. If every two years or so new leadership is needed, that alone is symptomatic of an unhealthy church. Time, effort and resources will have to be spent again to activate a search committee to find the person that is the right fit for the congregation. It also makes it harder to find quality applicants, because news gets around that this church cannot keep its pastor. Potential applicants begin to assume that this is a difficult congregation with much internal strife.

In 2004 *Christian Today* conducted a survey on congregational health. Seventy percent (70%) of the congregation responded that they have experienced situations of conflict, 69% lost members, and 25% lost their leadership. The stark reality is, there is an exodus of members and pastors from churches in North America for a variety of reasons, and many are in a state of risk: their families falling apart, and personal health threatened from stress and burnout.

The fifth challenge that church faces to it mission is the lack of an intentional, dedicated, conflict management and resolution system. Since this is what this book is about, in general and this chapter in particular, there is no need to elaborate on this point here; it will be sufficiently addressed in several ways throughout this work.

In summary then, these five pivotal subheadings we just covered, can also be viewed as the rationale or the compelling "why" conflict has to be managed and resolved at the local church level. There is where the commission to global evangelization is deployed. These five are not the only reasons, but they are surely most significant ones. Other researchers and writers may express them differently or even find additional ones that they consider to be of primary importance. Why a conflict management system (CMS) is needed?

The Work of the Church Compels A CMS

The work of the church makes having a conflict management system compelling. For this and other reasons, the local church must learn to deal with conflict effectively. The church is tasked with reconciling humankind to God and to each other through the redemptive message of the gospel (2 Cor.4:1-8; 5:18-21). No other enterprise on earth is assigned this unique work.

The Great Commission does not order the world of humankind to come to the church, but it certainly orders the church to go to world, preach to them the good news of the kingdom of God, make disciples of them, then teach them to observe the teachings of Jesus Christ (Matt.28:19-20). For people to confess with their mouth the Lord Jesus and become saved, they must first hear the gospel that the church has custody of and is commissioned to take to them (Rom.10:9-10:9-14). We have already established that the church must be unified to do this work. Nothing aborts this mission assignment more effectively than a conflicted and divided church.

The work of the local church is not a Lone Ranger's job; it is teamwork. Jesus started His work of ministry by assembling a team around Him. He finally handed off the work to this team. The practice of handing off ministry work to the pastor, to few paid and volunteer staff is neither practical nor biblical. It is very old school. The days when the Parson does everything are long gone. Paul informs us that the Lord of the church has gifted the church with *apostles, prophets, evangelist, pastors and teachers*

(Eph.4:1-12). These are separate ministry offices, but some people are blessed and gifted with all five like the five-talent man. Perhaps, they can do all five excellently.

The five gifts or offices are often tagged, the five-fold ministry. But what is most important is the purpose of these ministry gifts. They are to be used to *equip, build up, and* bring to maturity the people of God, so they can *do the work of the ministry* (v.12). Here again the team ministry concept is reflected. Yes, the pastor must implement the vision and have the oversight of the work, but here he or she is also called upon to equip the entire church to do the work. Equipping them to resolve conflict is part of that ministry assignment. It will enable church members to practice their Christian duty of peacemaking and peacekeeping. Such approach positions the church to move together in unity as the Body of Christs; this is fundamental to everything else the church does.

Endeavoring to keep the peace and unity of the church at Philippi, Paul pleads not only with two fighting sisters to cease their combat, he also appeals to the whole congregation to help these sisters keep the peace. He calls them true yokefellows with him in gospel of peace (Phil.4:3). The picture given here is this—like oxen yoked together in one cause and purpose plowing a field, so are members of the local church; they are yoked together in the cause of Christ. And each member should pull his or her weight. There is no excuse for the *yoke* of Christ is *easy* but there is a learning process that we must all discipline ourselves to obey (Matt.11:29). If there is a learner there is a teacher.

For these and other reasons, this book advocates a lay ministry peacemaking and peacekeeping group at each local church. It is first and foremost *educational* and *practical*. Members learn certain educational content and put that content to practice. They live it out in their daily interaction with each other. I give the educational framework the functional name of *Resident Counsel* (RC). You may name yours something else, if you wish. But it is peace ministry that is based at your church. The RC is consisted of trained agents of peace, managers of conflicts, that are charged with educating the church in their peacemaking and peacekeeping duties, to resolve situations of conflict in the church, and prevent members and leaders from becoming destructive. The RC is made up of lay members, but it has pastoral supervision as all the ministries of the local church.

The pastor does not have to be in the hearth of conflict; he or she does not have to go to every church fight. If this dedicated ministry of lay leaders is doing their work right as agents of peace-managers of conflict, the pastor is relieved to use his or her energy to do other matters. The next chapter addresses the educational ministry of the RC more fully.

CHAPTER 4

A STRATEGIC PEACEMAKING PLAN

Every local church should invest in a peacemaking, peacekeeping ministry plan. In the previous chapter, we established that the uniqueness of the church in structure, polity, governance and mission warrants that we manage and resolve conflict at the local level, that the church cannot fulfill its mission to itself, the community and the world, if it is fragmented by conflict. This chapter shows that church conflict is a residential problem and it should be settled at the local level. Now, we look more closely at the nature of the plan that is the right fit and best suited for the task.

It is the argument of this author that the local church needs a conflict resolution plan to educate members in their Christian duties of peacemaking and peacekeeping, to help them resolve situations of conflict, to preserve the unity of the church from schisms, and guard the integrity of its message to the community and the world. That's the rationale.

Such a ministry plan should reflect these *ingredients*: ongoing biblically based peace education training for all members of the church, a dedicated rapid response team to manage and resolve conflicted situations, and an intentionally focused program to maintain the unity of the church and preserve the integrity of its witness to the community. These ingredients will not be discussed separately because each does not form a distinctive slice of the cake; they are mixed together to permeate the entire cake. Stated more succinctly and in a more discussion friendly manner, this dispute resolution plan for local churches has five pillars: it is *biblical, residential, educational, lay leadership driven,* and undergirded with *pastoral oversight.* These are the five pivotal hinges that this educational peace ministry swings. Each is further explored and discussed throughout this chapter.

The Plan Is Biblically Based

Not all Christian peace ministries are biblical; if it is not biblical, it is not authentically Christian and should not be a ministry in the church. The church is a divinely established institution with a unique global mission to reconcile people to God and each other (Matt.28:19-20; 2 Cor.5:17-21).

Jesus said, *on this rock, I will build my church*, and Peter informs us in his Pentecost sermon that *the Lord added unto the church those who were being saved* (Matt.16:18; Acts 2:47 NKJV). It is evident throughout the Scriptures that Jesus Christ came to reconcile us to God and to reconcile us to each other (Matt.5:23-24; Rom.5:1-6). For these and other reasons, the broad humanistic literature on conflict resolution and negotiation available today, is not suitable for the church's peacemaking and peacekeeping ministry. It is useful but on its own, it is not the right fit.

Having said that, let me hasten to say this—the secular, humanistic body of literature forms a worthy and useful knowledge base for a well-rounded Christian practitioner, though it cannot stand on its own for ministry purposes. Why is this so? The church is driven by a different set of values that are uniquely biblical and unapologetically Christian.

Authentic Christian dispute resolution, therefore, is not only anchored in Scripture, it runs on values that are reflected in biblical themes like: repentance, confession, forgiveness, reconciliation, love and mercy, the interest of others, restitution of property taken by fraud, and much more. To meet this need, Christian educators have generated their own body of literature rooted in Scripture and Christian experience to reflect Christian values. A purely secular or humanistic literature sprinkled with a few scripture verses won't do.

For this and other reasons, Christian universities, colleges, seminaries and divinity schools now offer dispute resolution courses for the church. But there is one major downside inherent in most of these programs. They are mostly offered at the graduate level and directed to the professional leadership of the church. They are not usually accessible to the regular lay person in the pews. That inaccessibility creates an educational gap that this book now seeks to bridge.

Christians, like other human beings, want to win in their endeavors of life. But, since they are tasked by God with the duty of loving their neighbors as they love themselves, winning cannot be purely self-centered; it must reflect the interests of others. In our justice and social justice relations, we are instructed to do “justly and to love mercy” (Micah 6:8). The mercy we desire for ourselves we must be willing to give to others. Jesus Himself teaches us, “Blessed are the merciful for they shall obtain mercy,” and to love our enemies, to bless and curse not (Matt.5: 43-48). Christian negotiation and peacemaking efforts, therefore, are uniquely different from the humanistic approaches of the unregenerate world.

But again, I must emphasize, the Christian dispute resolution peacemaker and peacekeeper practitioners would be foolish not to learn from the vast body of conflict resolution and peacemaking literature available. In fact, both the Christian and humanistic approaches have benefited from each other’s literature; we learn from them and they learn from us. Both sides respect the dignity of difference in the other's approach. Christian dispute resolution is value-drive and doxological; we practice this discipline to the glory of God. Apart from these two invaluable essentials, it cannot call itself Christian dispute resolution. Peace for the believer is profoundly redemptive.

The Plan Is Residential

Residential means, it is based at the local church; it is inhouse. Church conflict should be settled in the house, in the community of faith, among the people of God. Most business corporations, institutions and organizations of significance have inhouse dispute resolution systems as well.

Such system deals with workers' grievances, complaints, conflicts, so they don't get out of hand to the point of disrupting the smooth operation and productivity of the company. There are policies in place as guardrails to prevent certain behavior from happening. One such behavior is sexual harassment. Employees must stay within the guardrails of acceptable behavior and there is a mechanism to remind them of that. The system is there to prevent people from jumping tracks, and if they jump tracks, or accused of jumping tracks, the system manages that and bring it to resolution.

If the situation is beyond their inhouse resources, the system is still able to manage by getting the parties agree to refer the case to arbitration. Arbitration is generally an independent body representing the interests of both parties. Arbitration decision is generally binding and final. Organizations find it more cost effective using the arbitration system to settle intractable disputes rather than fighting them out in a court of law as a win-lose situation. Sometimes a case is already in court, and rather than go through a lengthy, expensive litigation process, the parties agree to settle it through the arbitration alternative.

Unfortunately, because most churches have no formal inhouse conflict resolution system (CRS), their common approach to conflict is reactionary because the organization is in crisis and must do something. This crisis response often takes one of two forms: leadership steps in to render a solution, and/or solution is imported from outside, usually a hired consultant. If the pastor is not the source of the conflict, now he or she is dragged into the hearth of conflict. This ad hoc, impromptu, off-the-cuff approach generally makes the situation worst, leading to the downsizing of a congregation, split and even loss of leadership. Why this approach does not work well and often left churches in a worse state?

First, because there are no dedicated, inhouse dispute resolution system with trained people, tasked with the responsibility of conflict management and resolution, grievances are left unaddressed until they reach crisis proportion. Intentionality has given way to ad hoc, reactionary approach. A thoughtful, preventive system in place is always better. It takes time to examine the problem within its context.

Second, the inhouse leadership that usually intervene is the pastor and/or board of elders or deacons. It throws the pastor who is already overworked in the hearth of conflicted situations. People have already stake out positions and the battle lines are already drawn. If the pastor or some respected elder is not well trained in dispute resolution, he or she is likely to take on an authoritative tone and posture which will serve as gasoline on an already combustible situation.

Third, by the time the church engages paid outside consultants to intervene, the damage is already done; some members have already left, or on the verge of leaving. The matter has already spilled over into the community to become the talk of the town, discussed on social media, and leadership tenure now hangs in the balance.

There are times that leadership saves the ship from sinking and they are to be credited for the respect, wisdom and skill they have garnered over the years. But most often leadership is not trained in dispute resolution. Trained lay leadership is indispensable in conflicted situations; they can serve as a firewall to pastoral leadership demise. The apostles of the early church deployed lay leaders to resolve the first serious conflict the church faced (Acts 6:1-7).

I have found that consultants brought in from outside to resolve church conflict can be very effective, helping churches navigate through difficult times. But there are three downsides why consultants have not made a significant impact, changing the culture of conflict bedeviling local churches. Here are the three downsides identified in the literature and experience: (1) As cited earlier, consultants are most often engaged when the situation already reached crisis proportion, when the damage is already done. (2) Consultants are effective, but too few to go around. (3) Peacemaking education is not high on the priority list of most local churches, so they don't budget for it.

The better approach is for each church to have its own trained conflict resolution counsel (CRC) in place. The CRC ministry or *Resident Counsel* can establish a relationship with consultants to come in once or twice a year with an all-members' workshop for the congregation and to sharpen the skills of CRC members. This way the local church can stay on the cutting edge of a vibrant peace ministry.

One key benefit to the local church having its own CRC is the fact that It is a *dedicated ministry* with *ongoing presence* managing and resolving conflicted situations, preventing them from derailing the church from its mission assignment. This sentence is loaded, so let's unpack it a little. I am using the term *dedicated ministry* in the same sense as when someone said, the fax machine is on a dedicated line. That line is not used for regular phone calls, so it cannot be busy because someone is on the phone. All this line does is to send and receive fax. The *Resident Counsel* is that dedicated, conflict resolution ministry for your church. You become good at what you practice.

The conflict management and resolution team of the local church is a body of five to seven people (depending on the size of the congregation). They are trained and tasked with the responsibility of dispute resolution ministry of the church. The team has *ongoing presence that is why it is called Resident Counsel.* The team members are trained as *Agents of Peace-Managers of Conflict.* They can spot conflicts in its early stages of formation and prevent them from becoming destructive to the organization. The team is accessible to the congregation, so Individual church members can come to them to address their grievances. This way the matter does not spread and infect the entire church body.

Ongoing presence means something. The New York Police Department (NYPD) gives us insight into this abiding presence concept. They report that an unoccupied police car left on the side of a highway has just about the same effect on drivers' behavior in reducing speed as the occupied police car. This method of policing is also confirmed in other areas of the country. Writing for the *Daily Comet,* Jean-Paul Arguello attest that the Thibodaux police in Louisiana deployment of "Ghost Units is not so dumb after all." This "high-visibility" approach to policing "reduced crashes 10 percent from the previous five years." The presence of a peace ministry in the local church, however, is more than a symbolic gesture of peacemaking. Residency truly matters! It has visibility, intentionality and proactivity working for peacemaking and peacekeeping as Christian duties.

The Plan Is Educational

A church conflict management system that is lay ministry driven, calls for a particular education mix that draws from both the science literature and the community of faith literature. Furthermore, the plan should be part of the total Christian education program of the local church. The focus should be on the acquisition of peacemaking and peacekeeping skills as well as Christian formation. Why Christian formation? Useful education involves head, heart and hands. Head is the intellect; the heart is love, compassion and mercy. Hands refer to doing or practice. Fervent spirituality is critical.

As stated earlier, secular organizations have their own conflict management system (CMS), but these systems are not the right fit for a church community in content and practice. However, they provide a useful knowledge base for the Christian practitioner. The church has a *theology of conflict, a different ethical process, training content and pedagogy*. The church's theology of conflict may be varied on the one hand, due to respective faith traditions, but unified on the other due to Christology. They all seek to anchor their peace theology in the peace theology of Jesus, which has much to do with Christian practice. It is a theology that expresses itself in love for God and neighbor (Mark 12:28-30).

Destructive church conflict is an inside job, because churches don't normally fall apart due to outside pressure. There is no institution that is prone to self-destruction as quickly as a church, especially if they sense hypocrisy in their leaders and each other. People will turn upon each other and upon their leaders in short order. Church people forgive but forgiving their own does not come easily. It appears forgiveness for those outside the church comes quicker and easier. For example, church members related to the Emanuel Nine, South Carolina church shooting, wasted no time to forgive the shooter that they had welcome to their Bible study. That church members find it more difficult to forgive their own, is an issue for further study, perhaps a dissertation.

The peacemaking effort should be part of the Christian education program and teaching ministry of the local church. In the *Great Commission,* Jesus commanded the church to make disciples, and the charge includes: "teaching them to observe all things that I have command you" (Matt.28:19-20 KJV). The Christian duties of peacemaking and peacekeeping are included in that command to teach. Perhaps, church folks fight because they were never taught peacemaking as a Christian duty. We just assume they already know that, but the culture of conflict in local churches says otherwise. Most church members have never had a workshop, a seminar, or any training in dispute resolution or peacemaking.

For that reason, this book comes with a curriculum (sold separately) to bridge that gap. The curriculum is called, *Agents of Peace-Managers of Conflict: Basic Training in the Resolution of Conflict for Local Churches*. The basic program is for the whole church. All members should take the course to advance their own peacemaking Christian duty at home, at work, and most certainly to help the church guard the integrity of its witness to the community and the world. Outsiders are not a threat to the church.

The church will choose five to seven members that complete the basic training to form what I call the Resident Counsel on conflict resolution, providing they meet other qualifications set by the church. Only large churches will need a seven-member counsel. The *counsel* members will go on to do the intermediate and advanced study as members of the counsel. They are trained as agents of peace-managers of conflict. Once this ministry is up and running, the church can say it has a conflict management system in place (CMS). It will deal with situations of conflict that rise in the church to the glory of

God. Like everything else, it will take time become proficient at this work.

The Plan Is Lay Leadership Driven

This section answers the overarching question, who leads the *Resident Counsel* team (RC) or Conflict Management System (CMS)? There are two choices of leadership: 1) the pastor-led conflict management system (PCMS), and 2) the lay-leaders conflict management system (LCMS). This book advocates for the lay leadership approach. I will show you why the pastor-led approach is not favored. But before we proceed, for the sake of clarity, CMS and Resident Counsel (RC) or dispute resolution team (DRT) are interchangeable names for the same group.

So, the conflict management system (or team) for the church are lay members. This CMS is not pastor-led in its daily activities for many reasons. Some of those reasons are highlighted in this section. It should also be noted that the CMS is not taking on the counseling ministry of the church. For example, if church members Susie and her husband Tom are having marital problems at home, that falls under the counseling ministry of the church. However, if Susie and Tom's behavior pose a scandal to the church, then her situation overlaps with the CMS as far as her membership and her office position in the church are concerned. The marital relation troubles go to the counseling ministry department.

Another example, a church member is upset because the board of deacons cancelled her week-end gambling trip to Las Vegas in the name of the church. Now, she and her group are angry and lining up supporters to make a big stink. Rather than the deacons fighting it out with them, the conflict management team picks up the case. The intervention provides counseling education concerning individual responsibility and the mission of the church. The mission, as stated earlier is doxological (to the glory of God). A church trip to Las Vegas that is missional is okay, but one for gambling could not be to the glory of God. We now turn a pastor-led CMS.

Why the pastor-led conflict management system (PCMS) is discouraged? First, pastors themselves are often what the rest of the church is fighting about, asserts Speed Leas. Leas argues that "the pastor finds it difficult, if not impossible, to get and keep enough distance to be helpful as the leader of the process for healing unless it happens on his or her terms." Leas prefer the pastor educate and teach from the pulpit, but delegate most of the conflict "educational and reconciliation [responsibilities] to capable leaders and members of the congregation" (Leas 2001, 20-44). Leas is not a singular voice on this issue; it is well documented in the literature that many a church conflict are caused by leadership. Some pastors have moved from showing authority to become authoritarian.

Perhaps, it is for this and other reasons John F. Halverstadt, a prolific writer and expert on church conflict, does not push the pastor in the center of conflicted situations, he prefers to draw upon the "communal power of conflict management" (Halverstadt 1991, 91). What does he mean by *communal power*? Halverstadt postulates that God has invested much in the congregation and that collective power should be drawn upon for dispute resolution. The core ingredient of conflict settlement is the paradox of "fighting for God's shalom" (p.189-99).

Drawing upon the communal power is important, that is why this book argues for educating the entire congregation in their peacemaking and peacekeeping duties. But you cannot always bring the entire congregation to settle a conflict, you must delegate that task to a capable small group. That is why this book further argues for a *Resident Counsel* of trained men and women in dispute resolution to take on that responsibility.

Second, a pastor-led conflict management system (PCMS) is discouraged, because pastors tend to lead or perceived to lead from a position of authority, God given and unquestioned authority some leaders tag it. Most church members don't accept the notion of unquestioned authority, so that alone is conflict producing. Inappropriate choice of words can inflame a situation just as wrong attitudes do. When tension is high, behaviors can be perceived as saying, "Who dare you question my authority!" Many clergy persons have unwittingly fallen into this authority trap with adverse outcome for the congregation and their own leadership tenure. An untrained and inexperience leader is walking on thin ice in a highly conflicted situation that can serve for his or her demise.

Yet, authority in leadership is indispensable but it will not serve you well in some conflicted situations. It is a two-edged sword, it can cut for you and cut against you at the same time. Speed Leas' observation, cited earlier, that *pastors find it difficult, if not impossible, to keep their distance to be helpful leaders of the healing process unless it happens on their terms* is an authority issue with two implications. For one, the pastor has too much at stake and operates from insecurity or from a position of "power" or "force." James Carter asserts that such power is often defined as "the measure of a person's potential to get others to do what he or she wants them to do, as well as to avoid being forced by others to do what he or she does not want to do" (Carter 1992, 79-88). Carter further asserts that conflict can be used "positively" for the greater good, but too often it is used for the "sake of power results from both the use and misuse of power." Misuse occurs when power is used to "manipulate," "control" and "intimidate people" (Carter 1992).

A third draw-back to a pastor-led conflict management system (PCMS) is *leadership style.* The twenty-first century, to a large extent, has adopted secular business models, titles and even the behaviors that accompany them in some cases. As a result, some pastors carry the title of CEO and behave in keeping with their secular counterparts from whom they borrowed the title. But although the church may use business principles, we have already established that it is unlike any other organization on earth. It is a divine institution and it has its own titles for its leaders clearly established in the New Testament of which CEO is not one.

Rick Warren asserts that "For twenty-five" years he "taught pastors that the church is a Body, not a business, an organism, not an organization!" Warren goes on to say that the church is a "family to be loved, not a machine to be engineered" or a company to be managed. Pastoring is an art. It has nothing to do with being a CEO. It's all about servanthood and authenticity and taking risk in faith" (Warren in Erwin Ralph McManus 2001, 6-7).

Warren is not alone in his position against church leaders assuming the title and behavior of CEOs. In responding to the Mars-Hill church leadership fiasco, Todd Pruitt posted a seven-point article about lessons pastors can learn from the disaster. Point number five said, "You are not a CEO." Pruitt argues that the "biblical metaphor of shepherd given the overseer of God's people" is used in both Testament and should not be "dismissed" for entrepreneurial convenience (Pruitt 2015).

The title CEO as a substitute for pastor, may sound innocent but one could argue that if the church has any chief, it would be Jesus Christ Himself. The apostle Peter to whom Jesus gave the keys of authority for the whole body of believers, identifies Jesus as the Chief Shepherd over His church; that makes pastors under-shepherds who are accountable to His higher authority (Heb.13:17; 1Pet.5:4). Secular CEOs are not accountable like that, so they can dismiss people without a second thought. Church work is more than a job and paycheck.

The fourth and final reason a pastor-led conflict management system (PCMS) is not the preferred approach—most pastors are already overworked or overextended. Conflict management and resolution is an emotionally exhausting and time-consuming process. It is a discipline that demands its own training and skills. The church will be better served, if this responsibility is designated to competent men and women from the congregation. A few decades ago, Arnold Kurtz of Andrew University wrote on pastors' overload in his article, "The Pastor as Conflict Manager." He recommends that the pastor workload be reduced or that conflict management be "institutionalized." I understand that to mean, other capable individuals of the congregation be charged with that responsibility.

The literature reveals that pastoral overload not only lead to conflicts of its own, it contributes to "fatigue" and "burnout" (Jenkins 2002). In a follow-up study done on pastor burnout, it was found that 74 percent of the 161 pastors who responded to the survey, related their greatest stress to excessive demands placed on their time; 47 percent felt drained carrying out their duties to their congregations, and labeled "interpersonal conflict" as exerting the highest toll on their leadership (Jenkins 2002). There is no question that burnout is a huge ministry problem today.

What are the arguments for a lay-leadership conflict management system approach? The converse of the four arguments against a pastor-led system can be used to support a lay-leaders' system, but rather than repeating them here, I will add few new ones.

First, a lay-leadership conflict management system (LCMS) anchors conflict at the root of the problem. Conflict is either sparked by leadership as "abuse from pathological ministers" (Greenfield 2003,149-64) or sparked by dissatisfied members, referred to as abusive members," "clergy killers," and "pathological antagonist" (Greenfield 2003, 23-43). For reasons cited earlier the middle of conflict is not the best place for the pastor to be. Destructive conflict is like a virus in the body; the whole body must take the responsibility to repel it. We repent, confess our faults or sin to one another and pray for one another that we might be healed (James 5:16).

It is evident from the literature that church conflict is an inside job. Church people have not been taught how to deal with conflict, how to protect the integrity of the gospel and the viability of their own local church organization. But, if a Resident Counsel of trained lay leaders is tasked with that responsibility, the congregation stand to be better served as the pastor focus his or her energy in other areas of service. This approach also anchors the solution where the problem is.

This concept of anchoring the solution where the problem is, may seem strange, and perhaps, you still don't see the point. Let's go at it another way. In Chapter 2, I stated that peacemaking and peacekeeping are Christian duties. That means, no member of the church is exempted from this activity. I illustrated the point by recalling when I was a healthcare professional in a major medical center and hospital. The policy of that institution then was "safety first," that safety was everybody's business. For that reason, all employees and staff members received the same safety training. You may be a surgeon but if you spot water on the floor, or a broken chair, or a piece of appliance with frayed electrical cord, you could not ignore it and say, that's not my job! Once you spot that unsafe situation, it becomes your job or duty to act. As a licensed Social Worker (when I was working as one), if a client reported to me that he is going to kill his wife, I had a professional duty to warn. In New York, the public duty toward terrorism is—it is everybody's business, so "If you see something, say something."

Back to the hospital illustration. In addition to all employees trained as safety first agents, the hospital also had a dedicated security staff, including a rapid response team. In like manner, the local church should train every member to carry out his or her Christian duties of peacemaking and peacekeeping, but at the same time, the church also needs a trained resident counsel of lay leaders to handle conflicted situations that could derail the entire ministry of the church.

Second, a lay ministry approach to conflict settlement follows the biblical mandate to equip the priesthood of believers to do the work of the ministry (1Pet.2:9; Eph.4:11-12). It is the ideal way to bring followers of Christ to Christian maturity. But the leadership of many churches have neglected to do so in peacemaking. It has never been a priority. The longstanding tradition in some mainline churches that only the pastor is called to do ministry is a long-discarded relic of the distant past, though some may still hold on to those dead dry bones. Peter refers to the priesthood of believers doing ministry with the oversight of one under-shepherd who is under the Jesus Christ the Chief Shepherd (1Pet.2:9). Educating believers in their peacemaking and peacekeeping duties come under the pastoral teaching ministry.

Third, a lay ministry approach to conflict settlement utilizes the gifts of church members to enhance the teaching role of the pastor (1Cor.12; Eph.4:7-13). Both passages cited here deal with spiritual gifts given to the Church by the risen, ascended Lord through the blessed Holy Spirit. All spiritual gifts are given for the edification of the church. The under-shepherd has the pastor-teacher a role to equip and guide the members into Christian maturity.

The Holy Spirit was poured out upon both male and female in the Upper Room at Pentecost, the birthday of the church. God ordained this day for a reason; Joel, the prophet spoke about it in his prophecy, implying that the entire church body is called to do ministry.

Fourth, the lay ministry approach to conflict provides residency. This is a point that much has been said already. Residency moves the church from just reacting to conflict in crisis to a more intentional and abiding approach. With residency dispute resolution is not a stopgap, quick fix, imported solution. With residency the solution mechanism is always there to prevent conflict from becoming destructive through education and leveraging the communal power of the community of faith. William Ury refers to this approach as the "Third Side" (Ury 2000, 7). For example, think of a street fight between two individuals or two groups—there is always a larger context of people looking on and often step in if things seem unfair or seriously getting out of hand; that's the third side.

Ury asserts that the conventional approach sees and treat conflict as two-sided, we versus them. But in reality, conflict is a three-sided phenomenon; "there are always others around...that constitute the third side of any dispute." The third side is the context or community; "it serves as a container for any escalating conflict." "Within the container...conflict can gradually be transformed from confrontation to cooperation" (Ury 2000, 7). If the third side can work for a street fight that is often unplanned, how much more will it work for the community of faith, where members have been trained to practice peacemaking as a Christian duty, plus having a resident counsel staffed with trained Agents of Peace-Managers of Conflict (APMC).

The Plan Has Pastoral Oversight

Since we have been discussing a lay leaders' conflict management system (LCMS) as the preferred approach over a pastor-led conflict management system (PCMS), you are probably asking, what then is the pastor's role? It has been loudly hinted and implied all along, but let's address it directly here to ensure there are no misunderstandings.

The pastor performs his or her usual function of under-shepherd, giving oversight to the flock. The pastor will preach and teach on the subject as necessary to equip the church to do the work of the ministry. The work of peace is part of that ministry the pastor needs to prepare the members of the church to do. The pastor will be instrumental getting the lay-leaders' dispute resolution ministry established and off training-wheels but will then handoff the day to day function of the resident counsel to its members. The pastor, however, retains the oversight function and is available to the counsel for consultation. The *counsel* will also brief him or her on any matter critical to the life of the church including matters that may threaten leadership tenure that he or she may be oblivious.

The relationship between the pastor and the counsel is close but has trusted distance. The congregation must have confidence in the counsel that it is not the pastor's puppet. The pastor must have confidence that the counsel that is mature enough to be an impartial broker of peace to the glory of God. It is not in the pastor's interest to dominate the counsel because the day will come when the pastor is in serious hot waters, and this impartial counsel must stand as the third side between him and the congregation. The *council* must be mature and independent enough to impartially stand in the gap.

A mayor of a city that strengthens the police, fire-fighters, the sanitation, the EMS and first responders, is a mayor that is ready to handle a disaster when it happens. But woe be unto that mayor and city, that weakens and demoralizes these institutions. That is the way the pastor should view his or her conflict management and resolution team. Through the pastoral preaching and teaching role, he equips them well for the work of the ministry to the glory of God.

Summary

In this chapter we have discussed a strategic peacemaking and peacekeeping plan for the local church. We have shown that such plan is indispensable preventing destructive conflict from tearing up the church and derailing it from accomplishing its mission assignment. The church should embrace a strategic plan and invest in a peacemaking ministry to resolve conflict, preserve church unity, and guard the integrity of its message to the community and the world. There is hardly a spiritual formation investment more important than this. It is designed to prepare and build up each member of the church to protect the ministry of the church rather than trashing it.

A peacemaking plan educates the entire church membership on their peacemaking and peacekeeping duties as Christians. The plan includes the establishment of a *Resident Counsel* of trained laypersons to resolve situations of conflict that may arise in the congregation from time to time. They are to manage these conflicts and bring them to resolution without derailing the ministry of the church.

The peacemaking plan rest on five pillars: it is biblically based, residentially located, educationally implemented, lay-leadership driven, and it has pastoral oversight or supervision. Substantial reasons are given why a lay leadership approach is preferred to a pastor-led approach to conflict. Chapter 5 explores the biblical precedence for this approach.

CHAPTER 5

CHURCH DISPUTE RESOLUTION PLAN: A BIBLICAL PRECEDENCE (OT)

Lawyers and judges painstakingly look for precedence in the glut of cases argued before the courts prior to their time, because they want to draw upon the wisdom of others who stood where they now stand. They are slow to establish new precedence, because precedence last for generations and serves as the basis for other decisions that will affect the lives of many. The God of the Bible is the God of precedence, so the wise will pay attention to what He has done in the past among His people and how He did it (Psalm 44:1-8). Precedence serves as examples to succeeding generations how their forefather dealt with certain situations. Each generation will set additional precedence for others that follow.

From the preface of this book, we have been making the case for a conflict resolution plan with residency, one that is led by lay members. Why so? Church conflict is an inside job and it should be settled in the house, in the community of faith, among the people of God. But to do that effectively, a dispute resolution system of trained lay leaders is need at the local church. We looked at the pastor-led approach and pointed out why that is not the best approach. So, we settled on a lay leadership model with pastoral oversight or supervision.

Since the whole word of God is the final authority for Christian life and practice, we now turn to the question, is there a biblical precedence for this lay leadership approach to dispute resolution? We will look at certain key passages in both Old and New Testament in our effort to answer this question. While we are doing that, we also want to keep our eyes opened to the context in which God wants disputes to be settled. *I argue that God wants dispute or conflict to be resolved in the context of justice but restrained by love and mercy in keeping with his nature.* You want to hold this point in your minds' eye as we speed through the Old Testament (OT). There will be many rabbits of distraction running across our path and the temptation will be to follow them. But we won't be able to go after them, we want to remain focus as possible.

CONFLICT RESOLUTION IN THE OLD TESTAMENT

As we search for a conflict precedence in the Bible, there are two ideas we will not waste valuable space to entertain, so let's address them now. First, the people group of antiquity that are most frequently addressed here is the ancient Hebrews. Second, some people say that *the cultures of the ancient world were most violent, tribal and brutal*. The implication is that we today are more human and civilized than they were. The counterargument is, they were no more violent and brutal than the cultures of our so-called civilized world and no less human. The supporting historical evidence is overwhelming.

The ancient word sacrificed their children to appease the gods; they did beheadings and such vile things. But by nature, is modern and postmodern humans any better? I don't think so! Look at the atrocities of World Wars I and II, Nazi Holocaust, the Korean War, the Khmer Rouge Killings Fields of Cambodia, the two Gulf Wars, the Rwandan Genocide, the Bosnian Genocide, the Darfur Genocide and the millions of babies being aborted each year, to name few inhuman behaviors. Now, are we any better than the cultures of antiquity in their brutality to their fellow humans?

History shows that by nature we are no better. We have invented more lethal methods to bring about the demise of our human neighbors, but on the surface, it doesn't appear to be so cruel after all. We can kill a million people long-distance with a couple of nuclear warheads fired from an aircraft traveling many times the speed of sound. Because we don't see the pictures, hear the cries, we convince ourselves how wonderful we are. That's one of the lies we choose to believe. We have only proven that educated humans, even with religion, is the worst savage earth has ever seen. Yet, if the savage is tamed or transformed by the gospel of pace, he can do untold good for his neighbors.

The second thing we do not have the space to entertain, is the idea that the God of the Old Testament (OT) was cruel and violent and very different from the God of the New Testament. This book rejects that characterization of the Hebrew and Christian God. There is one loving, just and merciful God of both Testaments. The earth is His and all that dwell on it; He is the true Landlord and we are the tenants (Ps.24:1-2). When we defy His laws long enough and refuse to repent, He retains the right to evict us off His property by all necessary means and give it to other tenants of His choosing. We see this scenario at work in the OT. That does not make God cruel; it affirms His Justice, and His justice is always restrained.

Without question, God is righteous and just in all His ways and He wants humans to reflect these qualities of His to their neighbors. Jonah's knowledge of God's passionate caused him to refuse to go to Nineveh freely. He feared that his preaching would cause the Ninevites to repent and God would not destroy them (Jonah 4:1-3). The prophet Micah (6:8), among others, articulates God's requirement for us to "do justly, love mercy and walk humbly" before Him. But only people who have had a transforming experience of redeeming grace are truly capable of reflecting God's nature and become the salt and light God wants them to be in this world.

Insights from Family Conflicts

How then did godly people handle conflict under the Old Covenant, in the family units, and in the larger community of faith? Are there insights New Covenant people can glean from their approach to dispute resolution? These are the two fundamental questions that our Old Testament (OT) inquiry seeks to answer. We will not and cannot track down every family dispute and every dispute within the community of faith. Instead, we will look at few relevant stories to make the case.

The first conflict in the OT is a family dispute that implicates God Himself. The first family, our ancestral parents is unique above all families; they had no birth, infancy or childhood as we know these growing up stages of life. They started as adults, created with God's image and likeness. God was their parents, so they carried His DNA of mother earth and Father God as we bear the DNA of our parents.

They were mandated like everything else created, to reproduce after their kind. They would reproduce sons and daughters to rule over the earth for God. They were a righteous family, commissioned to rule under God and for God. For this reason, God slightly restricted them by a clear command what they were free to do and not do. They had a spoken law with a visible reminder (the word and the tree). When free moral agents have laws—that sets the stage for potential conflict, because a law is the intersection where two wills meet, the lawmaker's and that of the subject. In this case God and man.

Freedom without restriction is anarchy; rules are guardrails to keep people safe. Nonetheless, the first family chose to ignore the divine command. And by doing so they became rogues against God. They knew what the consequences of their disobedience would be before they acted. They were commanded not to eat of a certain tree, because they would die. By ingesting the fruit of a certain tree, it would reset their genetic makeup and change them into creatures of death and dying (Gen.2:16). A law can be the point of conflict between lawgiver and the one who is to obey the law.

Adam and his wife--their behavior brought them in conflict with God. The woman blamed the serpent for her behavior. The man said to God, "the woman you gave me" made me do it. The implication is obvious—God, you bear some responsibility for this because you gave me the law and this woman. The truth is, the man and his wife violated divine law and became a rogue with Satan (Gen.3:1-7). In love and mercy, God dealt with them. He covered their nakedness, punished the serpent, gave the man and the woman promise of redemption (Gen.3:15). He then expelled them from the garden. The expulsion was an act of mercy for without it, they would have eaten of the tree of life and live forever in their miserable, sinful state (vv.22-24). That would have been living hell on earth.

What is the conflict resolution lesson here? God is Almighty, but he limits Himself by His word. He could not revoke death and let them off the hook; God is holy and just. When God speaks, His word becomes law. God cannot violate His own law, but He can act in love and mercy and that's exactly what He did. God was setting a precedence for the administration of justice as we will see later. Again, expulsion from the garden was an act of mercy toward God's most exalted creature, and it was done in the context of justice restrained by mercy. Justice and mercy are qualities God require in human relationships. But note a second thing, the garden debacle was a family conflict; God is the parent.

Family conflict two, Cain killed his brother Abel. Cain was a cold-hearted, unrepentant murderer; he was quick to take life that he did not and could not give. He settled a family conflict destructively and with a weapon. God held him accountable; tried him and gave him life sentence. Cain pleaded for mercy, mercy that he did not give to his brother. And God showed him mercy by not immediately taking his life but giving him life sentence instead. Cain was given time to reflect, repent and cry-out for mercy.

What is God doing here? On the one hand, He is giving Cain what we call today, due process. On the other hand, God is upholding the sanctity of human life and laying the foundation that the administration of justice must be restrained by mercy, no matter how little that mercy may be. These themes of the sanctity of human life, justice and mercy run through the entire Old Testament (OT).

Family conflict three, Abraham and his nephew Lot. Lot's father was Abraham's brother (Gen.12:4-5). When he died, Uncle Abraham took Lot under his care and gave the young man a start in life. When God called Abraham to leave his kin folks and hometown, he took Lot with him. As Abraham prospered, Lot prospered. Eventually, they both had a sizable herd with herdsmen to care for them. It so happened that quarrel broke out between the herdsmen of Abraham and the herdsmen of Lot. From the implications of the story, Lot's group appears to be the aggressors, and the matter had the potential to escalate and get really ugly. But Abraham acted as a righteous, godly man supposed to act, graciously. His action is memorialized in history as an example to us all. He called his nephew aside and said to him, "Let there be no quarrel between you and me or between your herdsmen and mine for we are brothers" (Gen.13:8-9). Abraham had a nobility Cain did not have.

Abraham resolved the matter by not looking to his own interest alone but to the interest of his nephew. He said, our herds have become too great for us to stay together, we must separate. The land is before you pick your choice, if you go to the right, I will go to the left. If you choose the left, I will go to the right. Lot picked the best pastureland, the plains of Jordan. But there is this little caveat in the text that worth noting: "and he pitch his tent toward Sodom" (Gen.13:10-13).

They parted company without animosity, and they remained friends and family. Before we continue, I must emphasize these three conflict resolution principles in the story: 1) Abraham resolved conflict by looking not only to his own interest but to the interest of others (his nephew). 2) They parted company without animosity, holding no grudge, and 3) Abraham resolved conflict doxologically (that is to the glory of God). After Lot left, God appeared to Abraham and renewed his covenant with him (Gen.13:14-18). God was pleased with the way Abraham conducted himself. Do you take the interest of others into consideration in a dispute? This is one golden key in dispute resolution you should never forget.

Lot prospered but one day trouble came knocking. His tent was no longer pitched toward Sodom. He was now dwelling in Sodom, not in a nomad's tent but in a house. He was a resident of some stature. Perhaps, a respected judge who sat with other judges at gate of the city to settle disputes. On one occasion Sodom was overrun by a coalition of ten king and their armies, and the best of Sodom was taken including Lot, his family and all his belongings.

Uncle Abraham got news of this hostage taking of his nephew and family. He armed nearly 400 servants in his camp to go after them. He overtook them, won the victory and brought back Lot, his family and all his belongings. *Abraham is teaching by his life that righteous people don't keep grudges*. But that's not the only downturn and reversal of fortune that happened to Lot. Sodom and her adjacent sister city of Gomorrah were exceedingly wicked. It is hard to say why Lot did not relocate. Perhaps, he was heavily invested there. The Bible said his righteous soul was vexed due to the wickedness of Sodom (2 Peter 2: 6-9).

Before God destroyed the twin city, He visited Abraham and informed him what he was about to do (Gen.18). Abraham began interceding for the twin city with his nephew in mind. When he said to God, be it far from you to destroy righteous with the wicked, he was clearly thinking about his nephew. God agreed that if fifty righteous people were found, he would save Sodom. Abraham continued praying as if he were negotiating with God. He moved God to reducing the number from fifty to forty-five, then to forty, then ten. God agreed, if ten righteous were found He would save the city. Ten righteous were not found but God gave His word to Abraham to protect his nephew and family. Angels had to physically drag them out of the city to save their lives. Lot loss a lot of material possession when he fled Sodom, but that can be replaced (Gen.19:15-28). Thanks to a praying uncle that did not keep grudges.

Family conflict four, Abraham and his wife Sarah. Lot made a poor choice when he moved his family into Sodom. Now, Abraham is about to make a poor choice that will lead to a generational conflict for thousands of years. Despite God's promise of a child, Sarah could not see how an aged, barren woman as she with an aged husband could have a child. She felt surrogate parenting would be the way to go. She gave her Egyptian maid, Hagar, to her husband to impregnate and bear a child for her. Surrogacy was not immoral or illegal at the time, but it was not in God's will for Abraham and Sarah. Abraham should have said, no, to sleeping with Hagar but he did not. Hagar gave birth to a son whom they named, Ishmael. Hagar reneged on the agreement and kept her child. She used her son to advance her status in Abraham's eyes to the provocation of Sarah. This developed into a serious family conflict.

Eventually, Sarah indeed got pregnant with the child God had promised her. The child was named Isaac. In the process of time, Sarah went ballistic and demanded that her husband send away the slave woman and her child because she saw Ishmael conducting himself in what many Hebrew scholars believe to be a vulgar manner toward Isaac. Abraham resisted this painful demand but compromised when God stepped in and told him to listen to what his wife said. Abraham was faced with what we would call an ethical choice, a value conflict. A value conflict is a choice between two significant values. In this case, pleasing his wife and throwing out his son and son's mother. He had to choose between two evils. There is no good choice here, somebody has to compromise. When God stepped in on Sarah's side Abraham had to agree to a painful compromise. As hard as this compromise may seem; the conflict was settled doxologically. That is, to the glory of God.

Family conflict five, Jacob and Esau, Isaac and Rebekah. This became another generational conflict that is still impacting Middle Eastern cultures today. Abraham's son Isaac married a woman named, Rebekah. She had twin boys, Jacob and Esau. The fight between these two boys started in the womb. They were kicking and prancing to the point of great concern to Rebekah. She inquired of God as to what was going on inside of her. God told her that two nations were inside of her and the older would serve the younger. Esau was born first, and Jacob came second, clutching on to Esau's heal as if they were competing who gets born first (Gen.25:21-26). The first born of course is the heir and gets the birthright, the lion's share of the father's estate. That was the tradition and cultural norm. But Esau in the process of time made a childish trade but with great significance; he sold his birthright to Jacob for a bowl of stew. Selling the birthright is one thing, collecting it was another.

Since the birthright blessing is formally transferred by the father when he is close to death, how on earth Jacob is going to get what he paid for? Since, he is Rebekah's favorite and God already told her Jacob will rule over Esau, she came up with a deceptive scheme of how Jacob could trick his aged, vision impaired father and extract the blessing from him. With the help of Rebekah Jacob cleverly disguised himself as his brother Esau. The father thought he was blessing Esau when in fact it was Jacob in disguised. God intended Jacob to be the bearer of the covenant and did not need this deception to accomplish His will. Did a deception land Jacob in God's will? Technically, yes! But it will have grave consequences. It started a multigenerational conflict between the two brothers and their families.

Immediately after Jacob got the blessing, Esau came and went into his father to get the birthright blessing of his life, only to find out he was tricked out of it. He wept bitterly! From here onward he was determined to kill his brother Jacob for deceiving his father and getting the blessing by fraud. But clever Rebekah perceived the danger to Jacob's life and pre-emptively sent him away to stay with Uncle Laban. She calculated that when Esau's murderous wrath cools off, she could send for Jacob to come on back home. But Jacob found love and a life of his own and felt no urgency to return home. He was with Laban for over twenty years. Uncle Laban, a master deceiver himself, took Jacob in his employ for cheap. He exploited the young man. But his deception was a blessing in disguise for Jacob.

In later years conflict developed between Laban and Jacob. Jacob became Laban's son-in-law, but that old geezer deceived Jacob badly. In his attempt to cheat Jacob, Laban changed his salary agreement with Jacob ten times in twenty years. He tried hard to keep the young man poor, so he could keep him slaving for Laban. But God favored Jacob and prospered him greatly despite Laban's unjust dealings. Jacob's prosperity earned for him strong resentment from Uncle Laban.

The resentment was so strong, Jacob began to fear for his own safety. He gathered his wives and children, possessions and servants and left without giving Laban prior notice. Laban came home one evening and Jacob was gone with his two daughters and the grandchildren. Intending to do Jacob harm, Laban armed a group of men and went after Jacob. But God appeared to Laban in a dream and told him, tomorrow when you overtake Jacob be sure you don't say good or bad to him. In other words, look old geezer, I have that young man covered, so you touch Jacob, and you answer to me. Laban got the message, so he was forced to part with Jacob on mutual terms. What's the conflict resolution lesson here? Some conflicts are settled by fight or flight. Perhaps, flight was Jacob preferred conflict style, he used it with his brother and twenty-two years earlier, he used it again with his uncle.

Family conflict six, Jacob's daughter, Dinah, is raped. Dinah went out for a walk and the leader of a nearby community took her into his house and forced himself upon her. He told Jacob that he loves his daughter and wants his permission to marry her. This ethnic group was not Israelite like Jacob, they were uncircumcised. Jacob agreed to the marriage under one condition, they become circumcised as the Israelite community. They agreed but Jacob's son did not go along with their father's compromise, but they kept quiet. When the whole community of men were circumcised and healing, two of Jacob's son, Simon and Levi, strapped their swords on and slaughtered every male in that community and carried off their possessions for treating their sister like a prostitute (Gen.34:1-31). What is the conflict resolution lesson in this?

Jacob *mediated* and *compromised*, but his attempt at resolution failed because his sons did not agree. Jacob did not ask them about their feelings on the matter and they kept quiet. They wanted revenge to vindicate the honor of their sister. When you mediate for a group be sure to get everyone on board; all must agree with the terms and negotiated outcome.

Family conflict seven, Joseph and his brothers. This conflict evolved out of sibling rivalry and developed into hate and attempted murder. Joseph's brothers hated him for two basic reasons: 1) He was loved by his father who gave him a special coat as an expression of that love; Joseph reciprocated by being a tattletale on his brothers. 2) Joseph received special dreams from the Lord with leadership significances. The brothers thought that the paternal preference positioned Joseph to get the lion's share of their father's inheritance and his dreams of them bowing down to him confirmed their fears.

The brothers knew Joseph was destined to rule over them and they were going to have none of it. By an act of providence, they did not kill him because a better alternative presented itself. They sold him into slavery. These brothers colluded together to lie to their parents about their younger brother's whereabout. To make the lie more convincing, they killed a young goat, and soaked Joseph's special coat in the blood. They took home the bloody coat as proof that some wild animal destroyed their brother. They had their parents believing this lie for over twenty years until they were exposed.

Having suffered slavery and imprisonment—by an act of providence, Joseph was fast-tracked to the pinnacle of executive power as the prime minister of Egypt. It was now in his power to exact revenge on his brothers for their cruelty to him when they came down to buy food to survive a famine. Joseph refused to take retributive justice against his brothers. He forgave them with these words, "You intended to harm me, but God intended it for good to accomplish what is now done, the saving of many lives" (Gen.45:3-9,50:15-26). *What is the conflict resolution lesson here?*

Here we see the themes of forgiveness and reconciliation. Later, we will discuss these themes, among others, as core Christian values in dispute resolution. Joseph did not excuse his brother's wickedness, but it was not his wish to be revengeful. He could see that God was already rendering justice to his brothers. Joseph reflecting God's *Sholom,* chose not to revenge himself; he showed the character of God in the context of love, justice and mercy. Joseph is a type of Christ, betrayed by his brothers, sold by his own, but prayed for their forgiveness.

Moses And the Exodus

Conflict resolution is about fairness and justice. Without question, God is just but humans may not consider all His dealings toward them fair. God administers justice throughout His kingdom, but He greatly restrains His administration justice with mercy. His does not always meet out justice equal to what we truly deserve. As our loving heavenly Father, He spares us from the punishment we deserve, for our feeble frame He knows. Furthermore, He wants us to do the same—to be just in our dealings to our fellow humans, balancing justice with mercy.

Because God is just, a false balance is abominable to Him, but a just weight is His delight (Prov.11:1). God abhors the behavior of employers cheating their employees and the mighty oppressing the weak or the rich taking disadvantage of the poor (James 5:1-7). These are injustices that give birth to conflict, violence and war. Where injustice prevails, now and then, God overtly steps in through a human agent or an act of nature or both to remedy the situation. That was the case when the mighty Egyptian empire had a prolong brutal enslavement of the Israelites. He saw the injustice, He heard their cries, and He came down to deliver, using Moses as agent (Exod.3:7-10).

Conflict Between Moses and the Pharaoh

The emancipation of Hebrew slaves was a conflict between the king of Egypt and the King of the Universe, a conflict between created gods and the one Almighty God. Moses was God's agent of peace, but pharaoh was not willing to cooperate, so God had to prod him into compliance. The process of liberation was a teachable moment for all. God demonstrated His awesome power and glory yet by mercy restrained Himself, so as not to utterly destroy Egypt. Centuries later, Egypt became a place of refuge for the Christ child who grew up to model through life and death the true mercy of God (Matt.2:13-21; 5:7). The bridge you did not destroy yesterday, may save your life tomorrow when you are on the run.

The Israelites did not leave Egypt empty handed; that too was a form of justice. God ensured that they got some reparation for the decades of slave labor building the economy of Egypt. This is indeed a compelling insight into God's administration of justice that nations that retain slaves can learn from. Perhaps, that was what America intended after the emancipation of black slaves when they promised forty acres of land and a mule, but such reparation never came to fruition. The government of Egypt did not suddenly have a change of heart and voted in a cabinet meeting to give Hebrew slaves reparation or did the Pharaoh issue an executive order on the matter. It was forced upon them; God Himself decided that Israel was not leaving Egypt empty handed. It was the administration of God's justice that produced the reparation outcome. But note that God's justice was restrained by mercy; He gave reparation to Israel without utterly destroying Egypt for their cruelty. Throughout Israel's history, God used the experience of their servitude to remind them how to treat the strangers among them.

Dispute Resolution Delegated

We now turn to one of the most phenomenal dispute resolution models in Israel's biblical history; it is a gift to the world to this day. Moses was not an ignorant man. He had what is equivalent to university education and a West Point Military Academy training; he understood geography and mathematics. He was also educated in the ways of the common people. For God's work, He was an ordained minister and a prolific writer. We are still reading the five books he authored today. He knew God face to face and spoke to Him as a man speaks to his friend. He was well equipped for his job assignment.

But in spite of his extraordinary qualifications, Moses set out to do something that was greatly flawed after all. He single-handedly tried to resolve disputes for nearly two million people. He took his seat as judge from morning to evening, people stood in line all day in the desert sun waiting to get their cases heard. He was an aged man, well over eighty years of age, but he lacked the insight on leadership delegation that was necessary to make life easier for him and his people. It was a contemporary of his that made this observation on his leadership and recommended a change.

Moses' father-in-law, Jethro, visited him and immediately observed that something was wrong with this picture. Frankly, he was dumfounded that such a brilliant man who personally knew God could be doing such a foolish thing. Well intended but foolish. Jethro observed that Moses was wearing himself out and making things unnecessarily difficult for his congregation.

Jethro counseled Moses, pointing out to him that his singular approach of mediation or dispute resolution for so large a community was greatly flawed. It was not only exasperating for his people; he would suffer burnout in short order. Moses' approach was not sustainable. Jethro acknowledged God's mighty power, but counseled Moses to "select capable men from all the people—men who fear God, trustworthy men who hate dishonest gain—and appoint them as officers over thousands, hundreds, fifties, and tens. Have them serve as judges for the people at all times but have them bring every difficult case to you; the simple cases they can decide themselves." Jethro continued, by doing it this way with God's approval, "that will make your load lighter, because they will share it with you" (Exod.18:13-23).

Moses, the man of God, listened to his father-in-law's wise counsel, adopted and implemented the Jethro dispute resolution model (VV.24-27). With the codification of the law later, the plan was fully and officially implemented (Deut.1:5-15). Author, Max May observes that Jewish law has both the fingerprints of God and man (May 1940). Our Western jurisprudence with its lower, upper and supreme court litigation of disputes finds in roots in the Hebrew Bible.

What insights can be drawn from Jethro's recommendation to inform our inquiry on dispute resolution for the people of God in the twenty-first century? Moses can be viewed as the ordained pastor, the professional minister with oversight of the entire flock of God. But God resides not only in the pastor but in the entire community of faith. The people in Moses' congregation knew this all along; they even thought,

Moses took too much upon himself and that caused conflict between them and him from time to time. Community of faith members have skills, talents and gifts that can be drawn upon for the edification of the body of Christ. That was the essence Jethro tried to communicate to Moses. Jethro observed that Moses' own health was also at risk, if he insisted on carrying all that load by himself. Today, we call this health risk, burnout. Many pastors and ministry leaders have succumbed to burnout due to ministry overload. The priesthood of believers can be equipped to do the work of ministry. They are not saved to be pew sitters but to bear witness of Jesus Christ (Acts 1:8).

Moses was humble enough to take counsel from a man not identified among the covenant people or coming from the academy but out of the bush; in itself, a teachable lesson for ministry elite. It suggests that no pastor needs to carry the load of the ministry all by himself or herself. No matter how gifted or anointed the leader of God's people may be, the Jethro dispute resolution model is a humbling and teachable example of judicial delegation and leadership.

Finally, Moses' approach to dispute resolution was individualistic, but Jethro's was communal. The lay community can be trained and mobilized according to their personal integrity and giftedness to resolve situations of conflict and keep the peace. No pastor needs to shoulder this task singlehandedly. After all, peacemaking and peacekeeping are

Christian duties; they are the responsibility of the entire community of faith.

Dispute Resolution Institutionalized

With the formal giving of the Law, the Jethro model of dispute resolution was fully adopted as a divine command and thereby institutionalized as the model. Moses recounted how this ministry delegation happened to the next generation (Deut.1:9-18). Undoubtedly, it was God Himself who endowed Jethro with such wisdom because when you compare the counsel he gave to Moses to the preceding passage, they are exactly the same (Exod.18:13-23).

The Torah deals with the individual, communal, spiritual, and social responsibility of the people toward God and toward their fellow Israelites, including the stranger among them. People were not allowed to take matters in their own hand and punish anyone without due process. To a large extent, the Mosaic moral law became the basis of jurisprudence in the civilize world, especially the Western world. It influenced the formation of the United States Constitution. Justice cannot be justice unless the law is viewed and understood in a moral context (Dworkin 1997, 1-25). Only a God who is moral can issue laws that are moral; the Torah reveals the moral character of God, His justice and mercy.

The Law mandated that six Cities of Refuge must be established throughout the land of all Israel (Num.35:6, 9-34). They were safe places where those guilty of manslaughter could flee and find protection from families who were hot for revenge without due process. These safe places gave refuge to the offender and opportunity for angry people who were wronged to cool off and think rationally until the investigation and due process were completed. If the death was accidental, the offender would be acquitted but had to stay in the City of Refuge until the reigning High Priest died, then he could return home. However, if the perpetrator was found guilty of premeditated murder, he would be taken from that safe place and be executed. Sanctuary cities in the United States find their roots in the biblical Cities of Refuge but have greatly departed from the original purpose.

Furthermore, the City of Refuge as part of the institution of judicial proceedings, was an attempt to mirror the moral character of God, showing that He is just and merciful. These cities also illustrate God's preferred way of resolving conflict, that He wants conflict settled in the context of justice restrained by love and mercy. The one word that captures this moral and ethical character of God for His people is *Sholom* (Scotts1973, 97-98).

The Torah, therefore, reflects the character of God as holy, just, benevolent and true, and reflects the nature of man as sinful. The law was God's ideal standard to which people would strive to reflect the nature of God more perfectly. John Willis observes that the Old Testament is rooted in "social justice" based on three timeless principles: the sameness of human nature throughout the ages, the unchanging nature and character of God, and the fact that the way God acts among men, and the way he expects them to treat their fellows are basically the same" (Willis 1975, 65-87).

The period of the Judges clearly depicts how Israel, the people of God, was still a loose confederacy of twelve tribes held together by the Torah and the institution of the Priesthood. They frequently fell below God's required standard and enemy nations were raised up by God to chastise and move them to repentance and restoration, every time they cry out for deliverance. Samuel, the last of the judges, was not only a judge but God's prophetic voice, priest and moral arbiter to his people. He anointed both kings, Saul and David, for the throne. So, Samuel transitioned Israel to the establishment of a new institution, the monarchical period, the office of the king. The king was required to follow the Torah closely; the success of his leadership was dependent on his obedience to God.

The institution of the priesthood had custody of the Torah, the administration of worship, approving health certification and resolution of certain family disputes. The godly kings like David and Solomon, at times, acted priestly and prophetically, but the priesthood and the office of the prophet were separate institutions from that of the king. The king could not usurp the prerogatives of those offices without serious repercussion to his reign. Saul stepped out of line when he disobeyed Samuel's instructions; he lost his throne and his life. David behaved wickedly when he committed adultery with Bathsheba and had her husband killed (2 Sam.11). God rebuked the king through Nathan the prophet (2 Sam.12). Like Saul, David would have lost his throne, but he humbled himself and sincerely repented and God took note of it (Psalm 51).

Unlike David, King Uzziah tried to usurp the office of the priesthood and was resisted by a group of priests. Rather that humbling himself and back away, he escalated the conflict and God stepped in and struck him with leprosy. He lost not only the throne but his life (2 Chron.26:16-21).

The king settled some domestic disputes. King Solomon's signature dispute resolution was the two women claiming to be the mother of the same child; when Solomon drew his sword to cut the child in two, one mother screamed and agreed to give the child to the other woman. Solomon concluded that the mother that screamed and was willing to give up the child to spare his life was the true mother. She got the whole baby. Dispute resolution requires knowledge and wisdom. The kings of Israel were more concerned with national security, so they dealt with conflicts involving other nations.

The Sum of the Matter

Destructive conflict has been a besetting sin for godly people since the paradise garden; no human being, no family, tribe, holy place or nation has been free of conflict. Adam, Abraham, Jacob's family, Moses, David, prophets, priests and kings, all had to learn how to manage and resolve situations of conflict. Some did well and reaped the fruits of peace and good relations, others failed and suffered the consequences of bad relations, violence and war.

We have observed that God wants His people to live in peace and enjoy good relations with Him and with their neighbors. God wants conflict settled in the context of justice, restrained by love and mercy in keeping with His holy, just and righteous nature. God gave His word: Torah, Prophecy, Writings as the standard for his people. He established institutions to help bring disputes to resolution: family, Priesthood, Cities of Refuge, prophetic ministry, elders and kings. The role of all these institutions was to bring the people of God in good relationship with God and their fellow humans.

The prophet Isaiah in his thundering diction announced what God wants from His people: "Stop doing wrong, learn to do right! Seek justice, encourage the oppressed, defend the cause of the fatherless, plead the case of the widow" (Isa.1:17). The prophet Micah sums up what God wants of His people: "He has shown you, O man, what is good. And what does the LORD require of you? To act justly and to love mercy and to walk humbly with your God" (6:8). Did the Old Testament with all its institutions achieve God's ideal? No, but it shows us that God wants human conflict settled in the context of justice restrained by mercy to reflect His nature; by so doing, dispute resolution will indeed be doxological; that is, to the glory of God.

Second, we learn from Abraham how a godly man can settle a family conflict by not just looking to his own interest but the interest of others. We learned much from Jacob and his family both negative and positive. Jacob seeks to resolve conflict using the avoidance mechanism of flight instead of fight. When his own daughter was raped, Jacob became the mediator and negotiated accommodation with the rapist but did not consider the feelings of his sons. It ended in disaster because accommodation reached did not reflect the interests of all the stake holders. Joseph teaches us the role of forgiveness in dispute resolution. These themes will be discussed again and again through this work.

Third, we learn supremely from Moses and his father-in-law, Jethro. Moses shows us the individualistic way of settling disputes and the accompanying risks. This approach has the huge downside of being time consuming and could lead to worker burnout. Jethro teaches, the *delegation* and *communal* approach to dispute resolution. Jethro shows us that lay-leaders and the congregation have a significant role to play resolving conflict in a congregation. This is a significant and leading precedence for the community of faith for all times.

CHAPTER 6

SETTLE IT IN THE HOUSE: A Biblical Precedence (NT)

Let us do a quick review before we move forward. This book advances a conflict resolution approach that has residency at the local church; it is a dedicated ministry run by lay leaders. It is not pastor-led but has pastoral oversight or supervision. It educates the entire church membership in their Christian duties of peacemaking and peacekeeping. It manages and resolves situations of conflict that rise in the church, thus preventing conflict from becoming destructive, fracturing the unity of the church and derailing it from its mission assignment. This team of trained lay leaders is referred to as the *Resident Counsel*. The members of the counsel are trained as *agents of peace—managers of conflict*; they seek to safeguard the church and the integrity of its message to the community and the world.

We have examined the Old Testament to see if there is any precedence for such approach to dispute resolution. In our examination, we found Moses doing what is equivalent to a pastor-led approach to dispute resolution. He single-handedly tried to resolve the dispute for a massive congregation of over a million people, a task that would have surely led to the condition we now refer to as burnout. His father-in-law wisely counseled him to do it differently by using lay leaders to share the load of the ministry (Exod.18). The Jethro Plan was sanctioned by God and adopted (Deut.1:5-15). We now turn our focus to the New Testament (NT) to see if we can find a precedence there as well, using the chapter title, *Settle it in the House.* Why such a title?

I never had the privilege of seeing my mother and father fight or had a serious argument. They had disagreements now and then, but to this day I have no idea who won, because it never came across as a win-lose conflict. There was no prolong argument because my mother's words were always few. My father was not the argumentative type, so he would briefly express his dissatisfaction and the matter was over. My mother generally kept quiet, so both of them would never speak at the same time.

Many years later after my father's death, a few of us adult children confronted mother as to why she kept quiet. She said, it takes two to argue, so if one kept quiet there was no fuel to feed the argument, it must die. "No matter the disagreement, we would never go to bed without settling the matter, so it always got *settled in the house*."

My mother and father were really good together; they had twelve children and raised eleven. I used to hear people back then say, "what happens in this house stays in this house." This statement has an upside and a downside. On the downside, the statement could represent a family philosophy of secrecy, used as a justification to coverup abuse, incest, domestic violence and a world of dysfunctional family behaviors. But on the upside, it could be a healthy practice for healthy families with almost biblical implications. For example, the apostle Paul instructed the church at Corinth to settle their disputes in the church among the believers, not among pagan unbelievers in the public law courts (1Cor.6:1-8). In this chapter, we will learn that settling conflict in the church house can teach profound, positive, biblical lessons. The practice can unify the church, even move a congregation to a higher level of spiritual maturity. We will return to this concept later.

The New Testament (NT) teaching on the resolution of conflict can be arranged into two broad interdependent categories: the life and teachings of Jesus, and the teachings of the apostles and the early Church. The word *interdependent* is very important here because the Bible is like a brick house, each brick reinforces the other. If you remove the fall of man in

Genesis, then there is no human sin to necessitate redemption and the coming of a Savior to die. So, there goes the resurrection and the second coming of Christ. The whole thing would just fall apart.

This would also be true with most biblical themes, including a God of peace seeking to resolve disputes among His people. Peace and peacemaking are not New Testament (NT) inventions. The God of the Hebrew Bible is introduced to us as a relational Being and He created humans in His image and likeness. There is a particular way God wants humans to relate and He began laying the foundation principles in the Torah as we have already seen. That is where we first encounter love for God and neighbor. Shalom was practiced by the people of God long before the apostles. The New Testament has taken those principles and advanced them many steps forward for the new life in Jesus Christ. In other words, the whole Bible is the self-disclosure of One God, the unfolding of one revelation. It fits together as the pieces of one puzzle; if you remove any part, the puzzle is unsolvable and makes no sense at all.

The Life and Teachings of Jesus

The New Testament Church started as a local Jesus movement in first century Jerusalem. It later conquered the Roman Empire and became a global institution. This was inevitable because the mission statement of the Church embraces a global vision

(Matt.28:19-20). Rome already had the infrastructure in place for the movement of its military, as well as trade. The gospel followed the trade routes.

The corporate culture of the Church is rooted in the New Testament understanding of the kingdom of God, first made clear by Jesus Himself. The kingdom culture is not new, but it has some new and unique elements. The kingdom finds its roots among the ancient people of God. Love, truth, righteousness, justice, mercy and peace are among the core values of the kingdom, and they are not New Testament inventions (James 3:13-18). They were divine requirements for the godly life set forth in the Hebrew Scriptures (Exod.20:1-17; Deut.6:1-9; Mic.6:8). These divine requirements were brought to perfect fulfillment in the Lord Jesus Christ (Matt.5:17-20).

Bruce Waltke asserts that the "unifying theme of the Old Testament is the breaking in of the kingdom of God" and this theme continues in the New Testament. This establishes a consistency and unity between the two testaments. God's revelation in both testaments calls people to the righteous life and to right relationship with God and neighbor (Waltke 2011, 80-82). Yet, there are difference between the two testaments. Jesus explains this difference in His famous Sermon on the Mount as He contrasted old expectations with new requirements. "It was said, but I say" became the mantra of change from the Law of Moses to the law of Christ (Matt.5:1-

48). Jesus ushered in the kingdom of God with a *New Covenant* based on the primacy of love toward God and neighbor (Mark 12:28-30; Heb.8:7-13).

Jesus' law of love removes the "eyes for an eye," tooth for a tooth," hate your enemy elements from resolving conflicted situations among the people of God. Conflict is still settled in the context of justice. But justice in human relationships must include mercy, forgiveness, love, peacemaking, neighborliness, and reconciliation (2 Cor.5:14-21). The administration of retributive justice, therefore, is left to God and human government (Rom.12:19; 13:1-4). But even here in human government, God wants the administration of justice restrained by mercy because that is the way He who wields absolute power and justice deals with humans. Jesus declares, "Blessed are the merciful for they shall obtain mercy" (Matt.5:7). He illustrates this requirement of mercy with the story of the Good Samaritan.

The change from the Law of Moses to the law of Christ sets a higher standard for human and divine relationships. Jesus taught that "unless your righteousness surpasses that of the Pharisees and teachers of the law, you will certainly not enter the kingdom of heaven" (Matt.5:20). This new era with its new standard of righteousness warrants a new narrative; that new narrative is the New Testament. In the context of dispute resolution, these are among the New Testament core values:

repentance, love, mercy, forgiveness and reconciliation. Christian dispute resolution, therefore, must not only take these core values into consideration; they are requirements to embrace and practice in daily life.

Furthermore, both Old and New Testaments teach that destructive conflict has a spiritual dimension. On the one hand, it springs from the depravity of the human heart or sinful nature, and on the other hand, it emanates from personified evil. With reference to human nature, the prophet Jeremiah gives us this diagnostic report: "The heart is deceitful above all things and beyond cure. Who understands it?" Only God holds the cure for a sinful heart. The prophet continues, "I the Lord search the heart and examine the mind, to reward a man according to what his deeds deserve" (Jer.17:9-10). In other words, God alone has the antidote for the deprave and sinful human heart, and He will adjudicate the deeds of all persons.

The NT further diagnosed human fallen nature and connects the etiology of conflict to a spiritual disease. The apostle James gives us this intelligence report, "What causes fights and quarrels among you? Don't they come from your desires that battle within you? You want something but don't get it. You kill and covet, but you cannot have what you want. You quarrel and fight. You do not have, because you do not ask God" (James 4:1-2). What is Jeremiah and James saying?

They are showing us the deprave, sinful condition of the human heart, and the source of human destructiveness. The inner sanctum of humankind is diseased. God promises a new heart. That new heart is received when a person is born again into the kingdom of God; he or she becomes a new creation in Jesus Christ (John 3:3-7; 2Cor.5:17). It is highly important that Christian dispute resolution workers understand this critical truth. It is one of the salient differences between the humanistic and the Christian approaches to the resolution of conflicts. Human nature needs transformation.

On personified evil—both testaments inform us that the spiritual dimension of conflict has a connection to that evil personification. Stated bluntly, there is a spirit being connected to destructive conflict who is capable of waging war with God and humans. The apostle John gives us this intelligence: "Then war broke out in heaven. Michael and his angels fought against the dragon...But he was not strong enough, and they lost their place in heaven. The great dragon was hurled down—that ancient serpent called the devil, or Satan, who leads the whole world astray" (Rev.12:7-9). Satan leads a well-organized opposition kingdom to the kingdom of God.

The apostle Paul exhorts followers of Christ on the spiritual dimension conflict with these words, "our struggle is not against flesh and blood, but against...spiritual forces of evil in the heavenly realms" (Eph.6:10-18). This spiritual connection of destructive conflict to personified evil is evident from the conflict in the paradise garden with God and our ancestral parents (Gen.3:1-8). This confrontation with good and evil was the mother of all destructive conflict for the human family.

It is important to grasp these two connections of destructive conflict: *human nature* and *personified evil.* It is not enough to say, "the devil made me do it." We are free moral agents; it is our own deprave and sinful nature made us do it. We cannot ignore human responsibility and accountability and blame it on the devil. Satan does not wield any authority over the people of God other than what we, like our ancestral parents, given to him. Jesus declares, "All authority in heaven and on earth has been given to me" (Matt.28:18). Jesus exercises this authority through His church on earth today (Matt.28:19-20; Acts 1:8). So, there is no reason the church should be held hostage to destructive conflict. If Satan had the audacity to start war in heaven against God and angels, with all certainty, he will continue that fight on earth against and through the church (Rev.12:13-17, 20:8-10).

Because of this dual spiritual connection of conflict to theodicy (personified evil), you can see why a mere humanistic approach cannot manage or defeat conflict that is bent on destroying. The approach must be profoundly spiritual as well, and firmly rooted in the word of God (more on this later).

The Apostles and the Early Church

Inasmuch as the apostles gave voice, arms and legs to the teachings of Jesus, we cannot honestly say that the New Testament (NT) has lift a formal, step-by-step model for the resolution of conflict. But it surely came close; it has given us some indispensable, fundamental principles that must be included in any Christian model or plan of dispute resolution. The wise practitioner will take them seriously.

Stated differently, the NT gives us a useful portrait, a preferred way how believers back then settled conflicts within their ranks. Undoubtedly, the life and teachings of Jesus shaped the way the apostles thought about conflicts and how they settled situations of conflict in the community of faith.

The person and teachings of Christ are at the very heart of the gospel and represent the standard for dealing with people in divine and human relationships. In fact, these two levels of relationships are interrelated—one affects the other. The apostle John declares, "For anyone who does not love his brother whom he has seen, cannot love God, whom he has not seen" (1 John 4:20). John asserts that one is a murderer if he or she persists in a hateful relationship with another (1John 3:10-12). The true mark of a disciple of Christ is love; love is a relational word (1John 2:9-10).

The primacy of love in human relationships is a dominant theme that emerges from the scriptures and informs the followers of Christ throughout the history of the church. It unveils how conflict was dealt with in the early Christian community. The primacy of love is beautifully captured in the Pauline epistles. First Corinthians thirteen is a good example; it reflects the spirit and the teachings of Jesus Christ concerning human relationships.

Paul did not depart from the theology of Jesus as some would have us to believe. He consistently follows the peace theology of Jesus. Theologian Graham Twelftree debunks the notion that Paul departed from the teachings of Jesus, that he neglected the miraculous which was central to the ministry of Jesus (Twelftree 2013, 26-27). The greatest miracle in the entire NT is the resurrection of Jesus Christ and it was the foundation piece in Paul's theology of ministry (1 Cor.15:1-50).

To Paul, the Christian faith stands or falls with the bodily resurrection of Jesus Christ. Paul sees the resurrection as an eschatological event; it guarantees the resurrection of all humankind, though all will not have the same eternal destiny and destination (1 Cor.15:22-23; John 5:28-29). It is absurd to advance a teaching that Paul was a rogue apostle who departed from the theology of Jesus on any subject, including war and peace. On the contrary, Paul thematically fleshes out the profound theology of Jesus that seems simple on the surface. He makes it clear that in Jesus God is reconciling humans to Himself and to each other (2 Cor.5 18-21). This bilateral relationship (God and neighbor) is reflected throughout the entire New Testament record.

The first potentially destructive conflict of the early Church is found in the book of Acts (6:1-7). The infant Church was accused by some of its members with unfairness, ethnic discrimination, favoritism, and even nepotism in the distribution of the temporalities of the church. The matter was potentially explosive. People of good will had given generously of their material substance, including money, to the Jesus movement (Acts 4:32-37). But now, the Greek-speaking Jewish members filed a complaint against the Hebraic, Aramaic-speaking Jewish members that their widows were overlooked in the daily distribution of foods. The implication here is that one group was attending only to their own interests to the neglect of others. It was a serious charge needing prompt attention and a wise solution.

The apostles at this stage of their ministry practice were not experienced in leadership; they had never led anything before. But with the help of the blessed Holy Spirit, they came up with a brilliant solution for handling this internal church conflict. They chose not an apostle-led group as the solution to the conflict but recommend that the congregation form a lay members' *counsel* of seven men, honest and respected, filled with the Holy Spirit and wisdom to take over that responsibility (Acts 6:3-4). The proposal pleased the congregation and they acted accordingly, choosing seven men and presented them to the apostles. The apostles consecrated them to service as they were chosen (v.6). The problem was solved to the satisfaction of all and the Church grew (v.7).

This conflict that was poised to be scandalous and most destructive, brought to light the giftedness of key lay members; they were chosen to form a *resident counsel* to resolve the dispute to the satisfaction of all. For the purposes of this book, let's name this group of seven, the *Stephen-Philip Dispute Resolution Counsel* (SPDRC) because they were the two most popular of the seven. Just as the *Jethro Dispute Resolution* plan provides Old Testament precedence for a lay leadership conflict resolution approach, SPDRC now provides us with a NT precedence. *They settled it in the house.*

So then, the twenty-first century local church is not without biblical precedence in terms of a lay leaders' approach to the resolution of conflicts. This first NT church conflict was settled in the house by believers of the congregation. They performed their peacemaking duty well. The following features of the *Stephen-Philip Counsel* are worth noting:

- The counsel was not apostle-led because it would have been an added responsibility, taking the apostles away from prayer and the ministry of the word and putting them in the hearth of conflict. This is an approach that every pastor should take note of.

- The apostles recommended a lay leaders' solution; they set the number of members for the counsel and stated their qualifications (pastoral oversight). The apostles did not sit back and watch the house burn down; they provided effective oversight.
- The apostles had the congregation choose the members of the counsel and the apostles consecrated them for their ministry assignment. This suggest congregational participation and pastoral authority. The solution was not forced upon them.
- The seven emerged as what I call, a *resident counsel*, charged with a specific task of dispute resolution, designed to keep the peace, preserve the unity of the fellowship and safeguard the integrity of its message to the community and the world.
- The congregation was satisfied with their choice and the problem was resolved. The solution was not imposed from top down; it was communal and that gave it a certain type of credibility.
- The Hebrew Scripture was the only Bible the Church had at this time, perhaps they knew of the Jethro Dispute Resolution plan offered to Moses (Exod.18:1-

27). It too was a lay leadership plan with pastoral supervision. Moses was the pastor of that congregation.

- The formal diaconate or board of elders that was developed later in the New Testament is often traced back to the *Stephen-Philip Dispute Resolution Counsel* (Avis 2006).

The second potential destructive conflict on record for the early Church—concerns whether the church members, including gentiles, should be forced to conform to Jewish dietary laws and the ritual of circumcision to be saved. This dispute started when certain unauthorized teachers came from Judea to Antioch with this erroneous teaching. Paul and Barnabas came into hot dispute with the group on these matters. The dispute divided the church at Antioch—they reached an impasse. So, they decided to send a delegation to Jerusalem to have the apostle address the questions for all the local churches (Acts 15:1-5). The Antioch church behaved with discipline and intelligence.

The apostles at the Headquarters Church in Jerusalem upon welcoming the delegation, convened a conflict resolution council to consider the question. After much deliberation, a consensus decision was reached, that conforming to Jewish customs and rituals were not required for salvation in Jesus (Acts 15:6-21). The ruling was placed in writing and delivered by hand to the local church at Antioch and churches everywhere. The local churches were relieved and joyful upon receiving the ruling (15:22-35). Church envoys from the Jerusalem church who were capable of answering questions accompanied the letter. Note again that is was the Antioch local church that asked for help. Be sure to read the full text of scripture on this one (Acts 15:6-35).

What insights in dispute resolution can we draw from this church conflict? The main insight is that a local church can become hopelessly divided in a dispute and without wise leadership, you have a split on your hand. In such case, the dispute has to be settled by an independent body and the ruling hand down as final. There are two types of independent bodies that can do that: *an arbitration body or the courts*. The church at Jerusalem with the apostles served as that arbitration body (the heathen courts would not be helpful here). The ruling was binding and final. The conflict was settled in the house. It would have been difficult for a public court of law to settle this dispute because it had to do with matters pertaining to the spiritual life, doctrine and practice.

Independent churches today are greatly at risk if there is no church body outside of the local church itself to act as arbitration. It is strongly suggested that a local church with or without a lay-leaders conflict resolution counsel, designate an arbitration body to which conflicts beyond the capability of the local church can be referred. If can be a group of distinguished board members or a group from the denominational headquarters, if the church belongs to one. Later in this book we will return to this critical issue of arbitration.

A third conflict of interest is the one with Paul and Barnabas (Acts 15:36-41). This dispute was over the young man named John Mark. He was a cousin of Barnabas. In a previous ministry assignment, Mark deserted the team and returned home (Acts 13:13). Perhaps, Paul fell Mark was unreliable and did not want him as part of the ministry team next time, but Barnabas wanted him. Paul would not compromise, and Barnabas would not compromise, and so they parted company. Barnabas taking Mark and Paul taking Silas (vv.39-41).

This personal ministry dispute is very interesting because it separated chief Christian leaders who were friends. Barnabas was in Christ before Paul, active in ministry and well respected by the apostles and the headquarters church in Jerusalem. A persecution against the church had broken out in Jerusalem scattering believers all over. Some believers (lay people), perhaps started the church at Antioch. Barnabas was sent by the apostles from the Jerusalem church to check out this new work to ensure they were preaching the right gospel and sticking to the apostles' teaching about Jesus. "When he arrived and saw what the grace of God had done, he was glad and encouraged them all to remain true to the Lord with all their hearts. He was a good man, full of the Holy Spirit and faith, and a great number of people were brought to the Lord" (Acts 11:19-24). This is the testimony of others about Barnabas; he was a good man!

Barnabas heard that Saul (Paul) who persecuted the Church was converted to Christ and now preaching the faith he once sought to destroy. Believers were afraid of him, thinking it was another ploy to get to them. But Barnabas went to Tarsus in search of Saul and when he found him, he brought him to Antioch and introduced him to the body of believers. The two men became friends and a ministry team (Acts 11:25-30). Later, it was Barnabas who introduced Saul to the apostles. While they were ministering in the church at Antioch, the Holy Spirit sanctioned them as a missionary team and the church commissioned them and sent them on their way (Acts 13:1-3).

But now after all this, these two brothers in Christ, ministry partners are separated in a sharp dispute over John Mark (Acts 15:36-41). It is a contention that worth careful contemplation because it is a teachable and insightful story on human relationships. It tells us that even when we are greatly anointed, we still have feet of clay. Our own sinful nature can get the better of us. Yet out of evil, good can come forth for God can turn around negative situations for His glory (Rom.8:28). Are there lessons to learn from this conflict? There are many lessons, but we will only highlight a few here:

1. No matter our leadership credentials and abilities, calling, vision and anointing, none of us is immune to destructive conflict. It can spring up to undo us at our unguarded hour and it can sever chief relationships, if we are not careful.
2. A young person like John Mark, called to the ministry, needs the nurture and validation of those who are senior in ministry. Some leaders, like Paul, may not immediately recognize the call of God on the life of some young person, while others like Barnabas will. Barnabas gave strong support to the young man, no wonder they called him the apostle of encouragement because he encouraged others.
3. Negative conflicts can have positive outcomes. Instead of one missionary team, we now have two teams and four missionaries (Paul and Silas, Barnabas and Mark).
4. If you have made a wrong call that upset the lives of others, fix it when you realize it is a wrong call. Paul later realized he made a wrong call and changed his mind about Mark. He endorsed Mark as profitable for the ministry. Later, Mark visited Paul in prison as a member of the ministry team (Col.4:10; Phm.24). Mark became one of the gospel writers. Paul's relationship with Barnabas was also renewed; Paul

speaks well of him as a ministry brother and colleague (1Cor.9:6).

Other New Testament Disputes

The New Testament is fraught with conflicts of various kinds: personality, ethnic, tradition and doctrinal. The conflict over the distribution of foods had ethnic overtones (Acts 6:1-7). The conflict that precipitated the Jerusalem Counsel was over Jewish tradition (Acts 15:1-35). The conflict with Paul and Barnabas over John Mark was personality (15:36-41). Paul was strong-headed and would not back down. The conflict between Paul and Peter in which Paul confronted Peter and practically labeled him, what we would call a two-faced hypocrite, was over Jewish customs and traditions (Gal.2:11-13).

It was not easy a struggle for the early church whose leaders were Jewish to overcome certain ethnic biases, despite the life and teachings of Jesus Christ. Not long after the Pentecost Holy Spirit outpouring, Peter had problems going to Cornelius' house on a ministry assignment (Acts 10). Cornelius was a gentile, a centurion who worked for the Roman government. God had to intervene to persuade Peter that is was okay to go to this man's house.

Despite Jesus' prior instruction that the gospel is for all humankind, and regardless of God's acceptance of this gentile man by angelic appearance, and the gift of the Holy Spirit and water baptism, Peter had to later explain his behavior to the other apostles before the church in Jerusalem (Acts 11:1-18). Jews did not go to the homes of gentiles for fear of being defiled; that custom persisted into the church. It is not easy to overcome entrenched tradition and ethnic biases.

Perhaps, this is why Jesus converted Saul of Tarsus, a Pharisee of Pharisees, an educated man, revealed Himself to Saul and tasked him with the assignment of apostle to the Gentiles. Paul understood the mind of Christ very early in his calling and was able to overcome the religious and ethnic biases that fueled his anger before his conversion. Jesus revealed to Paul (Saul, his Hebrew name) that gentiles are fellow heirs with the Jews in His kingdom, that in Christ there is neither gentile or Jew, bond or free, male or female, tradition or philosophy, circumcision or uncircumcision, except circumcision of the heart. All these things that once divide people have been removed by the death and resurrection of Jesus Christ. We are saved by grace through faith; it is the gift of God (Eph.2: 11-22).

Paul relentlessly drives home the truth of the gospel in an uncompromising and transparent way. He boldly declares that if any man or angel preach a gospel other than the gospel, he preached *let him be accursed* (Gal.1:6-10). Paul fiercely confronted the Big Fisherman (Peter) whom Jesus gave the keys of the kingdom when Paul perceived that Peter stepped out of line with the gospel. Without Paul, the New Testament (NT) would have been a very skinny book indeed. Of the 27 books comprising the NT 14 were written by Paul, if you credit Hebrews to him. With the exception of the apostle John, the other apostles did not write very much that we know of today.

Settle It in the House

Paul appears to overcome his Jewish biases quicker than any of the twelve apostles. He shows that in Christ we are all equal, that there is no big me and little you in the Body of Christ, that God is no respecter of persons; culture, gender, nationality, social status gives you no special standing with God. All these things we learn from Paul. Where do you think Paul got them from? He got them from the teachings of Jesus Christ of course, some by special revelation (Gal.1:11-12).

Paul demonstrated that the preferred place to settle church conflict is in the church, among believers—that, he learned from Jesus as well (Matt.18:15-19). Paul rebuked the Corinthian church for violating this protocol because they resorted to the heathen courts to settle their disputes (1 Cor.6:1-11). The apostle used very strong language which denotes strong emotion, shock or surprise: "If any of you has a dispute with another, do you dare to take it before the ungodly for judgment instead of before the Lord's people?" He continues his rebuke saying that if the Lord's people will participate in judging the unbelieving world and fallen angels, they should be competent enough to resolve disputes pertaining to things of this life.

What is Paul doing here? He is educating the local church, driving home to these Corinthians the protocol from Jesus that church conflict ought to be settled in the house. This concept eventually gave rise to church councils and church courts that were to follow. These councils and courts were primarily for disputes over doctrinal matters. Church courts abusively broaden the scope of their authority with the advent of Papal Rome, not in the interest of helping ordinary believers live out the peace theology of Jesus, but to weed out opposition and consolidate papal power through the Roman Church. In a sense that abuse precipitated the Reformation and set the stage for the relationship between church and state that was to follow in Luther's Germany, Calin's Geneva, Switzerland, and Henry VIII England.

In the twenty-first century, the civil court system has become really sophisticated; it is not heathen as first century civil courts or controlled by the church as medieval papal Rome. There are Christian lawyers that can argue Christian values before the courts today. That of course does not mean the courts will be sympathetic in the interest of the Christian, because everyone is equal under the law without regards for race, gender or religion.

At some point, the Christian of today will need the services of the courts on some issues, especially matters pertaining to real property, enforcement of contracts and the like. The law courts are important institutions of our society. But that does not take anything away from the position of Jesus and Paul and the NT that conflicts among believers ought to be settled in the church among believers. We will return to this issue of litigation through the courts later.

The church and its leaders as followers of Christ in the first century of Christianity, were frequently wronged, injured, dragged before the heathen civil courts, imprisoned and even killed. Yet other than the Corinthian situation that Paul corrected, we hardly have evidence in the NT of any church leader seeking remedy through the civil court, yet the church respected law and government (Rom.13:1-14).

The civil authorities beheaded John the Baptist, carried out the crucifixion of Jesus, executed the apostle James and would have done the same with Peter but God intervened (Acts 7:54-8:3, 9:1-9,12:1-24). Paul was arrested in Jerusalem and ushered from city to city to be heard by different civil authorities and when due process was delayed, he appealed to Caesar and was sent to Rome as a prisoner to appear before Caesar (Acts 26:24-32). Perhaps, the book of Luke and Acts were written as treatise for his defense. Paul's case was not a church member to church member dispute or church leader seeking redress through the civil courts. His case was a civil matter from the beginning. Other people disturb the peace by violating Paul's civil and religious rights. When he was not getting due process through the civil courts, he appealed his case to Caesar which was the right of any Roman citizen to do. Church disputes were generally settled among believers.

The Diaconate or Board of Elders

The diaconate or board of deacons was added to the leadership of the church at some point in the apostolic era; we are not sure at what exact point, but definitely after the Stephen-Philip dispute resolution team was installed in the book of Acts (6:1-7). Some scholars have traced the beginning of the diaconate to this group. Undoubtedly, the deacons or elders became an important office in the everyday life of church. It maintained order and resolved problems pertaining to Christian life.

It would be inaccurate, therefore, to conclude that the apostles and the early Church had no conflict resolution protocol in place. Our discussion up to this point, clearly reveals that there was a preferred way of settling disputes, though not very formal. This preferred way is rooted in the peace theology of Jesus Christ; that conflict should not be settled with the sword, but peaceably among believers in the community of faith (Matt.18:15-19). But was this protocol followed?

The obvious answer is, yes. The apostles followed the teachings of Jesus concerning the resolution of conflicts. First, this is evident with the way the apostles resolved the first major church dispute; they established what I call, *a resident counsel* (Acts 6:1-7). Second, there is further evidence with apostles convening the Jerusalem council to resolve a fierce church dispute that started in the church at Antioch (Acts 15:1-35). Third, Paul and Barnabas did not litigate their differences in the civil courts; as Christian brothers, they settled their dispute over John Mark between themselves (15:36-41; 1Cor.6:9). Fourth, Paul reprimanded the Corinthians for departing from the established protocol of Jesus and the apostles. If there were no protocol, the apostle's rebuke would make no sense.

The Corinthian church was very conflicted and undisciplined on several fronts. Perhaps, the organizational structure was very informal at the beginning. The church was divided around their favorite preachers (1Cor.1-3). They disputed over the authenticity of Paul's apostleship, he not being one of the twelve apostles (Chap.4). They did not correct the problems of incest in the church (Chap.5). Members were having their disputes settled before the heathen courts and not before the believers (6:1-11). Sexual immorality was besetting the church (6:12-20). They had problems with the institution of marriage (7:1-40).

It is fair to conclude, therefore, that if an official board of deacons or elders was not in existent at this time in the church at Corinth, they would have brought better discipline and order to this church. This lay ministry office of deacons or elders was later added, perhaps.

Paul's first letter to the Corinthians was written quite early, about A.D. 55; perhaps from Ephesus. In the salutation, no mention is made of a single person in charge, not overseer, not deacons, not elders. Instead, the letter is addressed "to the church of God in Corinth, to those sanctified in Christ Jesus and called to be his holy people" (1:2). It is addressed to the whole congregation. As stated before, perhaps, this church had no board of deacons or elders as yet and that may in part account for the lose morals, discipline and lack of order in this church.

When this epistle (First Corinthians) is compared with Philippians, written about A.D.61, it was addressed "to all God's holy people in Christ Jesus at Philippi, together with the overseers and deacons" (Phil.1:1). This church had a leadership structure and did not have the problems the church at Corinth had. In this epistle, we find one of the cardinal principles of dispute resolution, *considering the interest of others* (2:1-11). Here Paul appeals to two prominent and influential sisters, Euodia and Syntyche, to settle their differences (4:1-3). He appeals to the entire congregation to help the sisters get there.

Furthermore, Paul's first letter to Timothy, written about A.D. 64, clearly shows that Timothy was perhaps a bishop or overseer over certain congregations. Paul's words to him, "As I urged you when in Macedonia, stay there in Ephesus that "you may command certain people not to teach false doctrine any longer" (1Tim.1:3-4). Timothy had to be in a position of authority to command anyone. In chapter three, Paul reviews the qualifications for overseers, deacons and elders with Timothy. This is an indication that, like Titus, Timothy had authority to appoint people to these offices. The qualifications are repeated in Titus (1:5-9, 2:1-3:11).

The preference for settling conflicts in the local church in the context of justice, love and mercy, clearly rises to the surface in the Pauline epistles again and again but in slightly different ways. In other words, Pauline theology conforms to the theology of Jesus. The idea that Paul was a rogue apostle going counter to the teaching of Jesus is erroneous and should be vigorously rejected. The participation of lay members in dispute resolution also rise to the surface again and again in conformity with Jesus manner of life and teachings. In the next chapter, we will briefly explore the post-apostolic and medieval history of the church in search of precedence (or the lack of it) in the resolution of conflicts.

CHAPTER 7

CHURCH CONFLICT: PATRISTIC AND REFORMATION YEARS

From its birth on the Day of Pentecost (Acts 2), the Christian Church has always been conflicted to one degree or another. Then and now, conflicts from outside forces have been referred to as persecutions. In its early history, persecutions were largely led by political operatives who were determined to silence the voice of the church. This attempt to silence the church, however, began as religious persecution with the stoning of Stephen and gathered momentum with Saul of Tarsus with the support of the Jewish religious authorities (Acts 7-8:1-3; 9:1-5).

In the early years, political persecution was sporadic; it began with the killing of apostle James by King Herod (Acts 12:1-5). Persecution of the church rose to imperial level about

AD 64 under Nero but was not empire wide until the AD 250s under the reign of Decius. It escalated to its worst under Diocletian who came to power about AD 303. Imperial persecution ended with the edict of Milan in AD 313 under Emperor Constantine. He was converted to Christianity and made Christianity the official religion of the State. Constantine was indeed a pivotal character for the church.

Conflicts within the Church were largely doctrinal but were more dangerous to the life of the Church because they assaulted what the Church believed and taught. Persecution from without purified and unified the Church by weeding out those who were not willing to suffer and die for what they believed. But doctrinal conflicts were internal fights over core beliefs that threatened to fragment and weaken the Church from within.

Through the immediate postapostolic and early medieval eras, the Church handled doctrinal conflicts through vigorous scholarly debates to reach a consensus on matters of faith and practice. At times, scholarly debate resulted in schisms and heretic labeling for those who would not go with the consensus decision of orthodoxy. This somewhat noble approach later gave way to violent autocracy under papal control. This chapter looks at how the Church dealt with internal conflicts in three major blocks of history: the patristic, medieval and post-reformation eras. Before we discuss the patristic period proper, however, it is important to briefly consider the importance of orthodoxy or purity of doctrine to the life and authenticity of the Church. It is for this reason ecumenical councils became the preferred way to settle doctrinal conflicts because they affect the life of the wider church.

The Preservation of Orthodoxy

The twelve apostles and others, during their lifetime strived to preserve the doctrinal unity of the Church in the face of many radical and heretical individuals and groups. The apostles used short, simple creedal statements that the common folks could easily memorize. These creedal statements capsulized what was commonly believed; they typically began with the words, "I believe" or "We believe" or "I deliver to you what I also received."

Paul correcting the Corinthians on their abuse of the Lord's Supper said, "For I received from the Lord that which I also delivered unto you..." (1Cor.11:23 KJV). It is evident here that Paul received a certain way the Lord's Supper was celebrated, including the explanation of its significance and he was conveying to others that very protocol as received. That's how a tradition or practice of orthodoxy is developed.

Again, in teaching about the Resurrection of Jesus Paul said, "For I delivered to you first of all that which I also received:

that Christ died for our sins according to the Scriptures, and that He was buried, and that He rose again the third day according to the Scriptures, and that he was seen by Cephas, then by the twelve" (1Cor.15:1-5). These are simple creedal statements hung together like beads on a string, simple enough for a child to remember. This simplicity was necessary because a sizable population of the common folks could not read or afford expensive handwritten books in the first century of Christianity. These common folks heard Jesus gladly not only because he spoke their language, but the fact that Jesus used a pedagogy or method of teaching that was relevant to their immediate situations in life (Mark 4:33-34).

The traditional rabbinic schools of thought hardly had anything new to say; they endlessly quoted their predecessors for authority. But Jesus came along as an original thinker and teacher. He prefaced his teachings with the words, "It was said, but I say" (Matt.5:21-48). His hearers said of Him, "He taught as one having authority" and "never a man spoke like this man" (Matt.7:28-29).

Simple creedal statements were used in the early years of the Church as place holders for the teachings of Jesus and were labeled "the apostles' doctrine" (Acts 2:42, 5:42,6:4). These themes the apostle preached again and again. They were later collected to form what we know today as the Apostles' Creed. The Apostles' Creed predates the New Testament (NT) canon and is believed to be “the oldest creed of the church” (Holcomb 2014, 25). The Creed captures what the apostles believed and taught about Jesus. And much effort was exerted to preserve its authenticity.

The twelve apostles and other prominent church leaders who made contribution to the NT canon, vigorously defended the purity of the gospel against the doctrine of false teachers. Paul for example, was not one of the twelve apostles, but was an apostle with no less authority; he always warned against false teachers. In Galatians, Paul boldly asserts that if any person or even angel should preach a gospel other than the gospel he preached should be accursed (Gal.1:6-9). He was acutely aware that the gospel he was preaching was consistent with the apostles’ doctrine because he got most of it directly from Jesus Christ by revelation (Gal.1:11-12). Nonetheless, Paul conferred with the apostles in Jerusalem so that they could be assured of what he was preaching; being satisfied, they gave him the right hand of fellowship (Gal.2: 1-10).

The apostle Jude was not one of the twelve but was very concerned about orthodoxy in his ministry practice. His epistle was written about AD 66. Jude expressed deep concerns about the preservation of the apostles’ teachings. He urged his readers, “to contend earnestly for the faith which was once for all delivered to the saints” for ungodly men” had “crept in unnoticed" among the saints preaching and teaching a false gospel (Jude 3-4 NKJV).

Jude's exhortation to *contend earnestly* for the unity and orthodoxy of the faith was not exclusive to Jude, it is seen through the period of history called, the Patristic period or period of the Fathers (church fathers). We will first try to determine what centuries covered in the patristic period. Second, we will name a few of the church fathers that rose to prominence in the leadership of the church during the period and made significant contribution to the faith.

The Patristic Period

The patristic period is not clearly defined in the history of the church. Some historians mark the period as post-apostolic and stretching from about AD 100 to AD 450. Others prefer to divide it into Ante-Nicene and Post-Nicene Fathers, meaning that these church Fathers lived and wrote either before or after the Council of Nicaea (325 AD). Still others mark the period from the second century into the seventh in the Western Church and into the eighth century in the Eastern Church. Because Emperor Constantine's conversion and reforms were so defining for the church, others prefer to mark the period as "pre-and post-Constantine" (Himes 2013, 61).

The patristic period was at best turbulent within and without the church. From within, the church continued to put out the fires of heresies in order to maintain orthodoxy, and from without it continued to contend with the chill winds of political control and imperial persecutions. Leaders of the secular state believed they had rule over all of life, including the Church. But most church leaders did not believe that Jesus intended the secular state to exercise control over the church that He is Head and only Lord. But since the secular state had an army and the power of the sword, some church leaders were willing to compromise and accommodate them without surrendering complete control.

When Constantine became emperor and converted to Christianity, he later made Christianity the official religion of the State. Constantine was baptized by Eusebius of Nicomedia, a prominent church leader who influenced his moderation toward the Church. It was Constantine who convened the First Council of Nicaea in 325 AD). Before we look at what motivated Constantine to convene this council, we need to take a quick look at few prominent church fathers that held the Christian faith together up to this point. In other words, who are the Pre-Nicene Fathers? We will only reference a few of them.

They were prominent church leaders like Justin Martyr (130-165), who became the patron saint for philosophers in the Roman Church, noted for the concept of the Son of God as the life-giving Word that implanted the truth in the minds of all people. He also identified Christ as the New Adam and Mary as the New Eve in whom creation is made New. He was executed during the reign of Marcus Aurelius for refusing to sacrifice to a pagan god.

Irenaeus (130-200), was bishop of Lyons from AD 178 to 200, and was widely known for his publications *Against Heresies*, which was a refutation of Gnosticism. Origen (185-254) is regarded as one of the most outstanding apologists of the Christian faith. He pioneered what has come down to us as a three-fold biblical interpretation: literal, ethical and spiritual. He is also known for his heretical views on universal salvation, that all will be saved including Satan. From Clement of Alexandria (150-215) who "explored the relationship between Christian thought and Greek philosophy" to Gregory of Nyssa (330-395) who spoke mightily and wrote in defense of the doctrine "Trinity" and the "Incarnation," the Fathers fought to defend the apostolic teachings against heresy (McMahon on *Historical Theology*-apuritanmind.com).

Another prominent church Father is Tertullian (160-225); he is widely credited as the founder of Western, Latin Christian theology, a major opponent of Marcionism, and the first to work out a system of doctrine of the Holy Trinity.

Athanasius (296-373) served as the bishop of Alexandria and was a key figure at the Council at Nicaea. He vigorously argued against Arianism. Arius believed that Jesus was not in essence divine but was adopted in the role of Son by God the

Father, therefore, Jesus was totally human. Athanasius argued that if Arius is right then salvation through God would be impossible and Christians would be guilty of idolatry for worshipping Jesus. The Council of Nicaea declared Arius a heretic and his teachings as heresy.

Athanasius stands as a pivotal character among the church Fathers because he lived before, during and after the First Council of Nicaea called by Constantine in AD 325. Arius' position on the subordinate relationship of the Son to the Father was ruled heretical. The Nicene Creed, as we know it today, is said to be the most significant creed in the history of the church. It is actually the product of two ecumenical councils, AD 325 and the other in AD 381 which was convened at Constantinople (modern Turkish name, Istanbul). The council continued to debate and settled once for all the relationship between the three persons of the blessed Holy Trinity (Holcomb 2014, 33).

There are several influential leaders that guided the church through what we now call the Post-Nicene period. Some bear the distinguished title of Church Fathers, like Eusebius, Ambrose and Augustine, to name a few. But none had the far-reaching impact on the life of both Western and Eastern Church as the spiritual and intellectual giant named, Augustine. He was Bishop of Hippo in North Africa, a man of the academy, versed in philosophy and theology, a brilliant thinker and prolific writer. He cemented the doctrinal thinking of the Church for all times to come. It is clear from history that major doctrinal matters that had wide implications were settled in one church council after another.

Church councils became the precedence for settling doctrinal matters with significance for the entire Christian faith. After the two councils that settled the issues of the Nicene Creed (325 and 381), there were many other councils down to Vatican II (1962-65). There was the Councils of Carthage and Orange (AD 419 and 529), the Council of Trent (AD 1545-63), to name a few. The question that remains however is this—how did local churches deal with nondoctrinal conflicts up to the Council of Nicaea? While the answer to this question is not clear, we have to assume that such disputes were settled in the local churches according to the directives laid down by Jesus and the apostles.

If doctrinal disputes which had implications for the total church followed the council approach established at the Jerusalem Council in Acts 15, we have to assume that other conflicts were settled according to the directives Jesus and the apostles handed down to the Church. Jesus had the local church in mind when he gave the dispute resolution directive in Matthew (18:15-17). When Paul chided the Corinthian church about church brothers going before the pagan court to settle their disputes, it was because they departed from the established Christian protocol of dispute resolution (1Cor.6:1-8).

We may therefore summarize the church's attitude toward conflicted brethren who were in error up to the ending of the patristic period (about AD 450) as follows: 1) They debated vigorously, but in love, anchoring their arguments in holy Scripture and the apostles' teachings. 2) They used the guidance of the Holy Spirit, their intellectual powers (including philosophy) and the pen to write their treaties of defense in an attempt to preserve the truth and orthodoxy of the gospel. And, 3) they worked to convince those in error to turn and be reconciled. (For more information, see C. Matthew McMahon, *Introduction to Historical Theology*: *The Patristic Period* at: apuritanmind.com).

The Medieval Period

Historians generally define the medieval years as that period of time running from AD 500 to AD 1500. It runs from the fall of the Western Roman Empire to the Renaissance and Age of Discovery. These were turbulent times but for our purposes, the thing of significance to remember is the ascendancy of the Bishop of Rome to the throne of the Caesars. This marks the beginning of the Papacy.

The Church taking the seat and helm of secular government was a paradigm shift for Christianity. God's interest was now merged with Caesar's; that was beyond what Jesus intended when He said that we should "give to Caesar what is Caesar's and to God what is God's" (Matt.22:21). This apparent unprecedented progress of the Church was actually the beginning of its demise. Political power was gained, morals declined, and theology and practice departed from the NT.

One of most significant shifts in the theology and practice of Papal Rome was that the peace theology of Jesus was replaced with the "holy war" or "just war" theory of conflict advanced earlier by Augustine (Yoder 2009, 13-14). The church became exceeding militant, wielding both the power of the sword and the power of the keys with little or no mercy. The sword punishes and the keys controls access to the kingdom of God. Access most often for a monetary price.

Conflict was no longer settled in the context of justice restrained by mercy. The church became the source of conflict; the church became accuser, prosecutor, judge, jury and executioner. The Pope had the so-called unquestionable divine authority over human life and was oppressive and brutal to those who dear to oppose. Conflict within and outside the church, legitimate or otherwise was crushed without mercy (Dewar 2009, 268).

Under the just war theory, the Roman Church ruled by the sword. It is this theory advanced by Augustine that gave rise to the Crusades and the Inquisitions. Kenneth Himes argues that the "Crusades were wars sanctioned for holy purposes," and were not viewed at first as "significantly differing from just war ethic" since the stated objective was to defend innocent civilians who were "pilgrims travelling to shrines in the Holy Land." The objectives were later changed to become the rationale for waging war "against infidels" who did not embrace the true religion. This premise, he argues resurfaced centuries later in the religious wars of Europe" (Himes 2013, 321). The abuses of the Roman Church undoubtedly laid the groundwork for the Protestant Reformation.

Reformation Period

History is clear on the abuses of the Roman Church that led to the Reformation. "The papacy that survived the medieval era was one that had endured serious declines in moral authority and political respect" (Himes 2013, 116). The church had loss its moral leadership and spiritual compass and like fish it was decaying from the head down. It was ripe for reformation and renewal, but to lead such change without the sanction of the Papacy was a life-threatening proposal for anyone that would have audacity to challenge papal authority. Such person would be making the ultimate sacrifice and perhaps effect no significant change to the evil, abusive bureaucracy.

Nonetheless, in 1517 an Augustinian priest and theology professor named, Martin Luther, stepped forward with such a proposal. He drafted a theses statement with ninety-five points, posted to the church door in Whittenburg as a summon to church authorities to debate him on matters of scripture, theology and morals. This is the spark that ignited the firestorm that we come to know as the Protestant Reformation. It was not Luther's intent to split the church but to reform it from within. The Papal push back was life-threatening to Luther but friends in high places protected him or more accurately stated, the Lord of the church had him covered.

The Reformation came to head because of centuries of ecclesiastical abuses under the leadership of the Papacy. Reasonable men were no longer able to debate issues of faith and practice according to the scripture and their conscience. The church authority became the conscience of the masses and ruled with brutal force. That moved Martin Luther to take a stand against the abusive church authority at the risk of his own life.

The Protestant Reformation was not a singular event in a short period of time. There was Luther (Germany), Ulrich Zwingli (leader in Switzerland) and the French theologian John Calvin who became reformer in Geneva. The protestant reformation had differing theologies in different geographical areas. The Reformation gave a moral cleansing to the church, gave back certain authorities to Christ that the Roman church had usurped, and it gave back the word of God (the Bible) to the common people that the Roman church had kept from them.

The Roman church remained violent for a long period of time in its attempt to assert control and regain territory lost, but the Protestant movement kept advancing and spreading like leaven in a batch of dough. For good or evil, the Protestant Reformation opened the door for the rise of numerous denominational and non-denominational groups, such as we see today. Perhaps, that is the diversity the Body of Christ needed all along, where no one man can wield authority over human life in the kingdoms of men and for the kingdom of God.

The Protestant Reformation was not a clean, peaceful protest within itself. Like the Roman church, the movement was also violent as it tried to find its own identity. It was violent against those of its own who were deemed to be unorthodox. Influential church leaders retained some of the leadership styles they had learned from the Roman church, but the violence of the Protestant movement was nothing equal to the level of abuse deployed by the Roman church. The Reformation served for the furtherance of the gospel and a significant return to the word of God.

The Contemporary Church

Protestants and Roman Catholics today still have much to learn from each other; both have a noble and a tattered past.

Generally speaking, they have grown to respect each other and even accept each other as the people of God, even though elements in both camps think the very opposite. Though both groups have much in common in some areas of doctrine and Christian practice, they are still light years apart in other areas. Perhaps, that's the unity and diversity in the Body Paul speaks of (1Cor.12:1-31). Despite the differences, Protestants and Catholics are under the headship of Jesus Christ (Eph.4:1-16).

Furthermore, the Protestant arm of the Christian Church is not a monolith; it is also diversified into many denominations and independent groups, some of which are light years apart in doctrine and practice. It is no exaggeration to say that the Roman Catholic church speaks with one voice through one Pope, but Protestantism speaks with many voices. Some see this as an advantage for the Protestant camps while others consider it a profound disadvantage.

One downside is the fact that Protestant local churches are more beset by conflicts resulting in schisms after schisms. This undeniable reality is the concern this book is trying to remedy in some small way. The Roman Catholics have their own challenges but those are not my concern here.

The Sum of the Matter

We have seen that the Western church became extremely militant under Papal Rome and Protestant groups adopted a similar militancy, though less so in scope and severity. The contemporary church may have literally lay down the sword but has not fully returned to the peace theology of Jesus in the resolution of conflicts as recorded in the New Testament.

For sure, we have not fully mastered "the love thy neighbor as thyself" requirement of Jesus. The church is still divided by doctrine, race and national origin. In the United States, partisan politics has become another divisive element; the Republican party is almost synonymous with certain element of the evangelical church. Perhaps, this is a sign that the contemporary church, like its medieval counterpart, is ready again to ride the beast of world government as the apostate church (Rev.17:1-18).

Yet, as we look back over that paths the saints have trod, we observe that the larger Church body worked hard to settle doctrinal conflicts, from the Jerusalem Council (Acts 15) to the formation of Nicene Creed to Vatican II. Church councils have been used to settle major doctrinal conflicts. Today we may call some of these smaller councils Synods, Conventions, Annual or Biannual meetings, General Assembly, Convocations and so on. But we are less consistent with how we settle conflicts at the local church level where it matters most; it is where the fire of destructive conflict does its greatest damage. It's as if the local churches are left to fend for themselves.

The members in the pews of the local churches are fighting and airing their dirty laundry in the public square, in barber shops, beauty salon, social media and in the secular courts. It is shameful enough that churches should have dirty laundry, but to hang them out for public viewing is most disgraceful. When the church is so disgraced and tainted, its work and witness to the community becomes an *impossible mission*. Some local churches are fighting their pastors publicly and pastors are fighting their congregations publicly. Others are asking, how have we gotten here? But the better question is, how can we stop and how can we fix this?

There are many answers to the first questions. Chief among them is the fact that the members of local churches have not been taught their Christian duties of peacemaking and peacekeeping, and these local churches have no internal system to manage and resolve situations of conflict biblically and in the spirit of Christ. Most churches hardly have a peace strategy to preserve the unity and safeguard the integrity its message, worship and mission to the community and the world.

Some people are undisciplined in their behaviors; they tend to run wild in the face of rumors and scandals pertaining to their own church. Yet, Jesus and the apostles, the Scriptures and traditions have left us with precedence for dealing with conflict in the local church. Every church member has the duty of peacemaking and peacekeeping. We ought to love God and neighbor in word and practice.

I hope that your church with the guidance of this book will start a peacemaking and peacekeeping ministry to deal with conflict. In the next chapter, we will try to understand church conflicts more closely, so we can remedy it more effectively in our local church ministry.

CHAPTER 8

UNDERSTANDING THE NATURE OF CONFLICT

What is conflict? Conflict is a slippery and even difficult word to define. Almost any definition you come up with is inadequate. It is like trying to define love. Everyone thinks he or she knows what it is, yet each one gives a different definition. It's like the four blind men who were asked to describe the elephant: one running his hand from the neck over the back down to the hind part of the animal said, "It's like a mountain." Another feeling its long trunk says, "It's like a rope." Still another runs his hand up and down the legs of the mighty beast exclaimed, "The elephant is like a tree!" The fourth man feeling only the giant ears of the animal flapping left and right explains, "The elephant is like a fan." Are they all wrong or all right? Each of the four men experienced a different part of the same animal. Explaining conflict is similar; it is very experiential and subjective.

Conflict is a word used to describe many experiences thrown together, some good and some not good at all. But one thing is true, we all know when we are in a conflicted situation and if it is getting better or worse. Conflict therefore can have feelings of joy come from winning or feelings of discontent, frustration, betrayal, anger and even rage. If they continue to push your buttons, it could get really mean and ugly; beyond this is the war zone. In this chapter, therefore, we are not going to rush to settle on a neat, clean and shiny book definition. I am going to trust your judgment, that you already have a good sense of what a conflict is, especially destructive conflict. We will be raising and answering several questions about conflict and each answer will clarify the nature of this beast.

But just in case you try to define it, remember what a definition is. I was taught that when you define a thing, you must first put it into a class, then distinguish it from everything else in that class. For example, a chair is a piece of *furniture* with a back, four legs and a flat area for one person to sit. The class is furniture; the description is everything that is said after the word furniture. But not everything is as easy to describe as a chair. Somethings have complexity and not easily describable or categorized. Jesus, the master teacher, realized that complexity when He tried to define the kingdom of heaven to different audiences.

To make himself clear to His hearers, Jesus used illustrations or figures of speech (parables, metaphor, similes) that were familiar to his hearers. These are association sayings, descriptive stories, stories going from the familiar to the unfamiliar, from the known to the unknow, from the simple to the complex. Considered together, they constitute a method of teaching, a pedagogy called, the law of apperception (i.e. using the known to introduce the unknown).

When speaking to fishermen, Jesus said the kingdom of heaven is like a net thrown into the sea that gathers all kinds of fish and when it is full the fisherman keeps what he wants and throws back into the sea what's left (Matt.13:47-50). In ministering to investors, Jesus asserts that the kingdom of heaven is like a treasure buried in a field. When a man finds it, he covers it again, rushes home and sells all that he has and buys the field (Matt.13:44). Why? He that owns the field also owns the treasure.

Ministering to housewives Jesus said, the kingdom heaven is like yeast which a woman hides in three measures of meal and it works its way through the whole batch of dough (Luke 13: 19-21). To lovers He said, the kingdom of heaven is like ten bridesmaids with their lamps waiting for the bridegroom to arrive, five wise and five foolish. The wise took extra oil for their lamps but the foolish took none and were shut out of the wedding because they had to leave the wedding party to buy oil; the bridegroom arrived before they got back (Matt.25:1-13).

What is Jesus doing telling these descriptive stories? He is using what was familiar to His audience to teach spiritual truths. That is why the common people heard Him gladly; He spoke their language. Other teachers of the Law gave them nothing new, just quotes from their favorite teachers going back as far as they could. Jesus got them right where they lived. They understood Him! "No one ever spoke the way this man does," they said of Him (John 7:46). Like Jesus, let's use a few figures of speech: similes, metaphor, parables, stories to get a better understanding of the nature of conflict.

Conflict Is Like Fire

Conflict is like fire; it should always be used in a controlled way. If fire got out of control, you are in trouble. The same is true of conflict. Conflict can serve an organization well in providing different perspectives to a situation; it can stir vigorous debate. It prevents leaders from just having yes people around them. It challenges us to do things differently. It shakes us out of complacency and wakes us up to new realities and possibilities. Conflict can push an organization to change and grow or it can avoid conflict at all costs, stagnates and dies.

For these and other reasons, healthy conflict is good and should be encouraged and embraced. Speaking on leading change in organizations, John Potter, asserts that "transformation always fail to achieve their objectives when complacency levels are high" (Potter 1996, 4). In other words, people are inclined to settle in their old comfort zone, if they are unchallenged and have no sense of urgency to do anything differently. Conflicts stirs the nest and opens the gate to change and new possibilities.

But like fire, conflict needs to be managed, so that it does not become destructive. Wise leaders of organizations have a system in place to prevent conflict becoming destructive. Workplaces have fire extinguishers and a rapid response security force. But better yet, they have a system (a team of specialists) in place to deal with interpersonal conflicts. Some organizations label this body, *the ethics or grievance committee.* It handles conflicted situations like sexual harassment, workers' complaints and dissatisfactions. It functions as a kind of guardrail to enforce policies and keep people on track.

In his book *Firestorm,* Ron Susek points out something that is all too familiar—that like fire, "conflict between people generally start from a small spark." These "sparks can smolder, often for years, in a deep emotional memory bank before erupting into a firestorm. To assume the sparks will vanish is a grave mistake, he warned (Susek 1999, 17).

A firestorm is no respecter of persons or property; it will consume everything in its path. As I am writing this, wildfire devoured several communities in California. The town of Paradise was totally consumed, many lives lost, homes and businesses destroyed. Paradise looks like it sustained a nuclear blast. It has been often said, "fire is a good servant but a bad master." The Granite Mountain Hotshots was an elite team of 20 firefighters of the City of Prescott. They were fighting a wildfire near Yarnell Hill, Arizona that was started by lightening on June 28, 2013. On June 30th the wind suddenly changed direction and trapped all 20 of them in a firestorm. Only 1 escaped to tell the tails, 19 were devoured by the fire. That is the nature of unmanaged conflict; it is destructive.

This book is based upon research done for a doctoral dissertation that grew out of a New York church conflict. The church was founded in 1994 and was doing well but just below the surface a conflict fire was brewing and when it burst open, more than half the congregation was gone with the associate minister. This schism was bad and not so bad. It was bad because it twisted the truth, demonized good people and sever relationships for personal ambition. It was not so bad because another congregation was birth out of that destructive conflict. The apostle Paul asserts that some of the bad things that happened to him served for the furtherance of the gospel.

About five years later, the same church split again because of personality conflicts and people jostling for power and position. These two schisms drastically downsize the church and brought the work of the ministry to a paralyzing holt. The church at the time had no conflict management system in place and so the fire of conflict consumed everything in its wake. It's like a house fire and there are no sprinklers, no extinguishers, and no one remembers to call the fire department of the city.

When the conflict fire was over, only the pastor and a few members were left standing. As they walked through the ruins of years of hard work, they were shocked and wondered what just happened. Could brothers and sisters in Christ really behave like that! What can we do to prevent the destructive power of conflict from ruing another congregation, they asked? They had not a clue what to do.

There was no peace ministry in that church. Peace as a Christian duty was preached but not with any fervency and it was not put into practice. To this day, the second schism remains puzzling because there was not one significant thing people were fighting over. Some people did not have personal grievance, they were just supporting their friends to destroy the church. People turned upon each other. It appears that they cast just about everything they learned about Christ-like behavior to the wind. It is as if they were carried along by some sinister spirit. No one that left has every returned in penitence.

Some say, there were smoldering ambers from the first schism that were not fully resolved but kept burning quietly beneath the surface. In other words, there were secret sympathizers that wanted to go with the first group but chose to remain behind, but their hearts were not in it. That explanation seems unlikely because they did not leave and join them; they scattered in different direction and like Jonah waited for Nineveh to fall, they watched for the church to close but that did not happen. A couple of years went by and the experience gave rise to a doctoral dissertation. This book is based on that research project.

Yes, church people fight, and they could fight dirty too. Church conflict is indeed an inside job; churches don't really get destroyed from outside by the unregenerate world. Churches tend to implode; they fall from within. It is indeed an inside job and it has to be dealt with as such.

Conflict Is Like A Storm or Hurricane

Just as one parable does not fully explain kingdom of heaven, so conflict needs more than one figure of speech to explain its complexity. This time we will use a hurricane.

Most storms start at as a local, tropical depression and generally fizzle out, thus posing no threat to people or property. But now and then one picks up hurricane force winds and is no longer called a tropical cyclone or depression. It can move up to a category 1 hurricane, then a cat.2, then cat.3, cat.4 and finally a cat.5. From you hear this is category 2 hurricane, you know a catastrophe is in the making and you must get out of its path. With categories 4 and 5, you know you have a monster on your hand; the issue now is, how to stay alive in this destructive force coming your way.

Fire is a better analogy for conflict because you can control most fires by isolating them, managing them, then extinguish them as you do a conflict, except we use the word resolve in the place of extinguish. But you cannot do those things with a hurricane. Hurricane, therefore, is only like conflict because it has levels or stages intensity; we refer to them as categories. When the wind velocity of a storm reaches at least 74 miles per hour (mph), you have a category 1 hurricane; when it reaches 96-110 mph, you have a category 2. Winds 111-129 mph, you have a category 3, and winds 130-156 mph, you have a category 4 hurricane on your hand. Finally, with wind velocity at 157 mph and above, you have a category 5 monster to contend with. The higher the category, the greater the risk to human life and property. In that sense destructive conflict behaves like a hurricane.

Experts have identified stages that a conflict goes through with increased emotional intensity like a hurricane. Speed B. Leas in his work with churches in conflict, identifies five stages or levels that a conflict goes through.

There is Level 1: The people in the conflict "stay focused on the problem." Their language is generally direct, polite and with clarity. The goal is to resolve the problem. The language and behavior of the people in conflict are equivalent to wind velocity in a storm.

There is Level 2: "People become more self-protective." In other words, as things get heated up, people begin to look out for themselves. No one wants to be seen as the troublemaker, so protecting oneself becomes the focus and not the problem as in level 1.

There is Level 3: "People turn from self-protection and become more interested in winning. That is, they want to preserve their position in the organization. Now they are in different camps. They talk about us and them. They want to put their people in office.

There is Level 4: People are not just interested in winning any more, they want to get rid of someone. One group views the other as the enemy.

Finally, there is Level 5: People are dug in and fanatical about their position. They now feel as if they have a divine mission to get rid of those who oppose them (Leas 201, 16).

Levels of conflict are not always clearly marked, especially if you are not one of the primary parties in the conflict. You either hear of the conflict later or join it later. Perhaps, by that time, the conflict is already at level 3 or 4. For you the conflict made landfall as a category 3 or 4. People have already stake out their position and are trying to win you over to their side. People join sides for different reasons: to support their friends, to support a cause, it represents their interest, important people are on that side, that side is right, I have investigated the facts, and the list goes on.

Since there is a third side to conflict, perhaps it is better be part of that third side. The point is, the levels of conflict at times are not clear because you came to the conflict late. You arrived at the fight in the fourth rounds. A conflict could also be partly explained by a third figure of speech, this time as disease in the human body that is life threatening.

Conflict Is Like Cancer

Destructive conflict is like a cancer, a disease that infects the body with an assignment to kill. Anything that is destructive with an assignment to kill comes from an evil source. Two such sources were identified in a previous chapter as: Satan and human sinful nature (John 10:10a; James 4:1-3).

Some cancers are asymptomatic; they quietly work to destroy the body without notifying the owner. Symptoms are messages to tell us something is wrong, but a silent killer has no symptoms until it is too late. It reminds me of this pastor who took on an associate minister, but the associate had ambition of starting his own church. But he lacked the knowledge, experience and courage to go out and start one or seek help the right way to launch a new work. Instead, the associate quietly influenced individual members to himself by undermining the work of the church that he should have been building up. By the time the pastor became fully aware of the deception a schism was already underway.

The pastor stood defenseless because there was no clear-cut charge on anything, but there were several wild stories of dissatisfaction that were never expressed before the split. The truth is—someone had an agenda to start his own church and carried off part of an established congregation to achieve that end. It was the easy way. The person created a conflict and used it as a strategy to achieve a personal end. There was no concern whether the entire church closed as long as another open under his leadership. This is one-way conflict is like cancer; it seeks to destroy the host to live.

Some conflicts are like cancer because the people who lead them are not seeking therapeutic measures to heal the body; they are bent on destroying the body and generally for selfish reasons. In such cases, radical surgery is necessary. Surgery means separation. That is, separating healthy tissues from the infected ones. But be very careful how God's people are treated, even those that oppose you. They are not the cancer; it is the unrighteous behavior is the cancer. Be sure to make the distinction that they are not the cancer, even though they may have raised hell and separated themselves from your church. Don't treat them as they treat you, be Christ-like to them. No church is perfect. Even the member that publicly cursed and denied his Lord has the capacity to repent. If repentance has taken place, forgiveness and restoration should follow as Jesus has shown us in His dealing with the Big Fisherman, Peter (John 21:15-19).

Only the Holy Spirit, plus close adherence to the word of God coupled with much fasting and prayer can perform this radical surgery of separation. No pastor on his or her own can do it, especially if that pastor is the cause of the conflict by immoral living, fraudulent behavior or authoritarian leadership. Where such things are the case, gracefully stepping aside is perhaps the best solution, because both pastor and congregation need healing. Such stepping aside temporarily or permanently is much easier when prior provision is made for it in the by-laws of the organization. The church should be spiritually mature enough to quietly activate this provision without finishing off the failing leader and destroying the congregation. The purpose of surgery is not to kill the patient.

The surgery of separation is sometime necessary to save a congregation as amputation of a limb is sometime necessary to save a life. But no surgery like this should be a joyous or celebratory event. Some separations take the form of discipline, removal from ministry office or excommunication. When conflict expresses itself through an intransigent group that will not compromise. For group members, it is all or nothing. Here you have a schisms and separation is the inevitable solution. In this case, there is a staying group and an exodus group. Separation is always painful but not necessarily bad; it may save the life of the patient. The patient is the congregation; the staying group or leaving group.

Schisms are sometimes good, good for the group that stays and good for the group that left. Think of the Protestant Reformation; that was a schism, a great separation. But was it good for the church of Jesus Christ? As painful as it was—the protestant separation from the Roman church was a good thing. A split at the local church is not always a bad thing. Nonetheless, we must try to avoid it, if we can. If we cannot avoid it, we must manage it. Paul and Barnabas ministry team split over John Mark as a result, they ended up with two teams: Paul and Silas and Barnabas and Mark. A responsible local church will occasionally find itself disfellowshipping a member or leader for the sake of that person and for the sake of the larger congregation. I liken this act of discipline to a surgeon removing a defective body part to protect the body and save the life of the person. The surgery or separation is necessary.

But surgery should not be the first resort, doctors almost always try to save a limb from amputation; amputation is the last resort in most cases. Even so, when amputation has to be done, it is never a light joyous event. Amputation is done thoughtfully and with compassion. The same should be true when a member or leader that has to be removed from the Body of Christ. It should never be a joyous vindictive event. We should assume that the people that leave our church fellowship voluntarily or otherwise, are still the people of God. There should be no reciprocal demonization of each other, even though people might have behaved badly. The group that stays and the group that left need to search themselves and repent before God as needed because each group bears some blame.

Some *conflicts* are like *cancer* in the body not because they both begin with the letter "C" but the fact that they are both destructively progressive. They both have stages; conflict has five stages or levels, cancer has four. We have already looked at the five levels of conflict. Perhaps, there are comparative commonalities between the two (see Table 1). Doctors use staging as a way to describe the size of a cancer and how far it has spread from the primary site. The stages look something like this:

- **Stage I:** Usually means, the cancer is "small and contained in the organ it started in."
- **Stage II**: This stage generally means, the tumor is larger than stage 1, but the cancer has not spread to surround tissues.

- **Stage III**: The cancer is larger and has spread to surrounding tissues.
- **Stage IV**: The cancer has spread to another body organ; it has metastasized.

Table 1: The Conflict/Cancer Comparison

CONFLICT	**CONFLICT**	**CANCER**	CANCER
Levels	**Explanation**	**Stages**	**Explanation**
Conflict Level 1	People in the conflict stay focused on the problem.	**Cancer Stage I**	The Cancer is small and contained
Conflict Level 2	People become more self-protective.	**Cancer Stage II**	The tumor is growing; it is larger than stage 1
Conflict Level 3	People turn from self-protection and become more interested in winning.	**Cancer Stage III**	The cancer is larger and spread to surrounding tissues.
Conflict Level 4	Winning is not the goal any-more; they want to get rid of their opponents.	**Cancer Stage IV**	The cancer spread to other body organs. It has metastasized.
Conflict Level 5	People are fanatical about their position, acting as if they had a divine mission to get rid of their opponent.		

In conflict level 1 and cancer stage 1, the problem is contained. If a cancer is discovered at this point, treatment and survival chances are good; the cancer is contained, the conflict has not picked up steam as yet. It is at this point Jesus says, you should go to the offending party alone and try to settle the matter between you two (Matt.18:15). If you are successful, the conflict is resolved without it spreading and involving other people. The cancer is contained and eradicated.

But note well that two containment disciplines are required at this level: 1) when you learn of the situation, discipline your mouth, don't spread it to others. 2) Act promptly to talk it over face to face with the person and have it settled. Don't go into it over the phone, make an appointment to meet. You may find out it is just a misunderstanding, clear it up. If it is a disagreement settle it. If hurt is involved, acknowledge it, repent of it and forgive it and pray together. The matter is settled! Don't go talking about it with somebody else, because the wrong news is likely to get back to the person and open the wounds all over again.

The process is significant and should be noted. If your level 1 attempt to resolve the conflict does not work, you must go to level 2. Jesus said, take with you one or two witnesses and try again to settle the matter with the offending brother or sister (Matt.18:16). Heaven is observing the process and angels are witnesses at that end; you need witnesses at your end. Heaven issues an order in the word, so a judicial proceeding is taking place and witness are needed, because if it does not work due to one party refusing to cooperate, a verdict will have to be issued at some point as we will see later. Note that the second attempt that requires a witness or two corresponds with stage 2 on the cancer table, the tumor is growing.

But what do you do if your second attempt to make peace with this sister or brother does not work because of failure to cooperate? Jesus counsels us to go to a third step (Matt.18:17). That is, tell it to the church. This step is equivalent to conflict levels 3 and 4 because the conflict has spread to more people. On the cancer side this is stage 3 and possible 4, the cancer has spread to surrounding tissues and possibly to other organs. The cancer is metastasizing (spreading to other organs).

If the church cannot resolve it because one or two of the parties refuse to submit to the church—Jesus said, put him or them out of the fellowship (18:17). This is conflict level-5 where people are dug in, they refuse to compromise, refuse to repent, refuse to forgive. They stop behaving as Christians. On the cancer side, this is full-blown stage IV and radical surgery is warranted (that is separation). Churches are very slow to disfellowship or excommunicate people today and that perhaps contributes to the chaos and dysfunction of many congregations. They fail to exercise discipline or discipling.

Make no mistake about it, Jesus has delegated his authority to the Church to bind and loose and can hand back this unrepentant person to Satan for discipline because of his or her stubborn refusal to submit to the authority of Christ (Matt.18:18). Here, the local church exercises the authority of the keys (Matt.16. 17-19). We will revisit this issue later.

Conflict More Formally Defined

We have used three figures of speech (fire, hurricane, cancer) to give a descriptive picture to help us better understand the true nature of conflict and perhaps arrive at a succinct definition.

Fire tells us that conflict is not a bad thing; it is very useful but has to be controlled less it becomes destructive. Hurricane gives us another snapshot of conflict. You cannot control a hurricane as you would fire but at least, it gives you enough time to prepare for it. Hurricane also comes in categories (1 to 5), conflict also has 5 levels of intensity. In other words, just as we prepare for a hurricane, we can prepare for a church conflict. Preparedness planning should be part of the Christian education training of every local church. This book uses several names for such a plan: peace ministry, dispute resolution system, conflict management system, and resident counsel and so on.

In the third place, conflict is likened to a disease in the body, such as cancer. By nature, cancer takes over its host and eventually destroys it. Survival depends upon early detection. By nature, destructive conflict, if not controlled, will destroy the church fellowship or renders it useless in accomplishing its mission assignment. Conflict spreads, cancer spreads. Conflict has 5 levels, cancer 4 stages. Radical intervention is often required to get rid of cancer: surgery, chemotherapy or radiation therapy. Including surgery, all intervention method chosen is to separate infected tissue from good tissues. Destructive conflict is dealt with in the context of discipline and the key word is separation.

Having all this information on the nature of conflict, how would you now define conflict? I have settled on two basic definitions, one general and the other specific. On the general side we have normal conflict. This *is serious disagreement or argument between two or more parties over interests or needs*. On the specific side we have destructive conflict. It is a fight in which the opponents are bent on winning, hurting, humiliating or even destroying each other because of their unmet needs or interests. In the general category, the conflict is healthy and often remains such, but at times it crosses over the line and becomes destructive. A conflict should be monitored at all times so that it remains normal and not become destructive. But no matter how hard you try, there is always the potential for a normal conflict to cross the line to become destructive.

This book asserts that a system must be in place to prevent conflict from crossing over the line to become destructive, and if it crosses the lines, the system will manage it and bring it to resolution. If the conflict is a hurricane, batten down valuable property and get out of its destructive path. If the conflict is a cancer, stay with the treatment until the last cancer cell is eradicated. If the cancer is a fire, work with it until the last amber is extinguished. This is the work of the conflict management system (CMS) or team. Destructive conflict does not have to split or destroy an organization. Church fights do not have to spill over into the streets to barber shops, beauty salon and social media to assault the integrity of the church and hinder its mission to the community and the world.

Effective dispute resolution calls for a smooth-running conflict resolution system in place at the local church, long before crisis starts. It is there to educate the entire church how to behave in a conflict crisis (hurricane, fire or cancer) while the *Agents of Peace-Managers* of conflict work these fights to resolution. These workers are part of the local congregation, that's why we refer to them as the *Resident Counsel*. They work to preserve the unity of the church and safeguard the integrity of its witness to the community and the world. In the next chapter, we will discuss some of the major causes of conflict in the local church, so that we can prevent some of them from happening. If a rancher knows weak areas of his fence, he can preemptively have them fixed that his cows don't get out to cause havoc to his neighbor's property.

CHAPTER 9
CAUSES AND SOURCES OF CONFLICT

What cause church folks to fight? Frankly, the fact that they fight is not new; church folks have been fighting a long time. The apostle James who lived in first century Israel rhetorical asked his congregation, "From whence come wars and fightings among you?" (Jas.4:1 KJV). The surprise lies in a second fact—that in the 21st century, church folks are still fighting. James' question was previously addressed under two subheadings: 1) *that destructive conflict has a spiritual connection to personified evil, and 2) that conflict has a causative connection to human sinful nature* (vv.1-5).

The conflict war that goes on in human nature, is undoubtedly a spiritual disease inherited from our ancestral parents' encounter with theodicy in the paradise garden. There was a third party in that garden, an evil, intelligent, reasoning personality that incited them to rebel against God because he knew their loss would be his gain (Gen.3). We will explore these two causative connections to human conflict in this chapter: the theodicy personality side and the sinful human nature side.

It is clearly self-evident from numerous biblical texts that destructive conflict in the human family is an evil, traceable to the encounter our ancestral parents had with Satan in the paradise garden. The encounter was most destructive because it resulted in one hundred percent fatalities for humans. The apostle Paul gives us the statistics on this, "For as in Adam all die..." (1Cor.15:22). It was Satan and humans versus the Triune God. Adam and his wife wittingly joined forces with Satan to their own banishment and death. If this garden encounter with Satan was the mother of all destructive conflicts for the human family, the father would be the conflict that precipitated the fall of Lucifer himself, the angel we now know as Satan (Isa.14:12-15; Ezek.28:13-15; Rev.12:7-12).

Destructive conflict is a dependent cause of human sinful nature, according to the apostle James (4:1-7). It is inherently connected to and motivated by our sin nature which is fundamentally self-centered. So, we cannot correctly say of all destructive conflicts, "the devil made me do it." The devil is not directly responsible for all the wrongs we do including destructive conflict, indirectly, perhaps. For this and other reasons, God will demonstrate to the whole world that even when the devil is safely locked away in prison, humans will continue fighting God and each other, because they possess a sinful nature that is in revolt against God (Rev. 20:1-3,7-10). Of course, Satan is the beneficiary of human evil actions, but humans are responsible for their own actions. The issue is insightful and tempting but this chapter cannot take the discussion down that street a second time; our focus here is the practical side of conflict. We want to better understand the situations from which conflicts are most likely to develop in a church or faith-based organization. That is our focus here.

But I must further caution that, this book is not intended to fix every conflict. Our concern here is church conflict, how to have a peace ministry all year round, how to educate the members of the local church in their Christian duties of peacemaking and peacekeeping. We want to show how to build a rapid response team of trained *Agents of Peace-Managers of Conflict* to deal with conflicted situations, to maintain the unity of the church, to preserve the integrity of its message to the community.

Therefore, the better we understand how conflict develops and manifests itself in the church environment, the better able we are to deal with it effectively and overcome it triumphantly. Yes, there are principles in this work that are applicable to personal conflict, family conflict and conflict in the workplace, but those areas are not our primary focus. So, when I speak of *causes and sources of conflict*, I am referring to conflict in the community of faith, things church people fight about and why they fight. Even here, the deeper inquiry is not so much on the *what* but on the *why*. The research on which this book is based, surgically dissected the very anatomy of some living conflicted churches and studied the autopsy of some dead ones to provide a healthy way forward for other churches.

If church people fight over just about everything as some assert, then this book won't be big enough to cover all those issues. The literature on church conflict has a glut of material on that. I don't want to take you into the deep wilderness of abstraction and verbiage. So, our primary focus is on why church people fight. First, we will discuss nine major sources of church conflict. Second, I will drill down on nine minor reasons conflict erupts in congregations.

Minor does not mean insignificant by any measure. Being a pastor for over forty years, I have presided over a few conflicted churches. So, I want to share my observations on why church people fight. I will hang my observations on nine pegs or headings. These are by no means exhaustive and they do overlap in some areas. My aim is not to knock down the observations of others, the findings already written in the literature, but perhaps to add to them in some small way or arrange a few somewhat differently.

SOME MAJOR SOURCES OF CHURCH CONFLICT

Even though some of the *headings* in this section are paraphrased, they are largely credited to Roy W. Pneuman (2001), from his excellent article on *Conflict Management in Congregations.* The meat under these headings, however, are largely my own, so any short comings or defects are all my own and cannot be blamed on Mr. Pneuman in anyway whatsoever.

People Fight Over V*alues and Beliefs*

The church is a value laden and belief driven institution. Values are convictions we hold dear; they are rooted in beliefs that are anchored in Scripture and tradition. Beliefs are what we hold to be true. That is why churches have declarations of faith. What is a declaration of faith? It is a statement of what the group holds to be true. For example, the Apostles' Creed and the Nicaean Creed are two of the oldest documents on what the apostles and the early church believed. These documents became necessary because people were believing and teaching differently from the apostles' teachings.

Our values and belief systems are formed overtime and they become part of the self. When they are threatened, we perceive them to be an attack on us. Muslims are taught from early childhood to revere the Prophet Mohammed and the Holy Koran and they observe how adults respond to disrespect of the prophet or desecration of their holy book. As a result, they fight back, and they fight back vigorously, sometimes violently. Contemporary Christians fight back at various degrees of vigorousness, but mostly short of violence. Why both groups fight? It is an attack on their values and beliefs, what they hold to be sacred and true. It is perceived as an attack on them.

For twenty-five years, John Johnson faithfully served as a deacon in a Bible based, conservative congregation; it was his life, what gave him meaning. He was living out his values and beliefs. Then, without consultation or warning to the church board and congregation, the bishop who never visited the church or the community, appointed a gay pastor to take over this historic congregation. The mild-mannered Johnson became enraged. He was now the chairman of the board of deacons and vigorously objected to the appointment, not only because he felt disrespected and insulted. But he saw the appointment as an attack on him and the congregation on several levels.

First, his own values and beliefs as well as that of the congregation were under assault and there was no way on God's green earth, he or they were going to embrace such lifestyle, now imposed on them by some ecclesiastical bureaucrat. Second, he thought the appointment undermined the Scriptures upon which his faith, values and beliefs are anchored. Third, the appointment departed from the tradition to which he adheres. And fourth, the Bishop did not even have the good sense or respect for the congregation to secure their prior feelings on this matter. Johnson resolved that unless the Bishop rescinds the appointment, he will have a dirty fight and a schism on his hand and the congregation was unanimous with him. Deacon Johnson and the congregation dug in for a fight.

Values and beliefs are even more fundamental than the preceding illustration with Deacon Johnson. People in the same church are not a Xerox copy of each other in values and beliefs. For example, another church in the same denomination as John Johnson's was divided nearly fifty/fifty on the same question of having a gay pastor. That church will clearly split down the middle to become two congregations. What is this fifty/fifty divide saying to us?

It is saying that on several issues, people in the same congregation do not always share the same values or have the same beliefs; some may hold their beliefs with deeper convictions than others. Some people do not even know how deeply they hold their beliefs until those beliefs are challenged or put to the test. Beliefs and values that are not deeply held are not bonded to the core self—people tend to feel that they are more at liberty to negotiate these without damage to the self or disservice to the Scriptures. These we are willing to debate vigorously and even vote on, but if our side lose, we will throw in our support with the majority. But convictions that we hold strongly, convictions that bond with the self and rooted in Scripture are non-negotiables. People will not give their support to any winning majority; to do so, is to make a compromise of conscience they cannot live with. Here people fight back vigorously.

People who don't understand what's going on here will quickly label Deacon Johnson and his group homophobic. But Johnson and his group had not previously taken any open position against the gay lifestyle; they never march with banners protesting gay lifestyle; they never written to any political or activist group about it. Because the matter was not about gays; it was about their core existential values and beliefs as anchored in Scripture. Just as a lawyer must practice law in keeping with the constitution of the United States, Deacon Johnson and his church see the Bible as the supreme standard of the kingdom of God and Christian life. A clergy cannot practice ministry in defiance of this standard. Deacon Johnson's values and beliefs are not irrational; they are rooted in a higher law, the law of God.

So, when you see a church fight, ask the question, what are they fighting over? Are they fighting over values and beliefs? The people involved in the fight may not know that is what they are fighting over. The peace agent then must first get the facts, understand the gravity of their beliefs and values. They are most often rooted in tradition and Scripture and they would rather go to war than concede on these core values and beliefs. The new pastor who moves the wooden pulpit that was situated in the center of the chancel area and replaces it with a plastic one off to the side, may wonder why the congregation went berserk that first Sunday they discovered it. It is not about wooden pulpit; it's about what it represents. The church was built around the *centrality and authority* of the word of God. These values the center location and the solid wood represent to the congregation; they prided themselves a Bible believing church. Symbols matter because they represent our beliefs and values, and people fight vigorously over them, especially when they are discorded or desecrated. A plastic pulpit off to the side is *anathema*; it is cheap, no weighty durability or centrality.

Unclear Church Structure

Pneuman refers to unclear church structure as "structural ambiguity," which means the church has "no clear guidelines about the roles and responsibilities" of professional and non-professional people, staff and committees. As a result, people not knowing where the boundary lines are located, keep crossing them and tripping over each other. The boundaries or roles are not clearly defined. This is not a personal problem as such; it is system's problem. The danger is responding to it by blaming. People tend to react defensively when blamed and that almost always precipitates a fight.

But this fight is unnecessary and can be avoided. Here is how. If someone with a little wisdom and authority walks in and listens to the complaint and says, "this is not a people problem; this is a system's problem, so stop faulting each other for when you do that you make the problem worst." The problem is the work system we inherited; it is a system that needs to be updated to match the changing times and needs of this organization. Now, let us focus on the problem and try to fix it together without becoming part of the problem.

Once the problem is properly contextualized, blame is removed. Once the problem is labeled systemic, the fight is greatly reduced, giving everybody a chance to work together to fix it. This does not mean that people are absolved of responsibility and accountability. If hard words were spoken and feelings got hurt, people need to immediately apologize and forgive and move on. This blame the system moment also gives an opportunity for everyone to save face, so the wise leader will insist that everybody takes advantage of it to clear the air and remedy any hard feelings.

Experientially speaking, to remove *structural ambiguity* the pastor should lead the way to review, revise and update the by-laws annually or biannually to reflect the current realities of the organization and its operation. A by-laws committee should be tasked with the responsibility of studying the issues and make recommendation to the board that will intern make recommendation to the annual or biannual corporate business meeting where the body will vote on changes.

Individual offices, staffs, departments and committees should have a more detail version of their guidelines. The church handbook should also have a condensed version of the role and function of each office and committee; all members should have access to the church's handbook, so they can see who does what. If your church does not have a handbook, write one and make it available to each member. Secular organizations often refer to the handbook as the policy manual.

If and when there is a territorial conflict, these written documents can be used by the governing board or the church CMS to quickly determine what lane each person was operating in when the collision (conflict) took place and bring it to resolution. But beware, the matter now is more than who crosses over into whose lane. Hard words were exchanged, egos are bruised, feelings are hurt. The conflict is not resolved until this emotional piece is dealt with. Don't be fooled; don't gloss over it because people say, everything is okay. Sometimes people say that out of their discomfort, but they don't really mean it. They have a hidden dagger to use at a more convenient day. It is important that the person surrender his or her dagger.

The discerning leader should spot this false peace and locate this hidden dagger. In other places I refer to this as *smoldering amber*, a hidden piece of wood still burning when everyone thought the fire was completely out. This hidden amber will reignite the blaze later to everyone surprise. The conflict resurfaces because it was not properly settled. Go back and review the resolution of conflict Jacob mediated and negotiated with Shechem, the leader of the community that raped Jacob's daughter, Dinah.

Jacob thought his sons agreed to the deal he made with Schechem, but in fact his sons did not. Jacob did not even ask them their feelings on the matter. He just assumed they agreed with it because they kept quiet. But later they avenged the honor of their sister by killing ever male in the Schechemites' community including the rapist. What was their reason? Schechem treated their sister like a prostitute (Gen.34:1-31). That illustrates the dangers hidden ambers pose to keeping the peace.

Conflict Over Pastor's Role and Responsibilities

If the pastor's role and responsibilities are not clear to the members of the church, it can become a source of troubling conflict. People frequently have unfair expectations of the pastor, so they need to be educated as to the pastoral function. Most pastors don't see themselves as employees of the church. They see themselves as self-employed serving the congregation. For tax and Social Security purposes, the IRS tend to view pastors as self-employed as well but that's a separate issue we can't get into here.

There are members who believe that the pastor must visit them with ever major headache and minor tooth ache they may have. They don't think he or she should have two days off each week as they enjoy from their workplace, nor should he or she have vacation, drive a good car and paid a comfortable salary. I have had people who remarked, he is working for God and will be rewarded in the sweet by and by. They certain don't expect that from their workplace because they have a family to care for but for some reason the man or woman of God that serve them is viewed differently. Some see the pastor as God's do-gooder; his work is totally altruistic or charitable.

Some church folks think God objects to proper compensation. These are the same people who want to sit in proverbial wagon while the pastor hauls it up the hill with them all seasons of the year. Someone has to inform them, that is the old school way of church operation. Most pastors now a days belong to the new school; they view the whole congregation as doing ministry with the pastor. Some churches are chronically traditional; they did not get the memo that there are new ways of doing ministry. As a result, they are unwittingly engaged in pastor abuse by clinging to unfair expectations. Other are well informed but they choose to be disingenuous and meanspirited to the man or woman of God.

The flip side is also true, if the pastor's role and responsibilities are not clear to him or her, there can be an over or underperform of those duties that could provoke complaint leading to conflict. To overperform is to step out one's role and end in conflict with other offices. To underperform is failure to do the duties of the office. For example, the pastor is frequently absent from the pulpit on Sundays because he or she is away on paid preaching assignments. If the shepherd is not feeding his or her own flock but is away making money, should the people not complain? Behavior like this will invite conflict with the congregation.

The pastor should understand the church's expectation and should understand his or her calling and ministry; this should be made clear early in the pastoral tenure. For example, if a pastor defines his calling under what is called, the fivefold ministry and understands the expression, *do the work of an evangelist* to mean, travelling around the country on paid preaching assignments—that could be troubling, if done excessively. This behavior has been a cause of conflict; we will return to it later.

Outgrown Governance Structures and Archaic Buildings

Outgrown governance structure has a close resemblance to *structural ambiguity* previously covered under *unclear church structure*; in fact, they greatly overlap but each provides a useful photographic angle to the problem being discussed.

With the passage of time, a congregation can outgrow its *governance* structure. In other words, the way the church was originally organized to operate and do business is outdated; even the building can be archaic and no longer relevant. In fact, it has become a source of conflict for some churches. Let's take an extreme business example to illustrate the point.

The Blue Elephant is a White owned restaurant in town that also serves African Americans customers. Without the colored only sign posted, the restaurant had a particular section including special restrooms roped off to which this ethnic clientele restaurant cleverly guided. Patrons are steered to the section the restaurant deemed racially fitting and appropriate form them. To add insult to injury, the Confederate flag is prominently displayed. The owners contend that this is the way they have always done business for a hundred years and they have no intention of changing now. They want to preserve their heritage and tradition, they argued.

The restaurant is a throwback to another time. You can readily see how this extreme governance structure would invite conflict with free citizens of a democratic society. Some people would not abide by this way of doing business; they would aggressively challenge such treatment because it does not fit the times. A church's governance structure may not be as loudly discriminatory as the restaurant example, but it can be outdated nonetheless in many ways and not necessarily along racial lines. Just as the restaurant owners need to re-vision the way they do business; a church needs to have a changed vision as well. Outdated church polity needs to be revised from time to time; the old templet is not fit for twenty-first century ministry practice.

Baptist Church of the Savior on Bradford Street in New York was one such church (name changed). It had a long history of stability. But subsequent to that period of stability, the community around it began to change and the congregation composition reluctantly reflects that change. It changed from White to Black and White, then completely Black, from male pastor to female, from many members to a few. Notwithstanding, the congregation retained a few powerful nostalgic members that held on to the old school status quo and steadfastly resist change.

The one-hour sedated Sunday service with pipe organ and few aged choir members singing Beethoven had given way to electronic keyboard, drums, guitar, tambourine, handclapping, foot-stamping dynamic worship for two or more hours. Thrown in was dialogue preaching with the congregation responding with "amen," "hallelujah," and "preach it." But the few older members that hold power for the past thirty years and control the purse string resent and resist the change and refused to share power. They have been living in a state of denial, refusing to accept that the times have changed. As a result, the fire conflict rages on. They always refer to a set of by-laws that have not been updated in fifty years; the church it was drafted for no longer exists, but some nostalgic members continue resist change with hindsight longing for the good old days. The few older members are writing the obituary of a church that died long ago. The new congregation needs to revise the governance structure.

Additionally, the historic, landmark building that once housed the congregation is no longer sustainable for practical and economic reasons. This once strong stone and brick structure built to last a few hundred years is fast deteriorating. Its towering steeple, choir loft that's no longer used, pipe organ that's no longer plays, ornamental stained-glass windows all fit for a museum. Its leaky cathedral roof further renders it a relic of the distant past that is no longer practical. Maintenance of the structure is far beyond the needs and resources of the congregation. But parting with this monstrosity is cause for strong interpersonal combat.

Today most large churches are more sophisticated with visionary leadership, but there are many churches of the old school that are dying because they are unwilling to change, and change is too conflicting for them. Jesus once said, you cannot put new wine into old wineskin. The old governance structure and even some physical structures are no longer practical for twenty-first century ministry. Rather than nostalgically clinging to these relics of a distant past, leaders will have to educate their congregation to let go and move forward and live or remain stagnant looking back and die.

A congregation of fewer members cannot do as much as when there were many members; its human and financial assets are more stretched. Staff members are at risk for burnout when they are used in different offices over and over again. The church must rethink its vision, redefine its mission and restructure its governance to face the ministry realities of the twenty-first century.

Pastoral Leadership Versus Church Tradition

Every church has its own personality and tradition. The personality of a church is either dominantly built around a strong influential leader or around that church's history and tradition. For example, Marble Colligate Church in NYC drew its personality from Norman Vincent Peale who was its pastor for 52 years. Long period of religious formation like this often becomes a tradition of its own. It would take another strong personality to emerge from Peele's influence upon the formation of that church.

Another example is the now defunct Crystal Cathedral. It was shaped around the personality of its founder, Robert Schuller. There are those who believe that the interrelated financial problems and leadership dispute that brought down that church could have been avoided.

Observers saw it coming; the symptoms were clear. They believe that when the founder retired and handed over to his son, he refused to let go. That prevented the church from transitioning to a new generation despite its financial woes. The style of leadership that was successful for the father could not be duplicated in the son's generation; the times were different. Perhaps, the son knew that as signaled in his sermon series, My Father's Shoes. He clearly stated that he has to walk in his own shoes. The change of vestment was another signal; the father dressed in an academic hooded doctoral gown, the son appears to prefer business suit, jacket and tie, a more contemporary style. Conflict developed, and the rest is history.

A new pastor taking leadership of a church that was shaped around the personality of his or her predecessor will need much wisdom, and more so, if he or she does not have the flamboyant and charismatic personality as that prior leader. Leadership style and the church's traditional style can indeed be a source of major conflict. Stated bluntly—a nominal, docile church that doesn't say, amen, hallelujah! Yes, sir preach it, is going to have a heart-attack with an animated, charismatic, hand-clapping, foot-stamping, drum-playing, guitar loving, tambourine shaking pastor who prefers all that over the old Hammond organ that carried the church through the Great

Depression until now. This pastor is heading for trouble, big trouble, for the times have changed.

If politics is an action that seems *sensible and judicious* for circumstance at hand, the pastor is better advised to have tea with those rich and powerful old ladies in the Women Society before implementing any drastic change. They have lived to see pastors come and pastors go. If the pastor refused this advice on the basis that he is Holy Spirit anointed, remind him or her that Stephen, Peter and Paul were anointed too but one was stoned, the other crucified and Paul was beheaded. The strange thing about it, those same old ladies will still show up in heaven and perhaps ask him to show them around since he was there way ahead of them. They will be loving on Jesus and winking at him out one eye. It's too late to walk out; he is stuck with them for eternity.

Untimely Change Implementation

In the previous section, we looked at dispute developed out of two major conflicting styles: the leadership style of the pastor and the traditional style of the church. Now, we turn to *untimely changes implemented* by a new pastor as a cause for conflict.

A young new pastor who is less experienced may be in too much of a rush to prove himself or herself and move to make drastic changes too quickly and experience a push back from the congregation and board members. It is best to get to know the people first, build relationships of trust before implementing significant changes.

I was called to be the pastor of a suburban Baptist church during my second year in seminary, but to my advantage, I was not all that inexperienced; this was my third pastorate. Despite my experience, I got pushback on a few immediate minor changes that I implemented. The pushback was mild but that did not really mean the majority of members were on board with me. They were just sympathetic with my ignorance and went along with the changes, but I did not know their real feelings until much later when they felt more comfortable to share them. I recall two incidents in that church.

First, certain deacons used to stand in front of the church building smoking on Sunday mornings. I did not think that speaks well for the church, so I requested of the deacons not to do that. They did cooperate but with some grumblings. I later learned that the previous pastor who shaped the personality of the church for 35 years smoked with the deacon at their monthly meeting in the church office. Those were the days before the connection of smoking and cancer was made.

Second, I had counseled with a member who had a drinking problem and kept falling back after every attempt at rehab. For this weaker brother's sake, I did not feel comfortable serving wine at the communion to him. The deacons did not say much when I changed the wine to Welch grape juice. But two years later when I accepted a new pastorate and moved on, they went back to serving wine.

Another church I was called to pastor—the chairman of the board of trustees was not a member of the church; this was allowed in the outdated by-laws of the church. On Sunday mornings he shows up at about offering time, takes custody of the offering and left. He did not worship with us. His wife was the financial secretary, so these were the only two people who knew about the amount collected on a given Sunday until the financial secretary gave her report to the monthly trustees meeting and at the annual business meeting.

The integrity of the trustee and his wife were never in question, but the picture was not a good one. When the pastor requested a change, the small group of officers around the trustees and his wife dug in and push back hard. That cause people to become suspicious and requested a business meeting where these officers could explain themselves to the general body. They boycotted the meeting and that angered the larger congregation and moved them to dissolve the board and elected a new board to represent the interest of the church.

Those officers who were voted out of office were sent letters explaining the action of the general body and requesting of them to turn over all financial instruments, including bank books and other documents. They refused. A second letter was sent, and they refused. The third letter threatened legal action but also gave them an option to turn over all financial instruments to the regional denominational headquarters and area executive minister. They did that so no legal action was taken in honor of their years of service and in interest of amending the riff. They did not return to church despite attempts to bridge the gap. With the conflict management tools available today, this conflict could have settled differently.

Ineffective Channels of Communication

Pneuman observes that "often communication problems are more a result of conflict than a cause of conflict. That "when a conflict escalates, members of one faction tend to avoid speaking to the other faction" (Pneuman 2001, 50). While it is true that factions don't normally speak to each other in a conflicted situation, the church needs to establish clear and adequate lines communication to its internal body and the external world. The following four actions will help a church reduce conflicted communication that plunge the entire organization into conflict.

First, a church must be transparent to its own people, don't lie to them, don't keep them in the dark because that will give rise to suspicions, speculations and a loss of credibility toward leadership.

Second, the church body must be educated on how to handle church information. Certain corporate information should range from public to privileged to classified. Public information is for everybody. Privileged information is shared with the entire church body, but they do not share it with non-members or inactive members. Classified information is only shared with top executive leadership on a need to know basis. Sensitive Information intended only for church membership should not be shared from the pulpit on a Sunday morning with a mix of members and visitors. Member should be asked to stay back an extra five or ten minutes behind closed doors to receive the information.

Third, the church must control its message to the external world. The church must enforce a strong social media policy by controlling what information can be posted. Members must know what information cannot be shared with non-members. This comes under their duty to keep the peace, preserve unity, and protect the integrity of the church.

Fourth, the church should have an officially designated public relations person who is tasked with communicating to the press, social media and the general outside world on church matters. The secular press likes sensational and scandalous stories; it satisfies the ear of the curious and gives the news network ratings. But the church does not owe the secular press an explanation for its operation and should push back hard at any wrongfully broadcast stories through its public relations officer.

Fifth, the church should have an attorney who works closely with the public relations officer. The attorney is not the independent counsel of the pastor against the church or the church against the pastor and other leadership. Counsel advises the church on its leadership concerning the law. If a riff develops between the congregation and the pastor that warrants going to court, the church's attorney cannot represent the pastor against the church. The pastor must secure his own private attorney and task him or her to have the matter settled peacefully out of court, if at all possible.

Church People not Generally Trained to Manage Conflict

It is a fact that church folks are not generally trained to manage conflict. But I am hoping that the time has come or is near at hand when it will no longer be true that church people "manage conflict poorly." Because this book endeavors to bridge the conflict gap by training and mobilizing an army of agents of peace and managers of conflicts in churches across the United States and the world. Every local church needs a peace ministry, a *Resident Counsel* to educate the local congregation and manage situations of conflict. Churches need to budget for this peace education training.

The culture of conflict that prevails in local churches, causing them to turn upon their leaders and upon each other, destroying the work of the church and disgracing the name of Christ has to change. Self-control is a fruit of the Spirit and members of the church out of respect for Christ will have to learn to control themselves in the storm of conflict. Jesus said, "Blessed are the peacemakers for they shall be called the children of God" (Matt.5:9). Self-discipline is required to be a peacemaker; one cannot talk peace and practice war and violence. The church must set the example for the community.

Dissatisfied Members Boycott Services

Pneuman speaks of dissatisfied members holding back their participation in the work of the church and declining their financial support until their grievances are satisfactorily addressed. I call it boycott!

Boycott is an economic strategy not to buy the products or use the services of a business until the owners relent on certain demands levied against them. A severe and prolonged boycott can ruin a business. The approach works well in the secular commercial world but is hardly every used as a unified strategy in a local church, except by a small-minded, mean-spirited few who want to punish the leadership. In most cases the intent is to starve the pastor by controlling the purse string. In this sense, it is evil. In fact, no one should hold the Body of

Christ hostage for any reason at all. It is Christ church; He purchased it with His own life blood and build it Himself (Matt.16:18; Acts 20 28).

The church does not belong to any special group of influential people; it belongs to Christ. There is no big me or little you in the body of Christ. This attempt to boycott is one additional reason the local church needs its own internal conflict management system (CRM). The church must continue its mission while seeking to bring conflict to a resolution.

Therefore, the CRM will find the lead antagonist and his or her supporters and address the grievance in the light of Matthew (18:15-20). Have the boycott called off and work with other leaders to find a solution to the problem. If this person or persons refuse to submit to Christ, the church should not rule out handing him or her back to Satan for discipline of the flesh (1Cor.5:1-7). This discipline option should only be used in extreme situations in which every effort has been made to work with the antagonist and the person refuses to repent and that rebellion like yeast is working its way through the congregation.

On the other hand, bear in mind that opposing persons and groups are not always wrong. The approach used may be wrong but fundamentally, they may be very well bringing to the attention of the larger body important issues for the benefit of all. The merit of their proposal, therefore, should be carefully considered and not heavy handedly dismissed.

SOME MINOR REASONS FOR ORGANIZATIONAL CONFLICTS

Using the word minor to identify a source or reason for conflict could be misleading. Minor as used here, does not mean these conflicts are less important or less damaging. In fact, these conflicts are more frequent and more plentiful but often they get resolved quickly without becoming a disruptive event. But now and then, you will find a few that are very persistent and can mushroom into a major conflict. So, it is best to adopt a metrological attitude toward them—begin storm watch early, because an insignificant tropical depression could become a major hurricane. A cancerous tumor detected early could be lifesaving.

Wrongful and Unfair Treatment

Some church people fight destructively because they feel they have been wronged or treated unfairly. A conflict like this is deeply rooted in the emotions and could fester into resentment, bitterness and even erupt into violence, as more frequently seen in secular organizations.

The Person who worked for many years, giving all to a company, only to be escorted like a common criminal off the premises one Friday afternoon and told your service is no longer needed may react violently. This illustration may be extreme, but it is one of the causes of violence in the workplace. People feel they have been used, wrongfully or unfairly treated. Such hurt runs deep!

Some larger church organizations of late have adopted secular business models and titles (e.g. CEO) should guard against adopting the non-Christian ways of hiring and firing without compassion. When people are let down by those, they thought should have been family to them—they can really become unglued. Even in small churches, destructive conflict can result from people feeling as if they have been treated unfairly or wrongly. Some will carry this feeling quietly and alone for a long time, then drop out of fellowship because they did not expect church folks to behave that ugly and unkind.

Not all offended members will drop out of fellowship. Some are more intransigent; they have deep generational investment in their local church and consider it an extension of themselves and will not leave without a fight. They will dig in and build a coalition to oppose and sabotage every program and leader until they are heard. The problem is—churches are often deaf until they are deep in a crisis they can no longer ignore. But a church with a *Resident Counsel* with Agents of Peace-Managers of conflict can prevent a crisis because these dissatisfied people have an impartial entity that will address the matter early.

Feelings of Being Dominated by Superior

Some church folks fight dirty and destructive because they have been made to feel by other members less than a person of value—they feel dominated by those with education, status, giftedness and office positions. Popular persons are always in the spotlight; their they exhibit their value, worth and self-importance, not always for the glory Christ but for the glory of self. Like Saul of Tarsus, they think they are the righteous, capable, orthodox ones doing God's service. Jesus calls our attention to this behavior and cautions us not to be like them for they have no reward to gain in heaven (Matt.6:1-8)

The Bible story of the Pharisee and the Publican further illustrates religious attitude that causes others to feel less than. The Pharisee lifted his voice and prayed saying, Lord I am not like other men or like this Publican (tax-collector) standing by me here. I fast three times a week, I give tithes on all my earnings, I give to the poor. The Publican feeling like a nobody, could not even as much as lift his eyes toward heaven, but just smooth his breast and said, "Lord have mercy upon me a sinner" (Luke 18 10-14).

When conflict erupts because of dehumanizing behavior toward another, it could be hard to resolve. Why? People that are selfish and Pharisaical in attitude hardly possess the insight and self-reflection to correct themselves and change. Some folks that are hurt will push back stronger than one will expect, while others quietly withdraw from the fellowship. It takes a well-trained agent of peace-minister of conflict to create a safe environment for the less powerful to express their hurt without intimidation. The pastor's office is like the principal's office, and people fail to be transparent with the truth for they do not feel safe. A *Resident Counsel* of their peers could be that safe place.

Suspension of Privilege or Entitlement Offices

Some church people fight back to defend privileged entitlements or territory that has been abridged or taken away from them. A church office or position of service can become an extension of the self, especially if the person has served many years in that position. To take that position away is to bruise that person's ego and it will become a cause for conflict because the person cannot emotionally separate from the office. The next true story illustrates this point.

For many years Henry served as a trustee of First Baptist Church. Henry did not have above a high school education, but he was no fool. He was popular, well liked and have some financial resources and was a generous man to those that speak well of him. He was a signatory with the treasurer on the church's account. The Pastor wanted each check to have two signatures to be valid. The pastor had appointed a new chairman over the board of trustee.

After a while, Henry and the chairman became good friends and the chairman did not see eye to eye with the treasurer. Henry refused to sign checks preventing the church from meeting its obligation and conduct business normally. The matter became quite troubling, moving the pastor to add another signatory to get around the problem. But Henry being an influential man with the chairman and other supporters on his side did not take it kindly and this gave rise to sabotage, a destructive conflict.

Henry went as far as taking legal steps to get the church closed. His legal claims did not have merit to stand in a court of law and would end up implicating himself as a former trustee who used to sign checks. Henry, the chairman and a few others with him left the church because they were not humble enough to repent and submit to the pastoral leadership of the church.

Much of the story is left out to protect the identity of those involved. But what was really going on with Henry? First, Henry knew better, but his ego was bruised when he learned that he could not hold the church hostage because another signatory took his place. Second, he allowed himself to be used by others with a larger agenda. What are the lessons? Have a treasurer who is bonded as the authorized signatory on *payment instruments. This is true of the United States Treasury. and most business corporations. Have term of office so no one person can stay in office indefinitely.

Undiagnosed Mental Health Problems

My young adult daughter stopped going to church for a while. Then on three separate occasions she asked me to preach on mental health. As a trained mental health Social Worker, the third request certainly got me curious as to why such a request. I told her previously that the Lord did not impress upon me the need to address the subject as this time. I can't just walk in and tell my congregation they are crazy. Her answer gave me pause. She said, the behavior of some Christians is nothing short of mental health disorder and perhaps, that is one reason some people don't come to church.

Well, I know some church folks have mental health problems just as they have physical problems but coming from the observation of a young person was sobering. The fact is, some strange behavioral manifestations in church are confused as being spiritual or under the influence of the Spirit. Certain aggressive behaviors that provoke conflict and thrive on conflict are mental health related. But we do nothing about it because in American society a person has to be dangerous to himself or others to be escorted off for treatment. That frequently happen when a crime is committed. Unlike physical illness, people don't readily seek mental treatment voluntarily. Perhaps the stigma of being labeled crazy, is one reason for not seeking help.

Christian clinical psychologist Kenneth Haugk addresses the mental health issues prevalent in congregations. People with aggressive and destructive behaviors that bring down leadership and tear up churches he labels, *pathological antagonist*. Haugh provides extensive information on how to identify these mentally sick, disruptive and destructive people (Haugh 1988). People who habitually, obsessively, relentlessly and destructively seek to destroy pastors and their ministries are referred to as "clergy killers" by Lloyd Rediger (1997). These are people with a destructive agenda; they very well know what they are doing. Marshall Shelly (1985) in his work refers to them as well-intentioned dragons.

But it would be a mistake to think that mental health problems are confined to the pews. There are mentally sick ministers, pastors who abuse their congregations as well; they are rude, manipulative and dictatorial. They use the Bible inappropriately to control their people; rather than having oversight of the flock they lord it over God's heritage. Guy Greenfield, himself, a victim of church abuse asserts that there are ministers who abuse their congregations and by consequence invite attack on themselves. He classifies these abusive ministers into several categories, including *neurotic, angry, narcissistic, overly emotional and attention-seekers, bully* to name a few (Greenfield 2001,127-38).

Dictatorial Leadership

As stated in the previous section, there are ministers who by their own abusive attitude to their congregations invite attack on themselves. Being dictatorial is one such leadership style that people resist strongly. The problem is this—when people offer critical feedback, instead of the dictator pausing to evaluate his leadership-style, he sees the criticism as a challenge to his or her authority. Like a matador before a bull, he sees red, rakes up dust and charge again with more force. This dictatorial response often escalates the conflict to a higher destructive level. The personal and interpersonal growth of a leader can be greatly enhanced by feedback. But the leader needs humility to accept feedback and lean from.

Some ministers are dictatorial because of deep-seated personality issues; they feel weak and insecure in themselves. As a result, they react to disagreement or contrary views as a threat. They have fragile egos that get bruised very easily. It is a psychological state that in many cases traceable to their early socialization; psychotherapy is often needed to correct this mental health challenge.

There are others who are dictatorial because they wrongly interpret scripture and that gives them a distorted view of their role as pastor. They are called and commissioned by God and are answerable only to Him, they will tell you. But they conveniently forget that the church validated their calling, presided over their commissioning, and credentialized them to do ministry. They confused authority with dictatorial posturing. They also confused their present and future accountability to God, as reason for parishioners to submit their authoritarian spiritual guidance. They often quoting passage like Hebrews 13 (NKJV): “Remember those who rule over, who have spoken the word of God to you...” (v.7). Or, “Obey those who rule over you, and be submissive, for they watch out for your souls, as those who must give account. Let them do it with joy and not with grief, for that would be unprofitable for you” (v.17). If the authoritarian personality does not balance these verses with other scripture passages on leading God’s people, he or she can easily jump the guardrails and lord it over God’s heritage.

The apostle Paul gives a proper ministry balance with these words, “For we are co-workers in God’s service; you are God’s field, God’s building” (1Cor.3:9). The church has its professional ministry offices, but one should always remember that the congregation forms a priesthood of believers that are all doing ministry (Eph.4:11-12; 1Peter 2:9). The church is like marriage in which two people submit to each other in love (Eph.5:21-33). When we quote this Ephesian passage, we often fail to note that the main subject is not marriage; it is the church. Marriage is only used to illustrate the bilateral submission of wife and husband in love. Verse 21 is often overlooked, but it is the key to understanding the passage. In essence says that members of the church, the Body of Christ, must submit to one another out of reverence for Christ; that includes the leader or under-shepherd. When this humility rules a congregation, destructive conflict cannot have a foothold among God's people.

Church Members Unable to Exercise their Gifts

Some church folks fight because they are called and gifted for ministry but are not given the opportunity to exercise such gifts. This is a frequent complaint in some local churches, but there are two sides to this phenomenon that worth looking at here.

First, there are pastors that are very insecure and controlling; they want to die in office with the baton still in hand. They are afraid to prepare a successor or encourage any young talent. These young talents know that pastor's functional vigor to do ministry is waning. He loves the people and the ministry, but like an old hunting dog, he has the memory of the hunt but not the physical vigor to do it. Yet, he is fiercely protective of his turf. People are talking quietly but they hold back out of respect. Pastor is no fool, he senses what is going on but just cannot let go. The whispering creates a feeling of animosity in one segment of the congregation. A conflict is brewing with the potential of becoming destructive. It takes a strong board with wise members to have a sit-down dinner with pastor on this matter. Even if pastor has seen God face to face, like Moses, he or she needs to make plans for a successor.

Second, there are men or even women who are upstarts. They want to launch out in ministry overnight without proper training and guidance; they don't want to submit to anyone. These upstarts would rather break-away with a few members to start their own little church rather than submit to mentoring and wise guidance. This has been a situation of conflict in some churches when upstarts are told that's not the way to go about launching oneself into ministry. Ministry work that begin like that tend to fail and the people scattered.

In some cases, these would be leaders return to their former church but with a loss of credibility. The church and the kingdom are better served, when the local church adopt a mentoring program to validate and guide those who feel a sense of calling to full time ministry. Relationship with a couple of seminaries or divinity schools is encouraged.

Unrecognized Service

If you have ever worked under a boss who takes credit for all your bright ideas to make himself or herself looks great in the face of superiors, but you never got any recognition, then you should know what it feels like not to be recognized for your work. And you feel that way even though, you get paid and, to some extent, you should make your boss looks good in the eyes of his or her superior. Church work is mostly volunteer work, a word of appreciation and a tangible gift now and then helps.

The Bible gives us this practical insight on encouragement, "As iron sharpens iron, so a man sharpens the countenance of his friend" (Prov.27:17). Encouragement is like gasoline to the engine of an automobile; you get more mileage. Church and ministry workers are largely volunteers, so a pastor must learn the relational art of recognition, appreciation and encouragement and use it sincerely to those in ministry with him or her. Give honor where honor is due; sometimes it is just saying thanks, your service is appreciated. At other times, a gift card—dinner for two.

Showing such appreciation and kindness to ministry workers is fine with the Lord of the church. He made His disciples breakfast on the beach after some of the most difficult days of their lives. The fish fry was not to rebuke anybody but to encourage them, event to reinstate Peter after his miserable failure. Perhaps, this meeting was the deciding event for them to opt out of the ministry vocation or commit permanently to the *Jesus Movement;* they all committed themselves (John 21).

When people feel unappreciated, they work with heavy hearts, heavy feet and a dull countenance. It takes the joy out of work and it infects others because apathy is contagious. People tend not to express this lack of appreciation feeling openly; they grumble quietly and speak in codes. A busy leader who is not very observant or possess relational sensitive can easily miss this. It manifests itself in sporadic unrest among the flock and the shepherd can't figure it out because no one is talking openly.

It can leave a leader isolated. It is a classic destructive conflict, but it is not the hurricane, fire or earthquake type; it is more like the cancer that is asymptomatic until stage four. It leaves the weight of a bad reputation upon a pastor. And it hurts because it feels very undeserved. The key is to cultivate an environment where appreciation is expressed frequently, and it will do wonders for collegiality and worker moral. Paul used the last chapter of Romans to give appreciation and recognition to ministry workers and co-workers; he called them by name. That is worker appreciation memorialized a part of the sacred scriptures for all times.

Leadership Compensation

Leadership compensation is one of the areas people fight about. In most cases, this happen because there is no system in place and the church is uneducated concerning what constitutes a pastoral compensation package. Ignorance in this area is volatile, a lethal cocktail. People compare the pastor's standard of living with theirs without taking into consideration that pastoral ministry is also a profession which requires higher education training and credentials as a secular professional discipline. Yes, some pastors have no higher education training, but look at the outcome of their ministry work.

The minimum education for an entry level pastor, used to be a four-year bachelor's degree and three-year of Seminary or Divinity School training with a Master of Divinity degree. Ministers with years of experience now a days have an earned doctorate degree. Yet, for all this some congregations do not give their pastor the professional recognition they accord a secular professional. Some even begrudge what the pastor is paid. And heaven's help him or her if he and his wife drive expensive automobile and live in an upscale part of town.

The board of deacons and trustees should be properly instructed on this matter of pastoral compensation because the complaint will reach them first. If the church does not have a board of trustees, then it is not properly constituted, and prompt effort should be made to correct that.

No pastor should be serving as bookkeeper and treasurer, but he or she must be knowledgeable about the church finances. The law in all fifty states require a non-profit organization to have trustees. The church by-laws should state how many, how they are elected, their function and their term of office. The number of trustees depends on the size of the membership. A small church (under 300 members), perhaps 4 trustees. A medium size church (301-800 members), perhaps 6 trustees. A large church (801-1500 members), perhaps 9 trustees, a very large church (15001 and over), perhaps 12 trustees. They should be spiritually qualified, preferable property owners with roots in the community.

One third of the trustees should be elected annually, so at no time will all the trustees be new blood. The trustee must leave office when his or her term expires; the trustee can be reelected but not until he or she is out of office for at least one year. Term of office is normally three years.

A pastoral compensation package must take into consideration the minister's training and experience. A recent seminary graduate with a Master of Divinity called to a small church, would not receive the same compensation as a pastor with ten years' experience, a Doctor of Ministry or a Doctor of Philosophy degree. But the lines of compensation and benefits are the same. The lines are:

- Basic Salary (weekly)
- Housing Allowance, if the church does not have furnished house with paid utilities for the pastor. If the pastor lives in his or her own house, he gets the fair rental value plus the cost utilities (monthly).
- Four weeks paid Vacation or more each year.
- Reimburse professional expenses (e.g. the use of personal car for church work).
- Retirement and health coverage.

Pastoral compensation should not be a secret because that will create suspicion and rumors and then conflict. Compensation should be reflected in financial statement manual of the annual church business meeting which is made available to the entire active membership.

Again, your church officers (trustees, deacons, financial secretary, treasurer, church clerk) should be well informed on these matters, so they can deflect any financial rumor that arise from members. The church that refuses to follow the law and these simple guidelines puts itself at risk.

Leadership Visibility

The lack of leadership visibility is another hotspot for destructive conflict to develop. If the pastor is hardly around, the flock will complain. This matter was addressed earlier but it is worth revisiting here.

If the pastor is frequently gone from his or her local church ministering somewhere else, is he not short-changing his people? This has become a pattern of behavior for some pastors, and their congregations are grumbling and complaining about it. It is not a matter to take lightly, because it cuts to the heart of the integrity question as well. Members of a congregation come together to hear from the Lord through the God-appointed shepherd over that flock. While they know that God can speak through anyone, they did not come to hear deacon Brown or some visiting clergy three to four times a month. They want to hear from their pastor.

If the pastor is absent frequently, say several times each month or even every other month, that could be considered short-changing the congregation or even abuse coming from the pastoral office. Church members are no fools; they know what reasonable ministerial engagement is. They also know that a pastor could be driven by greed, *prophesying* for profit at their expense. The pastor must do right by his or her congregation and keep his people informed. Hiding behind the Pauline expression *to do the work of an evangelist* is not enough scriptural fig leaves to hide pastoral negligence. It does not mean the pastor neglects his or her congregation running around the country. If one wants to do that, perhaps becoming a full-time evangelist is a better fit calling, not pastor. Shepherds stay with their sheep.

Perhaps, the pastor should prepare the congregation each year for the days he or she will be absent from the pulpit ministering somewhere else. A schedule published way in advance and made available to all members can help keep them in the loop, but still does not justify the behavior. Frankly, they should know where their pastor is, it should never be a secret. And this privilege should not be abused. It is the best way to prevent a conflict from starting. If these pastoral engagements are thought out properly, they can be seen as the pastor extending the ministry reach of the local church. As such, now and then some members of the congregation can accompany the pastor.

Conclusion

As this chapter has revealed, the sources of conflict are numerous; we cannot possible list and comment on all of them. But I have shown some frequent major causes of conflict at the local church. The truth is, just about anything can develop into a major destructive conflict, and that's why all members should be taught how to live out their Christian duties of peacemaking and peacekeeping and the church should establish a dedicated peace ministry. I give this ministry team the name, *Resident Counsel* but churches can name their peace ministry as they see fit. The important thing is that the church has such a ministry to work for peace, keep the peace and preserve the integrity of the church and its witness to the community and the world.

CHAPTER 10
GENERAL PEACEMAKING TOOLS

Christian dispute resolution tools constitute a body of knowledge, functions and practices that are social science based, on the one hand, and biblically conforming or rooted on the other hand. In other words, while the approach is uniquely Christian, it has partly drawn some contents from the general literature field which is in keeping with Christian biblical principles and most assuredly from the Bible.

It should not be surprising that some secular literatures have biblical contents because the West was largely shaped by the Judea-Christian heritage. The Church and the Bible predate the secular discipline of dispute resolution. For that reason, this chapter examines ten themes from the general field of dispute resolution, peacemaking and negotiation—themes that are in keeping with Christian values and useful to the Christian approach to conflict resolution but need supplementation.

The ten general themes are followed with the discussion of ten indispensable biblical principles for Christian dispute resolution (chapter 11). These 20 themes are principles (tools) used to resolve conflicts the Christian way. They are also reflected in the core curriculum that accompanies this book (sold separately) for individuals, school and churches to teach the course. Christian peacemaking practitioners must become proficient in the use these tools; they should demonstrate competence in all 20 themes. So, on the one hand, the Christian practitioner should have a solid knowledge base from the social science conflict resolution field and on the other hand, a solid knowledge of the Bible.

Competence, however, is not limited to the practitioner's ability to synthetize social science knowledge, biblical knowledge and best Christian practices. It includes mature Christian living or spiritual formation involving mind, heart and the Spirit. Resolving conflicts in a Christian context is not just helping clients get to yes or to achieve a winning outcome. In fact, it is not about getting to yes or about winning or losing. If you do get to these terminal resolution points, how you get there is more important than your arrival there. For the sake of peace, you may have to turn the other cheek, go the extra mile and even voluntarily surrender your rights. This is one-way, Christian dispute resolution is uniquely different from the secular approaches. Christian dispute resolution has a theology that reflects the peace theology of Jesus Christ, whereas the secular does not acknowledge any. Yet, many of their ideas are a carryover from the church and the Bible that shaped Western civilization. The church can reclaim them and strongly anchor them again in their original biblical values.

TEN GENERAL PEACEMAKING TOOLS

To emphasize, the ten themes that appear under this section carry core educational content that is necessary to function as a competent practitioner of dispute resolution. These themes or tools are also used by Christian practitioners but are mixed or supplemented with more sharply defined biblical principles.

A tool is an instrument used to accomplish something else; it gives you leverage to get more done with less. Almost every piece of literature on conflict resolution referenced one or more of these general themes: prevention, avoidance, negotiation, mediation, accommodation, leadership, collaboration, reconciliation, arbitration and litigation. They are also required knowledge base for any person wanting to do conflict resolution work in just about any context.

Destructive Conflict Prevention

We have already established that normal conflict is inevitable, and in some cases necessary for the growth and development of an organization. Now, we take this one step further to say, *destructive conflict is preventable*. When conflict is no longer for the general good but becomes a selfish, mean-spirited weapon to hurt, damage, sabotage, insight violence or provoke war, it has crossed the line of being constructive into becoming destructive. Destructive conflict is progressive, if it is not managed and brought to resolution.

The work of prevention must begin long before conflict crosses the line to become destructive. That is one reason, this book insists on a *resident conflict management system,* also called *a resident counsel.* When a housefire breaks out, you are better able to control it, if you have fire extinguishers on hand, rather than running to the store at this late hour to buy them.

The work of prevention contains and manages a conflict as fire fighters manage fire, stopping it from becoming utterly destructive. But how do you do that? We already agree that you must have a conflict management system (CMS) in place. We refer to it by several names but the preferred one is a *Resident Counsel* of lay-leaders who are trained as Agents of Peace-Managers of Conflict. This ministry group is your inhouse fire-brigade, your rapid response team. Let's ask the question again, how do you prevent a conflict from becoming destructive?

William Ury asserts that to prevent destructive conflict, the worker or peacemaker must be a "provider, teacher, [and] bridge-builder" Why a provider? Ury further asserts that conflict is about unmet needs, therefore, the peacemaker must find a way to meet those needs. Say, a hungry villager holds up a grocery store full of shoppers with an M-16 because he wants food to feed his family; the commonsense thing to do is to meet his needs. The need of a person or group can be anything. It may be a need for recognition, a need for justice, for jobs, the need for a community water well. The root cause of many conflicts is *unmet needs*.

But being a provider is not as simple as handing food and water for the villager's need. You may have met his needs today, but what about tomorrow when he is hungry and thirsty again? He is likely to return to the store with other villagers. But by that time the store owner may be armed so as not to be taken unawares again and without defense. Unmet needs or the lack of resources now turns into violence and even full-scale war. In this scenario, you can see the unmet needs of one individual or village has the potential for conflict, violence and war. Destructive conflict is progressive, if not prevented or intentionally contained.

The peacemaker, therefore, must look at the root cause, and see the need at a more fundamental level. The proverbial saying is applicable here, *give a man a fish, he eats for a day; teach him to fish, he eats for a lifetime.* The provider has to move from a one-day charity to become an enabler; he or she enables people to meet their own needs. This is where the peacemaker takes on the role of the teacher, helping people to solve their own problems. The shopkeeper gives a job so the unemployed person can earn his keep rather than robbing his store. A community shares water resources with their neighbor.

Conflicts escalate when people do not have the "proper skills or attitude" to defuse them. When people are frustrated, and they do not have communication or relational skills, they tend to become part of the problem they are trying to solve. That is like using gasoline to put out a kitchen fire. The teacher must teach self-control, communication skills, relational skills to problem solve. The villagers are hungry because they have not learned modern skills of farming and irrigation. The neighboring community has those skills but kept the information to themselves. As a result, the hungry villagers raid their food supplies. This is where the peacemaker becomes a "bridge-builder." A bridge provides access to the other side.

The bridge-builder is one who goes between to connect two sides. A bridge must serve both sides equally. The bridge-builder is an establisher of relationships; he gets people to put down their fighting clubs and talk to each other. Several years ago, New York Archbishop Cardinal Cooke upon his return from a visit to Cuba with Fidel Castro was asked by a reporter, "What did you hope to accomplish?" Cooke replied that he wanted to be a bridge between the two nations. The reporter asked, "Don't you think Castro used you on this trip?" Cooke replied something to the effect, *if you are going to be a bridge you must expect to be used, even walked on*. The peacemaker's job is to connect the two sides and get the dialogue going. In a church setting, all members should be trained as peacemakers and peacekeepers, but the CMS or resident counsel is directly tasked with that responsibility.

Conflict is not a Lone Ranger sport, by its very nature, it requires a partner to fight and a partner to resolve it. As I write this, United States' President Donald J. Trump and North Korea's Kim Jong Un are meeting in a second summit in Hanoi, Vietnam to resolve the conflict between their two countries. Whether they immediately solve the problem or not, they are willing to try because we all know that war or peace needs a partner. Peace begins with establishing a relationship.

Dudley Weeks builds his conflict model on the preservation of relationships that he refers to as "conflict partnership," a process with eight steps or skills (Weeks 1994, 1-31, 63). If members of the local church can be educated as peacemakers, enabling them to forge a partnership with each other, perhaps the culture of conflict will end. That's why the CMS has not only a provider and teaching role but a builder of relationships or partnership role as well. It will help to prevent conflict from becoming destructive. But currently very few churches have such a system in place, so conflict tears them up.

The Avoidance Path to Conflict Resolution

Avoidance is presented in the literature as another way of preventing conflict, but not always in a positive light because it includes "denial," "flight" and even "suicide." Some authors label them "escape response" because people use them when they are avoiding conflicts rather than solving them (Sande 1991, 23). Denial is a defense mechanism people deploy in high anxiety situations. It is an ostrich-like syndrome attitude of burying one's head in the sand and pretend the problem will go away. But conflict denied or neglected is like fire, it will not go away; it will become more destructive.

Others take to flight at the least confrontation. *Flight* and *flight* are biological defense mechanisms all animals and humans use when in the face of danger. They are our natural response to fear. Garvin De Becker tag them our "survival gift" because they prepare the body for adrenalin flight or to stand its grounds and fight in the face of danger (Becker 1997, 1-23). But one cannot take to flight from all conflicts, otherwise there would be no authentic resolution of them.

There are those who turn on themselves when they feel boxed-in and see no way out. Suicide is their ultimate escape. Perhaps, we know of people that fit into all three categories of avoidance: denial, flight, suicide. Tim Ursiny (2003) in his book,

The Coward's Guide to Conflict provides an excellent roadmap to navigate conflict for persons who are so afraid of conflict that they can see no useful purpose for it. Yet, as negative as avoidance may be portrayed in the literature, it has some positive benefits in the resolution of conflict.

For example, if you are in a conflict with a person with a gun and he is itching to use it, perhaps flight might be a safe way out. Denial is a type of avoidance; it is a mechanism that the body deploys sometimes to deal with sudden or overwhelming crisis. Suicide is extreme avoidance and some people resort to it rather than taking the lives of others or they feel a sense of hopelessness. If the man who murder the *Mother Emanuel Nine* in South Carolina had turned the weapon on himself, as bad as that would be—it would have been better than taking the lives of nine defenseless people in a church prayer and Bible study meeting. Others end their own lives when they perceive the world in closing in on them.

The Bible book of proverbs provides a wealth of wisdom and insight on how the principle of avoidance can be used positively to stay clear of many relational troubles. The dispute resolution team members of your church or organization should be familiar with the principle of avoidance, its positive and negative uses. Understanding why and how people use the avoidance principles will most certainly help the conflict resolution practitioner to become a more effective peacemaker.

The Negotiation Principle

Negotiation is a central principle in conflict resolution education and practice in both secular and faith-based organizations. It is a common, yet specialized principle, used at the dinner table and in sophisticated business and elite diplomatic transactions.

One child at the dinner table will offer incentives to the other to take his turn washing the dishes. Law enforcement people use the same principle to get hostage takers to release their victims. And business corporations will use it to cut multi-million-dollar deals. Diplomats use it to arrive at cessation of hostilities and war between nation states. From the mundane to the sophisticated, practitioners are using the principles of negotiation to get desired outcome. Negotiation is not a leap in the dark it is a real tool to leverage outcomes.

But what is negotiation, how do you define it? Broadly speaking it is a way of relating to competitors, friends or foes, to achieve a desired outcome. In reality, the word *negotiation* "refers to two very different processes: power-based negotiation (often called bargaining) and interest-based negotiation." The power-based negotiation can be observed between labor unions and management, often called collective bargaining. The process looks very adversarial, like two prize fighters trying to outdo each other, yet both need each other and prefer to negotiate rather than resort to *strike*, *sabotage* and *violence* (Dana 2001, 40-41). Frequent conflict between pastors and their congregations is perhaps traceable to power-based negotiation which is more adversarial. It is very easy to resort to ego power when threatened or when personal and professional territories are perceived to be invaded.

Interest-based negotiation is a type of win-win, non-adversarial dialogue based upon the interest of each side, so each side comes away with something. Each side must take the interest of the other into consideration and even help the other achieve their interests. It is not based upon greed which is win/lose, winner takes all. Dana asserts that people in organizations tend not to use this approach because it is perceived by some as "weak" (Dana 2001). However, what secular organizations consider "weak" is perhaps viewed by faith-based organizations as strong. In the first century, the cross of Jesus and the gospel were viewed by the secular world as the *weakness of God* and the *foolishness of God.* But to people of faith then and now they are the wisdom of God and the power of God unto salvation (Rom.1:16-17; 1Cor.1:18-19).

The Bible has much to say about the *interest of others*, and for that reason Christian interest-based negotiation goes much farther than secular interest-based negotiation. It is such a powerful approach that scholars and practitioners have labeled it a whole new approach and named it, the *reconciliation of interest* approach.

The skills of good negotiation are necessary and indispensable when dealing with conflicted situations, especially deal making in business. G. Richard Shell of the Warton Executive Negotiation Workshop asserts that "effective negotiation" is built on six foundations: "your bargaining style," "your goals and expectations," "your authoritative standards and norms," "relationships," "the party's interests," and "leverage" (Shell 2006, xvii-xx). An analysis of Shell's six foundations reveals that they are not so secular after all; it is the spirit or attitude that one brings to the negotiation process that makes the difference. A secular tool can be adjusted and sanctified for spiritual use.

Ken Sande (2004), a leading pioneer in the field of church conflict, includes *negotiation* as one of his six "peacemakers' response" to conflict (p.26). As noted in the beginning of this section, negotiation is commonly used by unskilled as well as people who are highly skilled specialist in the field; it is a very popular principle in all walks of life and a very effective tool in conflict resolution and peacemaking. At the heart of Christian negotiation is *process and outcome*. Process is how we get from point-A to point-B. If it is selfish, manipulative and devious to arrive at an advantageous outcome—both process and outcome would not be authentically Christian. The Christian conscience could not be at peace with such devious outcome; it is not doxological (to the glory of God).

The Mediation Principle

Mediation often involves a third party and it is often deployed as a conflict resolution strategy when the parties in a conflict are stuck, the relationship is so damaged that they stop hearing each other. An unbiased third party is brought in to facilitate communication and explore a common solution to the problem. While negotiation is primarily focused on interests, mediation is more focused on relationship. This can be easily seen in business or conjugal partnership.

In case of a marriage, the resentment and anger between wife and husband can become so bitter that they have to agree to see a marriage therapist or their pastor for counseling. The therapist becomes the mediator. The chief goal of the therapist is to create a safe environment that each can speak to each other without intimidation. The relationship is sick and needs healing. This could be a workplace conflict in which two valuable department heads are at war with each other and are bringing their respective employees along with them as soldiers. The war could bring production to a grinding halt if these two leaders cannot resolve their differences. Because of their value to the company, a third-party mediator is brought in to work with them to resolve the conflict.

Christians view Jesus as the mediator between them and God and for that reason, they generally approach God through Jesus (1Tim.2:5; Heb.12:24). The concept of mediation, therefore, has wide implications and applicability in Christian circles, but in every case, it involves a third party working with the ones in conflict. The Bible sees the repentant sinner in a state of enmity with a holy and just God who will hand down judgment. At the same time the Bible presents Jesus as the peacemaker who goes between to mediate a peaceful relationship for us with His Father (Rom.5:1-11; Eph.2:14-18).

Mediation principles sometimes intersect or overlap with negotiation or even used alternately at certain junctures in the conflict settlement process. The practitioner needs to be conversant with all the tools and use them as needed. A workman has wrench of different types in his toolbox which he can quickly access to complete a job. At some critical point, the conflict management process can be viewed as a quadrilateral in which the practitioner is playing one of or all four roles: "mediator, arbiter, equalizer," and "healer." As *mediator*, the conflict worker reconciles "conflicting interest;" as *arbiter* he or she determines "disputed rights." As *equalizer* he democratizes power, and as healer he repairs "injured relationships" (Ury 2000, 140-68).

The Principle of Accommodation

Accommodation is a strategy used in dispute resolution, but seldom as an independent tool. Like all other tools, you have to know when its use is appropriate.

It is often used with another tool as leverage. For example, the FBI *negotiating* the release of hostages may agree to give the hostage-taker food, drinks and cigarettes for the release of women and children. That concession of going along with the hostage-taker is a form of accommodation; both sides are getting something in return. That something is not always substantive or material. A district attorney can promise immunity to a person implicated in a crime to testify against his boss who runs the entire criminal enterprise. That promise of immunity is a type of accommodation to the little fish to get to the big fish (his boss).

Look at it another way, one person in a conflict may value the preservation of the relationship over the issue they are fighting about and chose to go along with his opponent. This is a type of accommodation, frequently seen in business negotiation, where the relationship is more important than having the advantage in the immediate deal being negotiated. One side deploys the accommodation strategy giving the competitor what he wants because the long-term benefit is more profitable than the short-term gain. Perhaps, the relationship opens the door to markets in China with unlimited possibilities. G. Richard Shell asserts that a person with a strong propensity to *accommodate* is a more likely team player, one with willingness to help other people, even when it goes against his own interests. "When the relationship counts more than issue in dispute, the best concession strategy is accommodation" (Shelly 2006, 13,166).

No all persons who negotiate a conflict are strongly inclined to accommodation; some are the very opposite. They will not move to the left or the right because the strategy is *all or nothing*. This extreme may be good for a powerful multi-national corporation but has rare usability for a Christian. A group a Christians taken into custody in a hostile country, may refuse freedom unless it is given to all members of the group is one example this extreme position could be applicable.

For believers, accommodation is a welcome principle providing it does not require doing anything antithetical to Christian values and the word of God. Peter and John were arrested and forbidden not to minister in the name of Jesus. Why? It made the Jewish authorities uncomfortable. They had innocent Jesus crucified and now they were even more afraid of Him. The two apostles refused to accommodate them and responded, "Whether it is right in the sight of God to listen to you more than to God, you judge. For we cannot but speak the things which we have seen and heard' (Acts 4:18-20). They refused to end this conflict with the religious authorities through accommodation.

The biblical principle of turning the "other cheek," going the "extra mile" in the face of conflicted situation is a type of accommodation. For the individual believer and the community of faith, the word of God is the standard or guide for Christian accommodation. For practical reasons, I will add basic common sense or wisdom. The word of God may not object to an action with stated clarity, but common sense tells you, it is not the safe or practical course of action to take at this time.

King Solomon's first test of wisdom is seen in the story of the two women claiming to be mother of the same child. Both women were sleeping in the same room, each with her baby at her side. One woman got up at midnight and observed that her baby was dead, placed the dead baby beside the other woman and took her living baby. At break of day, the mother found the dead baby but insisted that this was not her baby. Her baby is the living one the other woman had. In order to settle the dispute, the king decided to cut the baby in two halves. He called for his sword and as he raised it, one woman screamed and agreed to let the other woman keep the baby. The king gave the baby to the woman that screamed and was willing to give up the child.

In that fleeting moment when that woman screamed to save the baby's life and relinquished claim to him just to make him live, she was unwittingly accommodating the needs of the other mother. The king was wise enough to know that no true mother would witness the killing of her child, she would rather give him up and make him live. Sometimes the solution to a dispute lies in critical or creative thinking.

The Principle of Leadership

In the literature, leadership is not explicitly or independently addressed as a tool of conflict resolution, but it is implicitly woven into the other tools as threads to a piece of cloth or as ingredients to a cake. Leadership then is a universal principle in dispute resolution education. In this subsection, therefore, leadership is viewed on two levels: organizational and personal.

In an organization, secular or otherwise, top leadership may not be directly involved in the day to day dispute resolution process, but their support is critical at the beginning to get the process started, critical in the middle to keep the process going, and critical at the end to embrace the outcomes. In other words, when organization leaders observe that something troubling is afoot that could throw the organization into crisis, they should be the first to refer the situation to the inhouse CMS and give the process their support. Sexual harassment for example—leaders at the highest level should implement a clear policy against such behavior and ensure its enforcement at all levels of the organization.

We know there will be leaders who make referrals of persons in conflict to the CMS but only do so policy wise to cover themselves, so it does not come back later to inflict the proverbial *bite.* People often say, I am doing this because I don't want it to come back and bite me. Beyond this self-serving referral, they show no support or concern as leaders should.

Support does not mean meddling in the dispute resolution process which belongs to the CMS. But at least, protect the CMS from inquisitive employees who spread rumors to prejudice the outcome or ruling the CMS intervention may offer. Leadership support for the dispute resolution process can prevent the whole organization from going up in flames but their overinvolvement in the process can also produce the same disastrous outcome. That's one reason organizations need its own conflict management system (CMS), a dedicated entity that understands dispute resolution as fire-fighters understand fire and are disciplined to see the process through to the end.

The CMS people need the latitude to get their work done, but they also need leadership support that workers can know that they are behind the effort to fix the problem. In a church where leadership might just be the pastor, his or her word and attitude could serve as the life or death tool until the organization finds itself in a serious conflict. At that point, the flames are likely to devour both the leadership and the organization.

There are also leadership that grudgingly hand-off dispute resolution cases to the CMS but work quietly to sabotage the process. Such leaders only protect their own self-interest and that of their cronies. They sit on the truth by lying and cover-up, not knowing that they risk their own positions being consumed in the fire of conflict. Haman was one such character. He was the righthand man to the Persian King Ahasuerus, but his insidious use of power and greed led to his demise. By scheming jealousy, Haman tried to consolidate his own position and power, but ended up destroying himself upon the very gallows he had built for Mordecai, the innocent Jew Haman set out to harm (Esther 7: 6-10). Mordecai's only crime was being a Jew, which was no crime at all.

On the contrary, when leadership gives support to the CMS people, they can work with confidence and workers will be more hopeful of the fairness of the dispute resolution process. The Greyhound people show confidence in their drivers by adopting the slogan, "Leave the driving to Us!" It is a signal to passengers to relax and enjoy their trips. The entire company thrive with this confidence in their drivers.

Dispute resolution leadership. Within an organization that is well-structured, the dispute resolution process has its own leadership; they might be negotiators, mediators, arbitrators, and even litigators. In a church, however, the distinction between these two levels of leadership is often not discernable because there is no dispute resolution system; the pastor is the proverbial cook and chief bottle washer. Some pastors like to be in control of everything; they are the organization leaders, and they are always in the middle of every conflict trying to settle it. Playing this dual role has proven to be disastrous for many of them. For that and other reasons, this book advocates for a lay-leadership conflict management system (LCMS).

As pointed out earlier, pastors who frequently put themselves in the middle of just about every conflict that erupts in their church, often surrender their own health to burnout and shorten pastoral tenure. Pastors can learn from the apostles of the early church. They setup what I call, a *resident council,* of seven laymen to handle the day to day situation of dispute resolution (Acts 6:1-7). The apostles found gifted people in the congregation and tasked them with that responsibility. I think the Holy Spirit is trying to teach us something here. Just as this delegated approach to dispute resolution was hidden from Holy Spirit anointed Moses, it is perhaps, hidden from many pastors (Exod.18:13-27).

Pastors are encouraged to transition from a pastor-led conflict resolution approach, to a lay-leadership system in their local churches as the apostles have shown us. At first, pastors will have to lead this change but once it is off training wheels, hand-it-off to a guiding coalition of laypeople; it is a powerful and rewarding way to lead change at the local church. It is one way to develop leadership competence in conflict management.

On this matter of *leading change* and the concept of *a guiding coalition*, a helpful secular work is *Leading Change* by John P. Kotter (1996). The 21st century calls for creative leadership on several fronts and church conflict management is one.

The Principle of Collaboration

Collaboration is a powerful conflict resolution strategy, but like all other resolution tools, it is only powerful if you know how and when to use it. It is often used in the context of negotiation. The core essence of collaboration is sitting down with people you disagree with; together, you come up with solution to problem that is of interest to both sides. Both sides will need to agree that a problem indeed exist and agree to certain rules of the road leading to its resolution. The very act of just sitting down with the opposition is a positive step.

Professor Shell (2006) asserts that the collaboration strategy is often the "hardest to implement." That it "seeks to discover the underlying problem through good analysis and candid disclosure of interests, find the most elegant solution by brainstorming many options, and resolve tough issues using fair standards and criteria" (Shell 2006,11). Many consider collaboration the ideal conflict resolution strategy. But I would think a strategy or tool is only ideal, if it is the right fit for the problem at hand. Collaboration strategy will fall flat, if it is incompatible for the problem being solved.

One of the reasons some theorists regard collaboration so highly is the fact that it is more inclined to *creative solutions*. "When problem is a conflict, the challenge often intensifies" and so many of us are uncomfortable with conflict, we tend to gravitate to the first solution, but the "key for successful collaborative solutions lies in having patience for creating multiple potential solutions," then carefully working through the most appropriate (Shell 2006, 246).

In other words, in the collaborative process, there are more heads with good ideas to solve a problem; with patience to reflect and carefully consider the options, the best outcome will most likely be achieved. For the secular practitioner that is bargaining for the most favored outcome in deal making, all of what is said here under collaboration is well and good. But it may all fall short for the Christian practitioner. Why? The Christian practitioner places a higher premium on the relationship over closing a winning deal.

The Reconciliation Principle

The reconciliation principle hardly belongs under the secular domain because it is fundamentally a Christian principle; it will be discussed at length in the next chapter.

Secular dispute resolution has their own version of reconciliation; they call it, getting along or tolerance. You stay on your side of the fence and I stay on mine and we will behave with civility toward each other. That is hard reconciliation, but that is how secular society deals with difficult relationships, short of killing each other. Biblical reconciliation comes from the heart; it has to do with the quality of relationship between the two persons after dispute.

The Use of Arbitration

Arbitration is an independent body that people in dispute agree to have their case referred for resolution. It is agreed beforehand that they will abide by the ruling of the arbitration body. For that reason, arbitration is almost always final, and courts are inclined to uphold their ruling. Secular organization and enterprises prefer arbitration to litigation most of the time.

Arbitration is less time consuming and cheaper than fighting it out in court. Sometimes a case reaches the court and rather than going to trial, the parties opt to have the matter settled in arbitration. Courts most often offer a win/lose situation, whereas in arbitration, though one side may not get all it wants; it stands a better chance coming away with something.

Some church denomination not only have a church court, they have an arbitration body to which the local church can refer their cases should they reach an impasse. Most Baptist churches voluntarily belong to a convention, but each local church is autonomous, choosing their own pastor and managing their own affairs. For this and other reasons, many Baptist and non-Baptist have neither a CMS, nor an arbitration body. They are most at risk to conflict.

There are others that have an area minister like American Baptist Churches, USA to whom the local church can appeal for assistance in a dispute beyond their capability to manage. Denomination with a central government polity have a provision local churches can look to when they are conflicted. But even here an inhouse CMS is the ideal because by the time local disputes reach the denominational office, it already done its damage locally. The denominational office is, perhaps, better for arbitration. That is, when the local church cannot resolve the matter.

There are still other independent churches that belong to no larger body to which they can appeal for help, they can either establish an inhouse arbitration above and beyond their CMS or the leaders of few churches can come together and form an arbitration body. Most churches do not have this vision or priority and when struck by a serious conflict, they fall apart.

The Use of Litigation

When people are angry and don't want to talk with each other, they are quick to threaten litigation. I will sue you, talk to my lawyer! they often say. The fact, most small churches have no attorney as part of their general staff; an attorney is only engaged when the church is in a crisis, and by the time they engage one, the conflict like a cancer is at its highest stage (stage 4).

If you use the hurricane metaphor, the crisis has reached category 5, threatening everything in its path, even life itself before some churches engage an attorney. Lawsuit against a church, like any other organization is expensive. The church has a better chance, if it has its own regular attorney to ward off predator individuals and organization from without who may see the church as an easy target.

On the inside, members have a biblical precedence for not taking their church brothers and sisters to court for dispute resolution. Since all believers have a duty to be peacemakers and peacekeepers, the leadership of the community of faith is duty bound to create an environment for the practice of this Christian duty, so litigation against each other become unnecessary. If the local church embraces the approach to dispute resolution taught in this book, their *resident counsel* would have taught the congregation the biblical response to settling conflict inhouse and not in the secular court.

Yet, this book not saying Christians and churches have no use for the judicial system. To create and maintain an orderly, just and peace-loving society, we need the courts to administer justice. Christians need the courts to fight not only for retributive justice but social justice as well, serving as a voice for voiceless, the poor, the weak and powerless. But when it comes to dispute inside the local community of faith, Jesus has already mandated that such disputes be settled among the people of God (Matt.18:15-18).

The Sum of the Matter

The ten general tools or themes briefly covered in this chapter are widely used in the secular discipline of dispute resolution, bargaining and peacemaking. They are also used by Christian practitioners but in vastly different ways. In secular disciplines, these tools are guided by secular beliefs, values and processes with a high premium on wining, because secular enterprises are driven by winning and profitmaking. That is the way the marketplaces of this world function.

But when these tools or themes are used by the church, they are driven by Christian beliefs and values and processes that are biblically rooted. Furthermore, the church places a high premium on relationships over profitmaking. The recognition of this differentiation is critical to understanding Christian conflict resolution and peacemaking.

In other words, the communities of faith enjoined the general themes with Christian biblical values, thus making the process uniquely different, and in most cases, the outcomes as well. In the next chapter, ten additional value-laden biblical themes are discussed. Some of them overlap somewhat with the secular tools but in name only, not in values, not in process, and in most cases not in outcome. Using the same tool names (e.g. mediation, negotiation, accommodation) is not an attempt to synchronize secular themes with biblical themes but to show similarity and difference.

The Christian biblical approach does not ignore the social science foundation and best practices, yet it has produced an approach to dispute resolution that is uniquely and unapologetically Christian. It is an approach that is doxological but at the same time radical and practical. In the end it is all about human and divine relationships.

CHAPTER 11

BIBLICAL PEACEMAKING TOOLS

In the previous chapter, we looked at general dispute resolution tools that are used by both the secular discipline as well as Christian, but the way they are used in Christian organizations is fundamentally different. It is like two computers with the same hardware, but they have two different operating systems. They are programed with different data and they process information differently. Christian dispute resolution uses the ten general themes covered in Chapter 10 but not the same way the secular conflict resolution disciplines use them. When we use them, we are guided by Christian beliefs and values, so the process is different and in most cases the outcomes as well.

As Christian practitioners, we merged ten additional themes of our own with the ten general themes to make twenty in all. Our ten themes are anchored in Christian biblical beliefs and values, thus making our process and outcome biblically grounded and uniquely Christian. So then, Christian dispute resolution is not just about securing a win or win/win or win/lose outcome for the persons in conflict as secular programs do. In fact, it is hardly about that at all. Like other humans, Christians like to win but just winning is not good enough. How we win is as important as winning itself.

The how of winning has to do with process; that is how you move from problem to outcome. Did you win by lying, cheating, deception, destroying your competitor's reputation in the process? Did your competitor's interest matter to you at all? Or, if you lose, how did you lose, how did you behave? Some people know how to win but they are sore losers. As discussed earlier, Christian dispute resolution that is biblical, is guided by the peace theology of Jesus and is doxological at its very core; it is done to the glory of God. Both process and outcome must be pleasing to God.

The ten indispensable biblical themes that shape Christian conflict resolution as this author sees them are: repentance, confession, forgiveness, the interest of others, the love of God, reconciliation, accountability, restitution, church discipline and restoration to fellowship. The merging of these themes with the ten general themes of Chapter 10 produced a dispute resolution process and body of literature that is uniquely Christian. This body of Christian literature now benefits both secular and Christian approaches to conflict resolution, negotiation and peacemaking.

For example, the use of forgiveness is one Christian theme that is now widely used to heal conflicted relationships in the secular approaches as well a Christian. Looking to the interests of others is also an indisputable Christian, biblical theme drawn from Jesus and Pauline theology that is now popular in secular dispute resolution and negotiation (Matt.5:38-42; Phil.2:3-5).

The practitioner in Christian dispute resolution, in order to remain true to biblical Christian values, should know the content of all twenty themes and how to merge them to produce the new synthesis that is truly Christian, biblical dispute resolution in content, process and outcome. Just getting a hold of secular hardware (contents and methods) and sprinkle them with a few verses of scripture and call it Christian will not do. The hardware must be programed with Christian operating system and data. That is where the Christian biblical themes come in. These ten themes are briefly covered in this chapter. I say, "briefly covered" because each theme has enough content to be a book on its own.

Repentance in Christian Dispute Resolution

Biblical repentance is the changing of a person's mind, attitude, disposition and direction concerning a wrong or harm committed or done to another person or persons; this includes against God. The word repent is from the Greek, *metanoia,* which means a change of mind (Unger 1988, 1073).

The emphasis is on change, profound change, not shallow or peripherical. The person is so moved by what he has done, the hurt he has caused, that he has not only changed his thinking about it; he feels differently about it and has resolved not to behave in such manner to cause such hurt again. She has further resolved to remedy the damage caused. For example, if property were stolen, she wants to return it or give compensation for it. Repentance is a radical change going the opposite direction; without it, genuine peace is unachievable.

Destructive conflict almost always involves offense real or perceived, done by one person or group to another person or group of persons. This offense could be unfairness in some matter, injustice, violation of rights, loss or threatened loss of property. The person or group is hurt, and that offense has escalated to the point of becoming destructive. Accusation has been levied, feelings are trampled upon and battle lines are drawn. This could become really ugly because emotions are running on high octane and people are on edge. In some cases, violence is threatened and litigation imminent. Like the ancient Israelites, Christians often travel as a mixed multitude; there is the few among them that are extremists, they don't abide by the rules of the road. They are like the spark that starts the forest fire. They could be "well intentioned dragons" (Shelly 1985). Or, "antagonists" among the people of God bent on derailing the work of the Lord (Haugk 1988).

But generally speaking, when conflict erupts among Christians, the people of God, the rules to resolve it are markedly different from unbelievers, even though the hurt is the same. The rules of conduct among God's people and how you settle conflicts are defined by God Himself. Almost always, sin against persons is a sin against God. God is the unseen offended One in the equation of Christian conflict. So, how do we then get from conflict to peace in a Christian context?

For the Christian, the word of God is the guardrails from conflict to peace. If you follow a railway line long enough, you will eventually arrive at a station. Station here means, Stop! But how you get to stop is unlike how secularists get to stop. Their values and guiding principles are different, much different from those used by the communities of faith. The word of God is the guiding principle for the church; some will say, it contains our guiding principles.

The word of God is the whole Bible, but in the Sermon on the Mount, Jesus summarizes His theology of conflict and how we ought to deal with conflict (Matt.5-7). Peacemaking is a Christian duty (5:9). In our administration of justice, we are asked to be merciful (5:7). We are called upon to love God and neighbor. Neighbor refers to all human beings, including our enemies that did us wrong. We are commanded to bless those who curse us, do good to those who hate us, and pray for those who spitefully use us and persecute us (5:43-47). The biblical path to peaceful relations with our fellow humans is not for the faint of heart. But if you are faint-hearted, the Lord will give you grace and glory to get to the peaceful relationship He requires.

Jesus makes it our Christian duty to work for peace, not only for our benefit, but for the benefit of others who are directly and indirectly in the conflict with us. In a war—it is not only the soldiers on the frontline affected; their wives and children back home are greatly affected as well. If he does not return home, they are among the collateral damages.

Every destructive conflict, if not quickly and peaceably resolved God's way has collateral damages beyond the primary fighters in combat. For a church with hundreds or thousands of members, the consequences could be huge. Conflict should be *resolved God's way* because as indicated earlier, Christian conflict resolution is *doxological.* By that I mean, it must be settled to the glory of God. That's the guardrail and guiding light in Jesus' theology of conflict. The apostle Paul expresses it this way, "whatever you do, do all to the glory of God" (1 Cor.10:31).

For one reason or another, we all want to benefit, to come out on top in the resolution of a conflict. But what brings glory to God may not always bring us out on top. Nonetheless, God's glory is one guiding principle in Christian dispute resolution to follow. As the wise men follow the guiding star in search of the Christ child, so may we in our pursuit of peace keep God's glory in focus, for it will most certainly get us to that peaceful resolution that is pleasing to Him. If the outcome is pleasing to God, why then should it not be pleasing for us? If He says, "It is okay." Should we not say, "Yes, Sir!"

Furthermore, as we will see later, Jesus calls upon us to forgive each other because it is on that basis, He forgives us (Matt.6:12-15). So, God is in every Christian conflict, not as the causative agent but as the directional agent to lead the parties to a peaceful resolution for their benefit and for His Glory. But again, how do you get to the station of peaceful resolution? You follow the guardrails (God's word) in general, and the peace theology of Jesus in particular.

The first step, therefore, is to lead the parties in the conflict to acknowledge the hurt they have caused each other and the offence that it is to God. They are the people of God and they call Him Savior and Lord, now they are called upon to submit to Christ and to one another in true repentance (Eph.5:21). Put away your sword, acknowledge the truth, submit to Christ and each other.

This acknowledgement of the hurt they have caused each other and the offense that is to God are the beginning steps to true repentance. Whenever we wrongfully hurt others, we hurt God in the process and repentance is required. David was a man after God's own heart. A story from his life illustrates this concept of repentance really well. He committed adultery with a man's wife. To cover up the resulting pregnancy, he tried to pin the pregnancy onto the husband. When that scheme failed, he had the man killed and married his wife (2 Sam.11-12). People usually say, that's God awful!

Note that David violated three of God's commandments to do what he did: he coveted the man's wife, he committed adultery, he committed murder (Exod.20:13—14,17). Since, the dead man could not speak for himself, God spoke for him. God sent the Prophet Nathan to confront David concerning the matter (2 Sam.12:1-6).

David's own mouth indicted him (12:7). Nathan renders God judgment upon the king (12:8-12). Both adultery and murder were capital crimes. So, David stand guilty before God. God must now decide the king's fate which could be the loss of his life and his throne. David had only two cards left, and he can only play one: the arrogance card or the repentance card. With arrogance, he could proudly beat his chest and assert his kingly significance or in penitence throw himself on the mercy of the court. That is, God court of justice.

David did the latter, he quickly and genuinely repented. On his face before God, he cried out for God's mercy. He said, "I acknowledge my transgression and my sin is ever before me..." (Psalms 51). God punished him but did not take his life or take away his throne; he remained king for a long time, and a good one too (2 Sam.12:13-15). His predecessor did a lesser offence but was arrogant and unrepentant and loss his life and his throne in the process. Saul's son Jonathan died with him the same day; that is collateral damage.

God is no respecter of persons; there are no big me and little you in His sight. But repentance matters to God and it matters big time. Like David, your act of humility before God could save your life and everything else. It is a subject to fully understand because it could be the difference between life and death, promotion and demotion, heaven and hell. David understood God and the power of genuine repentance, a tool we should all seek to know well.

There is repentance toward God and repentance toward people. In repentance, we acknowledge the hurt we have caused others including God; we resolve to make restitution if that is required, and we resolve not to hurt the person or persons again in that manner. Even in human courts, penitence for an offense goes a far way with the offended as well as the judge and jury. Jesus said, "Blessed are the merciful, for they shall obtain mercy" (Matt.5:7). If you are settling dispute between Christians, repentance is a critical piece to understand in that process. From God's perspective, repentance is the starting point, and we better make it our starting point as well (Isa.1:16-20).

Arrogance causes some believers to terminate fellowship with one church and take up membership with another without repenting; such behavior normally hinders their prayers from being heard, and it puts a blight upon their personal flourishing (Prov.28:13). For some, it is the reason for their poor health; they carried sins that they have not repented of or seek forgiveness for. You can't trash one church and unrepentantly seek refuge in another without consequence. Without repentance, your blessing will dry up.

Confession in Dispute Resolution

Confession is part of the repentance process. In fact, repentance is foundational to confession and forgiveness. It is the core of taking responsibility for an offense. In Western jurisprudence, a confession is the ultimate proof of guilt, providing the person has good mental health and the confession was freely given. A good confession cannot be extracted under coercion or from one with severe mental health disorder. If anyone of the two is present, the confession is invalid.

In biblical theology, confession is a prerequisite to obtain God's forgiveness (Rom.10:9-10; 1John 1:8-9). The same rule is normally followed in life among people because there is no need for forgiveness, if the person is not guilty. Look again at *David's confession, referenced earlier; he acknowledges guilt and takes responsibility for the hurt he caused (Ps.51:3).

Confession is normally made to the person or group of persons that have been offended. Confession is also made to God, if He is one of the offended parties. Since, most human offences are not merely offenses against humans alone but offences against God as well, the offender should also confess to God and secure His forgiveness (Matt.6:12-15; Jas.5:15). Again, in Christian dispute resolution God is always involved. You cannot hurt people and just confess to God; God will not hear you. You must face the person you hurt. After that you confess to God and secure His forgiveness.

In dispute resolution, other words are sometimes used in the place of confession, such as: taking responsibility for the hurt we caused others, acknowledging culpability, agreeing to the wrongdoing, accepting accountability and the like. Genuine confession is almost always done with a promise or pledge not to repeat the offense. This pledge gives assurance to the hurt party or parties that you are not going to hurt them like this again. This promise makes it easier for the injured party to offer the gift of forgiveness.

Ken Sande offers a roadmap for confession which he labels the seven A's. Some of them are slightly paraphrased here; the words in quotes are his:

- "Address" the confession to all who are offended.
- "Avoid" qualifying the confession with self-justifying words (e.g. if, but, perhaps).
- "Admit specifically," avoid generalization. If you stole the money say so.
- "Acknowledge the hurt." Show that you feel the gravity of the hurt you caused.
- "Accept the consequences." Don't blame it on your parent, or the devil made you do it.
- "Alter' your disposition. Confession is part of repentance which means genuine change.
- "Ask for forgiveness (and allow time)." Because people hurt so deeply, they may need time to forgive (Sande 2004, 126-32).

It is never easy to sit with a victim face to face, look him or her in the eyes and say, "I am responsible for the hurt you have suffered. I did it, I am guilty! I am sorry for the hurt I have caused you and your family, please forgive me!" For the perpetrator, it is a freeing experience; it is really true that confession is good for the soul. For the victim it could be hell on earth. It is never easy to sit there and take all that in, especially when brutal physical harm, violation of one's person or great loss of property have been suffered. It is hard! but necessary. It is where the healing process begins on both sides.

For the victim it could be a mix of freedom on the one hand, and terrifying emotions on the other, depending on the nature of the hurt. Where trauma is experienced, physical or emotional, a victim may not be ready to face his or her abuser because, in some cases, they relive the trauma all over again. In such cases, victims have to be ready and the environment safe and assuring that they are not going to be victimized again.

Confession is cathartic, it unclutters and purifies the soul. It is perhaps the best medicine for guilt. For members of the community of faith, the Bible exhorts: "Confess your faults one to another, and pray for each other, that you may be healed" (James 5:16 KJV). When we do wrong and choose coverup over confession, we harbor a malignancy that do us harm, even stifle our flourishing. The Bible tells us, "He that covers his sins shall not prosper: but whoso confesses and forsakes them shall have mercy" (Prov.28:13 KJV).

Confess fully and truthfully. Confession is an opportunity to fully come clean all at once and truthfully. The sin we are confessing to, will give a sense of shame and that's a good thing. It is a signal that our conscience is still alive. That shame could also serve as a temptation not to confess fully and truthfully. But it is easier to face the shame once with a true and full confession than to do it piecemeal. If we try to make ourselves look good by not telling the full truth and nothing but the truth, our confession could be regarded as insincere. When people are called a second time before a Grand Jury because they lied the first time around or did not tell the full story, they are looked upon will less credibility. *Confess sincerely, fully and truthfully the first time around.

Forgiveness in Dispute Resolution

In Christian biblical understanding, forgiveness is connected to repentance and confession; the three are inextricably bound together, so the process of repentance is not complete until all three points are covered. A person asks for forgiveness in the context of acknowledging the wrong done, confessing the wrong and resolving not to repeat the wrong that causes injury to the other. The injured party could be God or human or both. Sin is an offense to God; like King David, we own up to it before God, we confess it, we resolve not to repeat it, then we ask for forgiveness be it God or human or both.

Forgiveness, therefore, is a bedrock principle in Christian conflict resolution. It is based upon the biblical truth that all humans are sinners, and as such, they have offended God and neighbor in their actions. Therefore, all humans need forgiveness from God and neighbor. God forgives us on the basis of our willingness to forgive our neighbor (Matt.6:9-15).

Neighbor means our fellow human beings: enemies, friends, strangers, family, anyone (Matt.5: 43-48; Luke 10: 29-37). Forgiveness then has a human side and a divine side.

Stated another way, forgiveness has a kind of reciprocity to it. On the one hand, it is a gift we give to others, and on the other hand, a gift we receive from others, God or humans. God said, if you don't genuinely forgive, I will not forgive you. If you want to be forgiven, you must forgive (Matt.6:14-15). Peter asked Jesus, how often should my brother wrong me, and I forgive him, until seven times? Jesus answered, not until seven times but until "seventy times seven" (Matt.18:23-35). In other words, don't keep a record of wrongs done against you, forgive always. True love does not "keep record of wrongs" (1Cor.13:4-6 NIV). Forgiveness is your gift to the offender; every time he repents and asks for it, give it to him. Because every time you offend God, repent and ask Him to forgive you, He grants you forgiveness. You must do the same for your neighbor.

Rising from the hell of apartheid, South Africa under the leadership of Nelson Mandla had to make a choice between revenge and forgiveness. The administration chose the path of forgiveness, but forgiveness as a ready discussed is a process. Archbishop Desmond Tutu was chosen to lead the country through the process of forgiveness and reconciliation. Tutu calls it the fourfold path to forgiveness. The following four paragraphs summarize the essence of that process as he sees it.

First, criminals used by the apartheid government to murder people, physically abuse them, confiscate their property, falsely throw them into prison were given a chance, without revenge or retaliation, to come out of the shadows, meet with the families that suffered loss and maltreatment. Both sides were allowed to “tell their stories.” The criminals tell their stories to unburden their souls and relieve their guilty consciences by admitting to the crimes they committed and tell where bodies were buried. Victims and families tell their stories by sharing the hell they have been through. In the end, they retrieved bodies that could be accounted for; they mourned their dead, gave them a dignified burial received a modicum of emotional closure (Tutu and Tutu 2014, 67-92).

Second, “naming the hurt.” In this process, people were given a safe environment to tell their stories in an unrushed manner, to unburden the depth of their emotional and psychological hurt, mourn, grieve so that they could gradually come to that place to decide to forgive the perpetrator of the atrocities levied against them. This was a grueling, painful and time-consuming process, but it had to be done for the whole nation to move forward (Tutu and Tutu 2014, 93-117).

Third, “granting forgiveness.” Where great trauma and lost had been experienced—this was not an abrupt or quick process, time had to be given for victims to grant forgiveness. After the facts and truth of the atrocities were told publicly and directly to the families who suffered loss and to the nation by the people who committed them—and after the families told their stories, mourned and grieved their losses—they were now at a place to grant forgiveness (Tutu and Tutu 2014, 119-43).

Fourth, "renewing or releasing relationship." What do you do with the relationship when you learn that the atrocities were committed by your own family: spouse, siblings, nephews and nieces, friends, cousins, neighbors? Now that you have decided to forgive, do you return to that relationship? This fourth path required much work with families to renew the relationship or release it (Tutu and Tutu 2014, 145-62). Some relationships could not be renewed; in such cases, they were released, so the parties could go on with their separate lives.

Undoubtedly, South Africa would have become a failed state had Nelson Mandela chosen the path of revenge over forgiveness when he came to power. But he had enough compassion, insight, foresight and grace to know that suffering is redemptive, especially when viewed from the vantage point of the cross of Christ. Archbishop Desmond Tutu was the right choice indeed to lead the Truth and Reconciliation Commission. He himself said, there is "no future without forgiveness" (Tutu 1999). Blood would have run like a river in post-apartheid South Africa had Mandela chosen the path of revenge over forgiveness. The minority white population would have fled the country with their wealth and that would have set the nation on a downward economic trajectory.

In Christian dispute resolution, it is critical for a person to get *confession and forgiveness* right, because without them individuals could be steering into the abyss of failed human relations which is nothing short of hell itself. Furthermore, forgiveness is a necessary perquisite to a third cardinal principle—namely, reconciliation.

Reconciliation of Relationships

In his book *Father, Forgive*, Andrew White speaking to his ministry team, states that "the biggest obstacle we have to overcome in our work of reconciliation is the people who refuse to forgive...If there is no forgiveness, then pain, hurt, bitterness and anger incubates in the human soul" (White 2013, 26).

The ideal end goal of forgiveness is reconciliation of relationships; it is the gold standard to achieve. Reconciliation is one step beyond forgiveness, but that one step could be light-years away. In other words, even though forgiveness is achieved, reconciliation of relationship is not always achievable. Yet, it is necessary to pursue it because of the transcendent reality present in Christian relationships that demands that worshippers settle with an offended neighbor before God can accept that person's acts of worship. But first, let's look at why I consider reconciliation of relationship the goal standard to achieve in Christian dispute resolution.

Christianity at its very core is about redemption, and redemption is about God reconciling humans to Himself and to each other (Rom.5: 1-10; 2Cor.5:17-21). For this reason, our Christian faith communities constitute a spiritual family, the family of God. We refer to each other as brother and sister and to God as Father (Matt.6:1-15; 1Tim.5:1-3). When we worship together or break bread around the communion table, we worship and fellowship as a spiritual family before God, our heavenly Father. He wants no hypocrites in this communal gathering. You must be free toward God and neighbor.

Therefore, there can be no relational barrier caused by grudges or ill-feelings against each other at the Lord's Table. We do ourselves great harm when we unworthily participate in this celebration, the apostle Paul cautioned (1Cor.11:17-34). Worshippers must be free toward God and each other to worship acceptably and fellowship in God's presence. There is no argument that acceptable worship is contingent on the quality relationship worshippers have with God and each other (Acts 2:42-47; 1John 1:6-7).

In view of this worship requirement, Jesus gave us this directive, "...if you are offering your gift at the altar and there remember that your brother or sister has something against you, leave your gift there in front the altar. First go and be reconciled to them; then come and offer your gift (Matt.5:23-24). This directive is important for at least two reasons.

First, Jesus is speaking in the context of His new commandment of love for God and neighbor. By His life and death, Jesus models the law of love. His law of love must now be demonstrated within the household of faith among the people of God. To do this, believers must not only be reconciled to God, they must be reconciled to each other as well. God will not accept offering from dirty hands and worship from hearts that are not right toward each other (Ps.24:3-5). God enacted this worship requirement from the very beginning. He rejected Cain and his offering. God knew Cain's heart was not right toward his brother, that he had murderous intent (Gen.4 1-12; 1John 3:11-12). Under the new covenant, Jesus demands righteous behavior that go beyond that of the Pharisees and Teachers of the law (Matt.5:20).

Second, as ambassadors of Christ, believers have an active and a passive mission toward those outside of the community of faith. The Great Commission states the active mission of making disciples, reconciling them to God (Matt.28:19-20; 2 Cor.5:18-20). The passive mission is to bear witness by being *salt and light,* modeling to the unregenerate world what a redeemed community looks like. The end purpose of the believer's passive witness is the same as the active disciple-making, to reconcile people to God and each other.

Reconciliation of relationships is indeed the gold standard of Christian dispute resolution and the ideal we should all strive to reach.

Now, what example is it to the world of unbelievers when church folks fight from the church building out to the parking lot, loud and vulgar as if they never met Jesus? They slander each other on social media, at the laundromat and at the beauty salon. There is no distinction between them and the unchurched. The problem is—they have not been reconciled to each other, and perhaps, they had a bad spiritual birth or were never birth into the kingdom of God at all (John 3:1-21).

In spite of what is stated in the preceding paragraph, the gold standard of being reconciled to God and each other can be achieved; it is what God wants. That is what we are to strive for in dispute resolution. But there are a few exceptions; there are times that this ideal standard is not achieved for it cannot and should not be forced on anyone. Genuine reconciliation comes from the heart.

Some people have been traumatically violated in relationships and do not wish to return to them, and it is neither wise nor advisable for them to return to such former situations. Being raped, beaten by reason of domestic violence—the releasing of the relationship is preferred to the renewing of the relationship in many cases. Forgiveness is achieved but reconciliation of relationship is not.

Christian leaders must face this fact, that there are times forgiveness is achieved but reconciliation is not. No pastor, bishop, counselor or priest has the authority to force any human being back into such relationships that put their lives at risk. If they do and it ends tragically, they should be held accountable under the law. I know this is strong language, but no responsible church leader can speak in hush tone in the face of rape, domestic violence, child molestation, sexual abuse and harassment. The letter of Scripture should not be used to force any member of God's family back into such situation. We must accept that some relationships are not reconcilable.

Archbishop Desmond Tutu who chaired the Truth and Reconciliation Commission for post- apartheid South Africa, shared the four paths to forgiveness (referenced earlier) that the country had to go through to be healed and remain together as a country. The final path was *reconciliation of relationships*. For some families, reconciliation of relationship was not achievable. The relationship could not be renewed; it had to be released. Now and then, the local church will come upon a few cases like that. The dispute is resolved up to the point of forgiveness, but the relationship cannot be renewed in the sense that people move back into same situation. The relationships, in some cases, have to be *released* and the people move on to their separate destiny.

Restitution of Property

In Christian conflict resolution education, training and practice, restitution should be seriously considered, especially where the victim suffers the loss of material property or sustains damages for which compensation can be offered. In many cases expensive litigious action could have been avoided if restitution or compensation were freely considered and forthcoming.

God has strong regard for property owners' rights, be it personal or real property. These rights are recognized in both Old and New Testaments. In fact, two of the Ten Commandments are about property and owners' rights: "You shall not steal" and "You shall not covet...anything that belongs to your neighbor" (Exod.20: 15,17;22:1-10). If anyone steals or is responsible for the loss of a person's property, restitution or compensation was required (Num.5:6-7). This principle of restitution is set forth in the Torah and was practice early in Jewish communal life and was true during the time of Christ. Undoubtedly, the practice is a carryover from the Judeo-Christian thought to Western jurisprudence.

When the tax collector, Zacchaeus hosted a reception at his house for Jesus and His ministry team, Zacchaeus made this confession: "Look, Lord! Here and now I give half of my possession to the poor, and if I have cheated anybody out of anything, I will pay back four times the amount" (Luke 19:18).

Note well that Zacchaeus made a *confession* and a *promise* which are in keeping with genuine repentance. Repentance always resolve not to return to the old habit of hurting the same person in the same manner again. Zacchaeus went one step further, pledging to return stolen property four times the amount required by the Torah (Exod.22:1—7).

Jesus responded to Zacchaeus' confession and promise of restitution with these words, "Today salvation has come to this house, because this man, too is a son of Abraham. For the Son of Man came to seek and to save the lost" (vv.9-10). Jesus did not ask Zacchaeus to make restitution to be forgiven of his sins but promise of restitution is a sure evidence of his repentance. John the Baptist had called people to "produce fruit in keeping with repentance" (Matt.3:8). Zacchaeus is committing to produce such evidence and Jesus bore witness to it. Zacchaeus' story is one example that Jesus embraces the biblical principle and practice of *restitution and compensation* for damages suffered, though not making it a precondition for His forgiveness. The only precondition to God's forgiveness is genuine repentance.

What is the lesson here? If you require forgiveness from a person you injured by stealing his property, you must also consider returning the stolen property. Fraudulent behavior must be remedied by restitution or compensation. Restitution should not be glossed over, it remains an important

Christian principle and practice today, though not often spoken of from pulpits sermonically. Ken Birch contends that unlike the legal system that connects offender's freedom to restitution in kind or with time served, for the believer, restitution is largely covered under forgiveness. Forgiveness is the "desire for the offender to somehow make amends for the wrong that was done, that leads to repentance" (Birch 2008, 1-20).

Birch's assertion is true to an extent, but I want to make it clear that forgiveness should not be confused with restitution. Let me illustrate—the offended person may forgive the thief but still requires the return of his property. Some offended persons may forgive the trespass and release the material debt as well, but this is not always possible. I may forgive and not press charges against you for entering my property, stealing my Mercedes from my driveway and greatly inconvenience my life. But that forgiveness does not mean you get to keep my $125, 000 Mercedes. If one had truly repented of his theft, he would want to return the stolen property. The Zacchaeus story appears to connect genuine repentance with the obligation to do restitution.

But it is true that other than genuine repentance, the Bible has not explicitly stated any precondition to receiving God's forgiveness nor human for that matter. But the same Bible teaches restitution as a practical matter to be considered. Human forgiveness is a gift given not just to the offender on the basis of God's forgiveness, but a gift the offender gives to himself or herself in order to avoid being held hostage by the situation. Does that mean the thief can keep the stolen property because he got salvation and God's forgiveness? No! You can only keep the stolen property if the owner gives it to you. Jesus said, "teaching them to observe all things that I have commanded you" (Matt.28:20). This is one of those things that pastors can lead believers to do the right thing.

Let's ask the same question another way. Should a pastor or church member who embezzled thousands of dollars from the church or his employer pays it back? The answer remains, yes! The church or employer may forgive the theft and chose not to prosecute, but that does not justify keeping the stolen property. Some form of arrangement should be made to return the stolen property or to pay back the sum that was embezzled. However, if the material debt is released by the owner, then the matter is resolved. I dwell on this issue because of the prevailing spirit of entitlement and lack of Christian conscience and ethics observed among some church folks these days.

Should you as a church member find yourself in such a predicament that you have to make restitution, you may want to confer with your pastor or some other spiritually mature believer to help you through the process. Depending on the gravity of the situation, you may even want to confer with an attorney to help you formulate a strategy to return the property or workout a method to repay in manageable installment amount. Let me further emphasize—borrowing money from friends or foes, banks or other financial institutions and refusing to pay it back is theft. The Bible instructs us, "owe no man anything, but to love one another" (Rom.13:8KJV). In other words, "Let no debt remain outstanding, except the continuing debt to love one another..." (13:8 NIV).

Not honoring one's debt has been the cause of many disputes and litigation before the courts. The guilty party has offended both God and the person or organization defrauded. It makes God look bad in the face of unbelievers when His children behave fraudulently. If a debt is not forgiven by the person that suffers loss, restitution or compensation should be made. God will not be party to anyone profiting from stolen property.

The Interest of Others in Dispute Resolution

In conflict resolution, *looking to the interest of others* is a major peacemaking tool or principle used by both Christian and non-Christian practitioners. People in dispute bring their differences to the table: different worldviews, issues, values and beliefs, opinions and convictions, solutions and interests. Each side has a view as to how the conflict ought to be settled.

The problem is—interests tend to be subjective and one-sided, not normally skewed to the interests of others. People in conflict are often like two boxers fighting for the same championship belt; each side is preoccupied with winning. Because of this self-interest on either side, it is difficult to agree on anything. Yet, each side wants to walk away with a good deal or the best deal. The Bible has taught us that the best way to achieve this is to consider the interest of your opponent and help him or her to achieve it.

The fact is, if you are able to understand the other person's interest and help him or he to achieve it, you stand a better chance of getting what you want, and you are more likely to settle the conflict in a satisfactory manner. This is an amazing secret, negotiators have uncovered. But you will even be more amazed to learn that this principle, popular in both secular and Christian dispute resolution, negotiation and peacemaking is taken from the New Testament (Philip.2:1-8). Here the apostle Paul declares, "Do nothing out of selfish ambition or vain conceit. Rather, in humility value others above yourselves, *not looking to your own interests but each of you to the interests of the others*" (vv. 3-4).

The larger context refers to the incarnation (i.e. God becoming man in the person of Jesus Christ). He stepped down from His high position to become human, not for His own benefit or interest but in the interest of entire the human family

(John 1:1-2, 14, 3:16-17). Jesus Christ through many unselfish acts of love has removed the hostility and settled the conflict between God and the human family (Rom.5:1-3; Eph.2:14-22). Christ's work of redemption is a work of conflict resolution. It has cleared the path for humans to be reconciled to God and neighbor. The cross of Christ is an instrument of peace between God and humans. The cross reconciles us to God and neighbor.

The Philippian passage (2:1-8) calls upon the church, the people of God, to model the humility of Christ by putting the interest of others over our own self-interests. There is no better way to negotiate peace or the cessation of hostilities between individuals, people groups and nation states than finding out what are the needs and interests of the other side and help to meet them. The interest of others is normally used in the context of negotiation. It has more leverage in Christian context because it seeks more than a mere win/win or win/lose outcome. That's the best secular negotiation can offer.

In the Christian context, *the interest of others* is huge because it also includes material property. Poirier asserts that settling a material dispute is more than a "Solomon compromise—cutting the baby in half...conflicts are about persons before they are about problems" (Poirier 2006, 159). A Solomon's compromise seems clever but not a good enough approach for Christian dispute resolution. It appears to be a win/win solution because each of the two parties got a half of the prize. But in fact, it is not a solution; it is a lose/lose proposition because the baby would be dead if followed. That would also intensify the hostility between the two women. The interest of others sometimes means giving up the whole baby to the other person who is not the rightful mother. You suffer loss but the baby lives. The Christian in dispute may have to give up the whole baby because settling for half is selfish proposition.

Love in Christian Dispute Resolution

Some may ask, "What love got to do with it?" Secular dispute resolution does not operate on the basis of love; nor does the negotiation of war and peace and multi-million-dollar business deals. They are not influenced by love. The closest secular negotiation comes to Christian love is their version of taking the interest of their competitors into consideration. So, America and Russia negotiate on the basis of interests whether it be military or trade, not love or even trust of each other. When they close a deal, it is normally a win/win outcome. We get something, they get something; love has nothing to do with it.

But this is not the case in Christian dispute resolution and negotiation; love of God and neighbor is foundational to what we do. Love is a driving Christian value behind our conflict resolution of conflicts. The process and outcome we seek are both anchored in the word of God; if it is not, it is neither biblical nor Christian. Jesus made love fundamental to Christian life in His famous Sermon *on the mount. He demonstrated this new commandment to love God and neighbor throughout His earthly life and ministry (Matt.5: 43-48). For example, He assumed the role of the lowest slave when He washed His disciples' feet (John 13: 14-16,34-35).

Jesus condenses the Torah, the Writings and the Prophets into two fundamental requirements for the righteous life: love for God and love for neighbor (Mark 12:28-31). Love is more than a cozy feeling toward another person; love is acting in mercy and compassion toward our fellow humans. It is treating them the way we would want to be treated if we were in their predicament. Love is a gift we owe to God and our fellow human beings. The Bible teaches that love is the greatest of all spiritual gifts (Rom.13:8; 1Cor.13).

Before you conclude prematurely that this standard of love is easy, let me bring to your attention the words of Jesus, "unless your righteousness surpasses that of the Pharisees and the teachers of the law, you will certainly not enter the kingdom of heaven" (Matt.5:20). The standard for the righteous life under the New Covenant is certainly higher and more demanding than that of the Old Covenant. But New Covenant believers have two major advantages over Old Testament (OT) believers: we have the law of God written internally, and we have the indwelling presence of the blessed Holy Spirit (John 16:7-16; Acts 1:8; Rom.8:1-15). Again, we rhetorically ask, what does love to have to do with the resolution of conflict? It has everything thing to do with it! But we will only highlight three in this section.

First, remember, we are talking about how we settle conflict among the people of God at home, at church, or wherever they might be. The people of God are the family of God. As such, church conflict is a family conflict. God Himself is the Father of this family (Rom.8:15-17). Every fight among believers is a family fight. The entire local church body is called upon to submit to Christ and to one another in love (Eph. 5:21-33). This principle of mutual, reciprocal submission to each other in love has serious implications as to how we care for each other, but it is often overlooked by not reading and obeying verse twenty-one ((v.21). The entire Ephesian 5:21-33 passage explains how the members of the church submit to Christ and each other. Marriage is only used to illustrate the nature and quality of that submission. The key is in verse 21.

Second, the people of God are in the kingdom of God as citizens (John 3:1-8; Col.). As such, we are called upon to model the *alternative culture* of the kingdom of God to the unregenerate kingdoms of this world, because it is God's agenda to redeem the kingdoms of this world; they will become the kingdoms of our God and of His Christ (Rev.11:15; Dan.4:3). How then do we model the culture of God's kingdom to the unbelieving world?

We model the culture of the kingdom by obeying and practicing Jesus' command to love one another. "By this everyone will know that you are my disciples, if you love one another" (John 13:34-35). The people of God bear witness to the unbelieving world of humans who Jesus really is. Jesus Himself sums it up with these words, "... let your light shine before others, that they may see your good deeds and glorify your father in heaven" (Matt.5:16). Therefore, church fights that spill over into the community at large damages the witness of the church and impede its mission. Frankly, it makes God looks bad when His children behave like the devil's children (1John 3:11-17).

Third, the people of God have a duty to those outside the community of faith. That duty, on the one hand, is to bear witness as salt and light. On the other hand, it is to make disciples of them for Jesus Christ (Matt.28:19-20). If we find ourselves in conflict with them, we should consider it as a witnessing opportunity to reflect Christ and share the gospel. The starting point is to recognize them as the image bearer of the divine. As such, we treat them humanly and neighborly, not as animals of the brute creation but as people for whom Christ died. They may not belong to our church club or our righteous group, but God has a vested interest in them (John 3:16-17). For that and other reasons, we hold ourselves to a higher standard of conduct, fairness and justice that they may want the salvation God has provided for them in Jesus Christ through the church (Acts 4:12; Rom.10:9-10).

We church folks sometimes behave as if Jesus is God's gift to the church and not to the world. But even a first grader can read the Bible text: "For God so loved the world that he gave his one and only Son, that whoever believes in him shall not perish but have eternal life" (John 3:16). So then, in the final analysis, what do we mean by showing love in our conflict resolution with neighbors? It is simply treating others the way we would want them to treat us if we were in their situation. Treat them with dignity, mercy and lovingkindness. That was what the Pharisees and teachers of the law lacked in the practice of their religious faith. The observation frequently moved Jesus to sternly rebuke them for their hypocrisy. He concluded one such rebuke with the story of the Good Samaritan, showing how a priest and a temple assistant ignored a wounded, half-dead Jewish brother on the side of the road. But a total stranger came by and helped him; he acted neighborly by showing mercy. That is the compassionate love Jesus wants to see demonstrated in and outside the church building.

When the opportunity presents itself to grab our enemies by the throat and demand our rights, love or neighborliness should bring to our remembrance the words of our Lord, "Blessed are the merciful for they shall obtain mercy"

(Matt.5:7). In our relationships to our fellow-humans, God wants us to act justly and to love mercy (Micah 6:8). Sometimes, like the Good Samaritan we go beyond the call of duty because binding up the wounds of the stranger and providing refreshment is not enough; he needs to be moved from the side of the road to a safe place, and his anxiety relieved by paying his bills in that safe place. This is the kind of Christian love that will *heal a fractured world*.

Accountability in Dispute Resolution

Some church and family conflicts develop in the context of inadequate or lack of accountability on the side of leadership or on the side of members. Both could be dangerous to an organization. God's people are not called to be rebels.

Moses had a conflict with his congregation and this conflict did not end well for him or his people because it precipitated the termination of his leadership tenure and the congregation loss a good man. Moses also loss his retirement benefits. What did he do?

The congregation had a critical need, a water problem. Instead of joining Moses in prayer over the need, they blamed it on him. They aggravated him to the point of disobeying a command from the Almighty Himself. The order the Commander in Chief to Moses was to speak to a particular rock and it would bring forth water for both people and animals. But in anger Moses struck the rock and said, "Drink you rebels" (Num.20:1-13). God disciplined him, not for what he said in anger, but for what he did—he struck the rock. He called the people rebels and they were rebels; God Himself called them rebellious. By striking the rock, Moses disobeyed orders and robbed God of His glory (V.12). The privilege to lead the people into their inheritance and retired comfortably was withdrawn and given to his assistant Joshua. (The rock he struck was loaded with spiritual significance or symbolism (1Cor.10:4). God held him accountable.

Congregational conflict could be very costly for both leader and congregation, if not handled properly, costly in money and leadership attrition. Congregations can drive good leaders over the edge and through the door. It is helpful to bear in mind that the pastor's ultimate accountability is to God (Heb.13:7,17). But not only to God; if you are a pastor and operate on the notion that you are only accountable to God—you are best advised to keep that conviction to yourself. Your governing board may think otherwise. Under certain conditions both leaders and congregation are called upon to submit to each other out of *reverence for Christ* (Eph.5:21). This submission is further illustrated with wife and husband in the covenant of marriage (vv.22-33). The church is the bride and Christ; the Bridegroom is the true Head.

A well-organized church has a governance structure in place that defines the powers and functions of its officers: how they are chosen, what their duties are, and how they can be removed from office. This instrument is normally the by-laws of the organization. In some churches, the pastor is the founder, CEO and bishop, beyond that there is no formal structure or written by-laws. Others do have written by-laws, but they are poorly executed. The checks and balances of the organization are normally stated in the by-laws or policy manual and implemented through the governing board. Where powers are not clearly defined, the church could be a risk during a serious conflict. With clearly defined powers and responsibilities come accountability. In this section, we will briefly look at leadership and membership accountability in the interest of surviving a serious conflict.

Leadership accountability-the pastor. In most Baptist churches, the pastor is accountable to the congregation via the governing board. This governing board is sometimes a single board or a joint board of deacons and trustees. These officers: pastor, deacons, trustees, financial secretary, church clerk and other officers' term of office and function are normally set forth in the by-laws. If that is not the case, perhaps the by-laws need to be updated. Pastoral tenure is not normally stated in the by-laws. An updated set of by-laws should keep the governance structure clear and smoothly running. A serious conflict will really test how well-written is your set of by-laws. If you are serious about accountability take the updating of the organization by-laws seriously. Well written by-laws are also very helpful in case of conflict with government authorities.

The pastor has a responsibility to his family and to his profession that he must guard and protect. A licensed, ordained minister wields a great deal of power that the rest of the church normally respects and honors. The pastor, however, can abuse his or her powers and bring himself into conflict with the governing board and the congregation. To avoid serious conflict, a relationship of mutual respect should be maintained. The pastor must also protect his flock from abusive members and abusive clergy persons including himself or herself. Some leaders are mentally and emotional ill, and they take out their pathology on their congregations. Some writers refer to them as "killer clergy" (Rediger1997, 101). *The governing board and congregation are also accountable to the pastor* and they have a duty to protect him and his family from unjust and abusive members or "clergy killers" (Rediger,1997).

Finally, the pastor is accountable to the Chief Shepherd for the entire congregation (Heb.13:17; 1Peter 5:1-4). There is a trilateral accountability that goes on in a church: the pastor is accountability to the people, the people are accountability to the pastor and for his family, and the pastor is accountability to God for the entire congregation. If these three levels of accountability are frequently reviewed, the church should do well even during the crisis of a conflict.

A church should be mature enough to deal with imperfections in their leaders without members becoming predatory, devouring them. A shepherd cares for his flock, but there is a way the flock also cares for the shepherd. So, there is reciprocity of care between leader and congregation which is very much biblical (1Cor.9:1-14). This care includes correction when wrong. Just as godly leader corrects those who err or stray from the path of righteousness, the leader should be humble enough to submit to correction when in error. This takes us to the subject of discipline.

Church Discipline in Dispute Resolution

Church discipline has to be understood in the context of the church as a family. The church is the people of God; the people of God is the family of God. In this family, God is Father. Jesus Christ is the Son and believers are the born again, adopted children of God (Eph.1:1-14). From eternity the Holy Spirit reigns with the Father and the Son. Throughout the church age, from Pentecost to the Second Advent of Christ, God dwells in the church through the blessed Holy Spirit (Eph.2:19-22).

As our earthly father who is the priest of his family exercises discipline over his children, God our heavenly Father exercises discipline in His family over His children (Heb.12: 4-

12). If we are not being disciplined by God, then perhaps we are not truly His children, we are illegitimate (v.8). That means, we belong to another father in the spiritual sense. Satan is the spiritual father of some people who claim God as their Father (John 8:44). Satan holds paternity over Judas and Cain to this day (John 17:12; 1John 3:12-15). All believers have a spiritual birth, a birth in God's family and kingdom (John 1:12, 3:3-7).

How does God exercise discipline over His own people upon earth? He does it through the church, but God has a people before the church was established, so we should find examples there. Indeed, there is precedence of discipline among His ancient people; at times, God exercised discipline personally but generally through the larger community. God personally disciplined Miriam for a destructive conflict she led against Moses, her brother (Num.12:1-16). God also disciplined Aaron's two sons for offering "strange fire" (Lev.10:1-7). But His preferred way of discipline is through the congregation under the guidance of its leadership. Discipline was never an isolated thing done in the dark, because God wanted discipline to be teachable exercise for the larger faith community.

God exercises discipline over His family through the authority established in His church. God did not give the church the power of the sword; Papal Rome assumed that authority against the peace theology of Jesus. God gives the minister of state the power of the sword to enforce discipline and maintain an orderly society (Rom.13:1-7). But the same God gives the church the power of the keys for discipline and to order His affairs in the faith community (Matt.16:13-19).

The church has the power to bind and loose on behalf of heaven. Spiritual offices including that of the pastor are given for the equipping and maturing of God's people to do the work of ministry (Eph.4:1-16). It is impossible to disciple a people without discipline. Discipline is critical to and inseparable from authentic discipleship. Jesus' work with His disciples is the primal example. The undisciplined disciple is an imposter, a false follower of Jesus Christ (Heb.12:8). True disciples of Christ are made in the crucible of a spiritual formation that is transformative (Rom.12:1-3).

Furthermore, the various names given to the pastoral office implies discipline. For example, "overseer" and "shepherd." Paul charged those given the leadership of the congregation with these words, "Keep watch over yourselves and the flock of which the Holy Spirit has made you overseers. Be shepherds of the church of God, which he bought with his own blood" (Acts 20:28). The task of the *overseer* or *shepherd* denotes careful and cautious discipline. This is captured in Peter's exhortation to those given such assignment, "Be shepherds of God's flock that is under your care...not lording it over those entrusted to you but being examples to the flock.

And when the Chief Shepherd appears, you will receive the crown of glory that will never fade away" (1Peter 5:2-4).

God's discipline is exercised through the church, the body of believers. The pastor leads but the discipline is not authoritarian or single-handedly imposed; it is done at the consent of the body of believers (1 Cor.5:4-5). The pastor with the body of believers are viewed as the *priesthood of believers* through which Christ is exercising discipline upon the individual or group of individuals that need to be disciplined (1Peter 2:9). Discipline includes disfellowshipping the unrepentant member (1Cor.5:1-5). The pastor and the governing board can act on behalf on the congregation and do so with transparency.

Jesus gave this directive to the church concerning dispute resolution: the individual in dispute with another should first try to settle it one-to-one. If that fails, take one or two other persons with you and try to settle it. If the person refused to settle it, tell it to the church. If he still refused to hear the church, the church should treat him as you would a pagan or outcast (Matt.18:15-17).

In other words, if the member refused to repent and submit to the authority of Christ church—the church may disfellowship the unrepentant member, hand him over to Satan (1Cor.5:1-5). Note verse 4, the church is called upon to disfellowship this unrepentant brother living in incest, hand him over to Satan because he is behaving as a child of Satan.

Handing the unrepentant church member back to Satan, some may consider hash discipline. But it has two purposes: one, to discipline the physical body through suffering, sickness and even death, that perhaps the soul can be saved (1 Cor.5:5); two, to prevent the sin spreading like yeast infecting the whole congregation (vv.6-7). The apostle orders the church to move collectively to excommunicate the brother; put him out of the fellowship. As the pastoral authority, Paul determined from Scripture and revelation that this incestuous lifestyle is contrary to the spiritual life in Christ. Genuine repentance that leads to a new birth experience is the first step to the new life in Christ (John 3:1-16; Luke 24:45-47; Acts 2:37-38).

Repentance is not only a necessary perquisite to the life in Christ, it becomes an individual and corporate devotional practice of the new life in Christ. A sinful lifestyle is not fitting for this new life (Rom.12:1-2; 2 Cor.5:17).

In the context of addressing the immorality of incest, the apostle Paul gives a litany of sinful practices that will exclude people from the kingdom of God (1 Cor.6:9-11). Some liberal scholars because they cannot get around the clarity of such text, seek to castigate Paul as if his teaching is contrary to the teachings of Jesus. The truth is, *all scripture* is *given by inspiration of God and is useful for teaching, rebuking, correcting and training in righteousness* (2Tim.3:16).

Some may say, Paul's directive to the church to disfellowship the incestuous brother is extreme. But is it? Jesus' directive in Matthew 18:15-17 give the same implication. If a member refused to correct a sinful matter after several attempts, the matter is be brought before the church. If member(s) refused to submit to the authority of the church, the next step is to disfellowship the member. That action is wrapped up in the expression, "treat them as you would a pagan or tax collector" (v.17). These two classes of people were outcast to the Jewish community. Now, the unrepentant church member is behaving like pagans and should be accorded the same treatment. A sinful, unrepentant lifestyle has no place in the Body of Christ because as yeast works itself through a batch of dough, sin spreads through the entire congregation.

But the Matthew 18 passage continues through verse 18, 19 and 20. Verse 18 says, "Truly I tell you, whatever you bind on earth will be bound in heaven, and whatever you loose on earth is loosed in heaven." This means, the ruling that the church makes concerning the unrepentant member is sanctioned in heaven. If the unrepentant member defies the ruling and leaves for another church in that unrepentant state—he or she will not flourish. When the member repents, the church body can reverse the process and restore him to fellowship. This reversal process is the loosing and heaven again sanctions this authority of the church. This is the church exercising the authority of the keys (Matt.16:18-19).

Now, most modern churches in America refused to exercise the authority of discipline and that is one reason the church is in the sad condition it is. Many churches and leaders have no moral authority to exercise discipline over their members. If moral authority is lacking, biblical authority is also lacking; you can't have one without the other. When the authority of the word of God is cast aside by a church, the morality of that church declines—in fact, that church has become an apostate gathering. The true church always in love submits to Jesus Christ (Eph.5:21-33).

As stated earlier, the power of the keys is given to the church and the power of the sword is given to the state. Both instruments are symbols of authority to maintain discipline and order. If a state fails to exercise the power of the sword, you have anarchy. If a church fails to exercise the power of the keys, you have an undisciplined and disorderly church. The ability to resolve conflict peacefully is one area of Christian life that the authority of the keys is exercised. Since the late 198s or there about, discipline in the local church has been on a steady decline. Maintaining membership size has taken precedence over quality Christian life.

There was a time when members used to get a letter of transfer or commendation when they move from one church to another or the second church would send to their former church to get it before extending the righthand of fellowship, but that practice is almost non-existent now a days. Members thrown out of one church for unchristian conduct, can move across town and receive the righthand of fellowship with no questions asked. If they raised hell in one church without repenting, they should not be given the righthand of fellowship until they show evidence of repentance. The standard of church membership has been greatly lowered, and church discipline has been cast to the wind. As a result, many churches have no moral authority to itself or to the larger community.

The aim of church discipline is to move the sinning member to reflection and repentance, to bring him or her to a deeper life of transformation, maturity and productivity in Christ. It may require the painful pruning of unproductive branches or parasites from a person's life as shown in the gospel of John (15:1-11). In some cases, discipline may require excommunication as previously discussed, depending on the gravity of the infraction and the attitude of the person. Discipline should not be mean-spirited or used to settle personal grudges; it should be administered in love and mercy with the intent to restore the member upon evidence of genuine repentance.

Restoration to Fellowship

Church discipline and restoration to fellowship after discipline are inextricable bound together. Discipline often removes or restricts a member from fellowship and the performance of certain services for a given period of time or until certain conditions are met. On the one hand, the discipline is a form of spiritual chastisement that isolates the infected member of the body. On the other hand, the intent is to move the person to repentance and restoration to fellowship after healing.

The discipline isolates and restricts the member to protect both the member and the larger congregation. It's like removing a rotten potato from a full bag of good potatoes. Or better yet, quarantining a contagious diseased person from infecting others. Discipline is a necessary experience but not joyous for those who administer it or for those who are the recipients of it (Heb.12:11).

If a church does not exercise its authority to discipline by correction, restriction or removal from service or fellowship, then there is hardly a need for restoration. For example, if a member goes up and down as a talebearer causing descension among the brethren, conducts himself in a manner that is not Christlike, discipline is necessary for his sake and the sake of the larger congregation. If a chair is broken, you tag it and remove it from service until it is fixed. The same is true for an electrical appliance with frayed chord, tag it and remove it from service.

But when a brother or sister is under discipline by restricted fellowship and service or full excommunication, there should be a plan for the restoration of that member to fellowship. When God disciplined Miriam for her infectious sin, she was removed from the congregation. But Israel did not march and leave her in the wilderness; they waited until the period of discipline was over and she was restored (Num.12:1-7). Like Miriam, the church member under discipline must show evidence of genuine repentance and healing before he or she restored to fellowship. There should be a plan of restoration, but the process should not be rushed or unnecessarily prolonged. Restoration should be done in a gentle manner.

The God who disciplines His people is the same God who said, “Comfort ye my people” (Isa.40:1). God is acting as the true parent who chastises in love and later provides comfort. After discipline has run its full course, the church should gently restore the repentant member to fellowship. The apostle Paul expresses it this way, “Brothers and sisters, if someone is caught in a sin, you who live by the Spirit should restore that person gently. But watch yourselves, or you also may be tempted” (Gal.6:1-4). In essence, don’t be harsh and authoritarian; discipline must be administered in love. The apostle James’ exhortation is applicable here: “confess your sins to each other and pray for each other so that you may be healed. The prayer of a righteous person is powerful and effective" (James 5:16).

One more thing to note, the Galatian passage (6:1) has a word of warning for the person or persons involved in this ministry of discipline and restoration—they must watch themselves, less they also be tempted. On the one hand, there is the danger of being too authoritarian and harsh, and on the other hand, too liberal and complicit. He who sets out to rescue a drowning person must be careful less he has to be rescued as well. Years ago, when tele-evangelist Jim Baker fell, another evangelist used language of discipline that was particularly harsh. He said that Baker was "a cancer to be excised from the body of Christ." Perhaps, it was a wrong choice of words, but the picture it conveyed was that of a surgeon removing and discording a cancerous tumor.

The problem is, you don't restore cancerous tumor tissues to the body; those tissues are forever discorded without consideration. To say that of a brother for whom Christ died was and is troubling. The statement was chilling and most unfortunate. Weeks later, the evangelist that spoke those words was himself caught in a salacious affair. Today, both brothers are restored to ministry and doing well. The matter serves as teachable example for us all in the context of sin, discipline and restoration to fellowship. The immortal classic hymn, *Rescue the*

Perishing, has a line that captures what our attitude should be to the fallen. It says, "Weep o'er the erring one, lift up the fallen, tell them of Jesus the mighty to save."

The next chapter deals with church conflict in a social media context, it is a necessary, urgent tool for the contemporary church; every local church should take notice.

CHAPTER 12

CHURCH CONFLICT AND SOCIAL MEDIA

In order to protect its name and brand from defamation as well as market share, every business or enterprise of significance has a social media policy that governs the conduct of its leaders, staff and employees. The church should be no exception.

This chapter looks at managing and resolving church conflicts in the context of social media. Social media can ignite or greatly exacerbate conflict situations of a local church to the point of that church losing its effectiveness to the community and the world. With emphatic urgency, this chapter shows you how to immediately activate some simple policy measures to protect your church or ministry entity in the digital age.

With the advent of social media, a church and its leaders can be defamed within a day, damaged to the point of little or no recovery in the face of a very wide audience of multiple millions. That is the downside of social media; the upside can be very encouraging and very uplifting, when properly deployed. The proper use has been hinted all along in this work, but the matter is so critical to the life of the church that I have decided to devote this short chapter to the matter.

Every Person a Philosopher and Reporter

Google and the Internet, smart phones, iPad and social media platforms have empowered the masses to know what's going on in society, report it, spin it and share it with a large consumer audience that will add or take away from it and share it again and again. It takes only one church member or visitor to a church posting unauthorized content on that church to start a damaging controversy.

Again, just about everybody coming to church now a days has a social media reporting device that can capture and deliver content seen and heard without hesitation, unless some policy with consequences is in place to restrain them. For good or evil, once the posted message and images have gone viral, reversing them is almost impossible. It's like emptying a large bag of feathers from a tall mountain on a windy day then try to recollect and bag them again. The best remedy is to have a policy in place to restrain anyone from doing it.

Social Media a Double-Edged Sword

Social media is like fire, if it is properly used, controlled and managed, it can do a world of good for the ministry of a local church. But just as fire out of control will devour everything in its wake and destroy you, so is social media. But such tragedy is preventable, just as destructive conflict is preventable. The social media piece in this chapter demands immediate action, if your church has no social media policy already in place. Don't wait for your peace ministry to be launched before you implement the simple social media measures suggested here. Do it now!

But before I share these simple measures, let me hasten to say that the purpose of this chapter is not to teach you how to implement social media for your local church ministry, that is a book in itself. This chapter is to help church leaders get out in front of this potential problem by putting some simple measures in place to prevent social media from destroying your church. I am talking about a proactive, yet temporary plan, until your church leaders can adopt a well thought out strategy for the long-term.

Simple Measures to Implement Now

Control the messages and images that represent your church. Not all sermons are for the whole world to hear. There are times that a pastor speaks directly to the flock under his or her care that the Holy Spirit has made him overseer. Jesus called his disciples away from the crowd from time to time for instruction and prayer. No pastor is called to shepherd the world. The pastor with the church is empowered to evangelize the world. But when people respond to the gospel message, the sheepfold is to nurture them. Discipline is a part of that nurture and it should not be done before the world.

Furthermore, sermons and teachings are the intellectual property of the pastor or persons that minister them. A policy in place how these should be used is wise stewardship. You can for bid individuals recording and posting these messages without your express permission. The alternative is to have the message officially recorded and edited and made available for all on CD, DVD or Online download, podcast and so on.

Control the images that represent your church. One way of protecting a congregation, is to control who records and post its images. There should be a level of privacy in a church worship that prevents anyone just to snap pictures and post them at will without authorization. The pastor and governing board should have a written policy on this matter. The policy will state what is allowable.

Church Conflicts are Family Fights and should not be talked about or posted on any social media platform by any unauthorized persons. All church members should be educated on this matter and help to enforce this policy. It is to safeguard the church and the integrity of its message.

Have an official Public Relations Person whose job is to speak to the media on church matters in the interest of the church. All lay leaders and church members should have access to this person. The pastor and governing board work closely with this media person. This is to allow the church to speak with one voice to the public. The church must control the message and the images that speak for the church, not the public.

The church should appoint a social media person who monitor the social media platforms to ensure that the church policy on this matter is not violated. Where violation is observed, the person that did the violation should be contacted forthwith to remedy the situation.

The Church should have an attorney to follow through with cases that are malicious and potentially damaging to the church. The attorney should act vigorously and expeditiously to have the matter settled in the interest of the church.

Policy Publication

A policy is self-defeating if it is hidden or unknown to the members of the organization. For this reason, the policy spoken of should be reflected in the by-laws of the church. The policy should be made available to all in short publication. It should be available on the church's website. A summary of it should be printed in all public events and attention called to it. It can also be shown on the overhead screen at all events. The publication is necessary for these reasons:

- It is a way of educating members of the church and visitors to the church as well as those that access church services and materials Online.
- People cannot claim ignorance, that they did not know.
- People that love Jesus and His church will help to keep the church scandal free.
- It serves as a warning to malicious actors, that there will consequences to their behavior.

Church Conflict and Social Media

In the opening paragraph, I stated that social media could greatly exacerbate conflicted situations—we already see how that is possible for the corporate body, defame the church and its leaders, causing the immediate community and the world to reject its message. But now we look at personal defamation.

One dissatisfied, disagreeable, antagonistic person or visitor may have a bad experience with someone related to the church and may take to social media to shame that person by airing what they consider dirty church laundry to discredit one person or group and implicate the church in the process. Or, two are more active members, instead of settling their conflicts the biblical way in the house, choose to fight it out on Facebook or some other social media platform. They probably started the process ignorantly, not intending to defame anyone, but it got out of hand, escalated, discredit the Christian message and reflect badly upon their church.

If there were a well-known social media policy in place with consequences, perhaps that would never have happened, and if it happens, chances are it would be picked up early and the church exercise discipline to have the matter corrected. The church has enormous power and leverage that it can use to counteract any social media problem. It can teach young people how to counter bullying and come to the rescue of another. If any church member is defamed, a wise social media church officer can direct a campaign to counter that defamation. Twenty-first century church ministry cannot be effectively done with a none-involvement social media attitude. Even if a church does not actively use social media to extend its reach and outreach, it needs a social media policy in place to protect its interest.

A Matter of Good Stewardship

All that has been said already can be narrowed down to one question, who has the authority and right to control the contents of the church that is posted on social media? The answer is the pastor and the governing board have that authority. If every Dick, Tom, Harry and Jane and Susie can post content in the name of the church, they control the messages and images that they want the public to see and here and that might not be in the best interest of the church. To allow content to reach the public that way would a high level of stewardship irresponsibility.

In an age when name and brand mean everything, the church must protect its name and brand. The apostles and the early Church were careful to do that in order to protect the authenticity and orthodoxy of the gospel against a sea of deception and distortion. The apostles had custody of the gospel and it was their stewardship responsibility to protect it. Paul enforced this stewardship responsibility with these words to Timothy: "You therefore, my son, be strong in the grace that is in Christ Jesus. And the things that you have heard from me among many witnesses, commit these to faithful men who will be able to teach others also" (2 Tim.2:1-2 NKJV).

The apostles received the gospel directly from Jesus Christ and the blessed, indwelling Holy Spirit brought back to their remembrance what Jesus taught them, and they tried to preserve that orthodoxy of the gospel the received. For that reason, the New Testament frequently refers to the apostles' doctrine or teachings. It is the standard by which orthodoxy was measured.

When Evangelist Philip preached out a work in Samaria, lead apostles (Peter and John) from the Jerusalem church went to Samaria to ensure that the infant church was conforming to the apostles' teachings (Acts 8:1-25). When Cornelius, the gentile centurion, received Christ, Holy Spirit baptism and was water baptized through the ministry of Peter—Peter, gave account of what happened to his fellow apostles at the Jerusalem church (Acts 10-11).

When Paul got converted and began preaching the gospel, the Jerusalem church sent Barnabas to check it out. He did and brought Paul to the apostle to Jerusalem where he received the righthand of fellowship (Acts 11:22-26). Why were the apostles kept informed of the gospel that was preached everywhere and sending reliable men to check it out? It was their stewardship responsibility to protect the Jesus name and brand. When apostles began to go off the scene, their teaches were captured in what has come down to us as *The Apostles' Creed*.

Throughout its history, the Church has had enemies of all types trying to corrupt its message and defame its leaders. The worst defamation comes from within the church itself. Therefore, the local church must be proactive in controlling its social media content. This has to be done wisely so as not to hinder the outreach of the church. There are members of the church that will have hundreds and thousands of social media followers that need to hear the message of the church, but the content they consume must come through a hub controlled by responsible, authorized social media stewards of the church.

For the church wanting to launch or finetune its social media ministry outreach, I strongly recommend the book, *The Connected Church* (Copyright 2017) by Natchi Lazarus.

CHAPTER 13

ESTABLISHING A RESIDENT COUNSEL

The focus of this chapter is not to introduce new material as such but *to help you with the implementation of* what is already written. It summarizes some key points and shows you how to get to work, putting that knowledge into practice. Your goal now is to prepare your local congregation to be a *peace-loving, peacemaking and peacekeeping church.* You will lead them to become agents of peace and better representatives of the Body of Christ. This peace mission includes, leading church members through a new level of spiritual formation and practice that will impact their ways of relating to others.

Changing the culture of a church could be a challenging undertaking; it will require patience and hard work. People are already settled in their comfort zone; they cherish their old practices as if they have the same value as antique furniture. Some don't mind change, but others will steadfastly resist change. They will tell you—this is the way we did it for decades; there is no reason to change now.

What they don't know is that such posture is typical of most dying churches. Thomas Rainer (2014) in his landmark book, *Autopsy of a Deceased Church* has these attitudes well documented. A church does not die overnight, so most people don't even observe that it is sick. Dying is a process but death is an event; the process is not as evident as the event. A church takes years to die. My hope is that this book has given you strong enough biblical and practical reasons or a compelling "why" you need to change. We will now take a few moments to reflect before we move forward.

Reflection on What We Must Now Do

Becoming a peacemaking church is not a program you put on for a couple of weeks in which some people take part and others don't. If it were a program, planners could feel a sense of relief when the program is over, that's not the case here. Becoming a peacemaking church is committing to a new lifestyle that will shape the individual and corporate personality of your church. In other words, everything you do will be shaped through the gospel of peace. It is not a program that has a begin and an end point. When Jesus said, *blessed are the peacemakers*—He was talking about a lifestyle change, a cultural transformation. It is not peace one day and conflict, violence and war the next. Each church, therefore, needs a sustainable strategy or peace ministry.

The goal for a peacemaking church is to teach each member how to fulfill his or her Christian duty as a peacemaker and live the life of a peacekeeper (Matt.5:9-12). Members will change for the better in the way they relate to each other at home, church and work, and how they relate to neighbors in the marketplaces of this world. A peacekeeper must learn how to settle conflicts. You will learn the skills of dispute resolution and train your people in the skills of conflict management and resolution; this includes the children. They should not be taking their cues and relational values from violent video games and television cartoons. We must teach them the skills of peaceful relations at home, school and most definitely at church.

Church folks must learn how to manage conflict, settle disputes without trashing the entire church. They must learn to stop shaming Jesus before the hosts of heaven and stop disgracing the witness of church before the community and the world. A significant percentage of church folks have not learned to control and discipline themselves, because they have not been taught or trained to practice the gospel of peace in relationships. We assume that by accepting Christ and joining the church they automatically become peacemakers but that is not the case. Peacemaking is a learned skill.

Self-control has to be taught, cultivated and practiced. Self-control (temperance) is the unpracticed, uncultivated fruit of the Spirit that is yet to be a spiritual discipline in the lives of many believers (Gal.5:22). In fact, many Christian are born again but not all are potty-trained. They sit in pews for years and have not grown to maturity in Christ. One reason is they have not been discipled to maturity. Making disciples is more than winning people to Christ and adding them to the church roster to increase head count; disciple-making includes, teaching them to observe all things Christ has commanded (Matt.28:19-20). That means guide them to maturity in Christ; today we call this kind of maturity spiritual formation. People are shaped into the image and likeness of Christ (Rom.12: 1-8).

The challenge is to train members to exercise their duties of peacemaking and peacekeeping, then choose five to seven (depending of the size of your church) of your best qualified members to form a *Resident Counsel* (RC). The RC is your inhouse security force; your rapid response peacemaking-peacekeeping team. It is like the hospital spoken of in one earlier chapter--it adopted a *safety-first policy* and taught all employees and staff this *safety-first* principle. But in addition, the hospital had a trained inhouse, rapid response security force. In like manner, all members of the local church are to be peacemakers; it is their Christian duty. But the *resident counsel* is the inhouse, rapid response, security force of the church. The ministry of this security force (*Resident Counsel*) is to manage and resolve situations of conflict so that they don't become destructive to the entire church and its ministry.

In other words, our attitude to conflict must change. Peace is more than a nice word; it is a relational attitude. It is reflected in our relationships toward our fellow human beings. We treat them as persons with of worth and value; they too bear the Divine image. When church members feel dissatisfied or heard a rumor, do they start a two by two whispering campaign infecting the congregation with misinformation? Or, they are trained to isolate this fire and put it out? People whisper because they have not been trained to take responsibility; they do not see themselves as stakeholders in the health of the organization, somebody else will put this fire out, not me.

The problem with whispering, no one knows how it started, no one wants to take responsibility to bring it to the attention of leadership. At times leadership got the misinformation but sit on it too long before addressing it, or they respond inappropriately. Their response add gasoline and make the matter more combustible. Conflict is like fire and if no one is trained to respond to it appropriately, you are likely to have frequent disasters on your hand. This is how church folks destroy their own church by becoming complicit in various ways: silence, gossip, slander, not knowing what to do. "My people are destroyed for lack of knowledge," the prophet warned (Hosea 4:6).

But both church leaders and members can be trained to respond differently to conflicted people and situations. When trained, they know what their Christian duties of peacemaking and peacekeeping are and what to do. With destructive conflict your church is on fire, it is an emergency! In a literal fire--they say, in case of emergency, break glass, pull the fire alarm, use the extinguisher to put the fire out. Don't just stand there, not knowing what to do or saying, it's not my job!

You may say, well my church is quite peaceful already, we have never had a situation that we could not manage. Thank God! You have been blessed, very blessed, if that is your experience. But that is like the State of Florida saying, we have had no serious hurricane in ten years, why worry about one now. Destructive conflicts are like hurricanes, they strike with very little warning. A category five conflict can hit your church anytime with very little warning. Like the five wise virgins, the congregation with wise leadership use this time to prepare. Disaster preparedness is wise planning.

If your ministry or church survives a serious conflict without significant damage, it will be a result of the disaster plans you put in place prior to that crisis. Take it from hundreds of fellow pastors, it is coming, and woe be to the pastor and congregation that are caught unprepared. This book provides you with survival knowledge, but as faith is dead without works, so is this knowledge without your implementation. Consider this book a conflict survival guide, a type of blueprint to get a congregation through troubled times. We hope that you will use it to launch a peace ministry in your church before the evil days come and the time of trouble is upon you.

You Need A Strong Why

You already have a strong why! Of course, you have to be inwardly won to this vision of a peacemaking church that the Prince of Peace wants, and the Prince of darkness strongly opposes. Briefly look back at what you have learned, that should strengthen why you need to do this now. Without a strong why, people often start projects and don't finish them. Such behavior has spiritual implications. Jesus warns against this type of mediocrity, myopic and half-hearted commitment to a project (Luke14:28-33).

We have looked at the problem in the previous chapters. The problem is the culture of conflict that has derailed local churches from their mission assignment, paralyzed their functions, fractured their unity and destroyed their influence and effectiveness in the community and the world. Most churches are like a sleeping volcano that can erupt at any time. So, don't get comfortable because it has not erupted since you are a member or pastor; you are due for the big one.

Destructive conflicts have destroyed the health of many pastors and forced them from the ministry. Some of them left very bitter toward church folks. Books have been written about this repetitive tragedy, yet many pastors and churches sit back feeling secured thinking, it will never happen to us. They convinced themselves that their churches have the nicest people in the world, and they will never be so destructive to the work of the Lord. They are singing the nice people song, not knowing Satan wrote the lyrics and put them to music. The autopsy report of congregations that song these lyrics is available for all to read (Rainer 2014).

Let's go back to Jesus little church of twelve. Anybody on the outside looking at Jesus nice little group would have thought, nice little group! They never would have imagined that one of them would have been a thief and a betrayer. Or, that the lead spoke-person of the group would have resorted to his cussing habit and ended up denying his Lord when he needed him most. Who would ever thought that a ministry team like Paul and Barnabas could have split apart by so sharp a conflict. It can easily happen to the best of us, anywhere, even at your church, unless you put in place the barricades to prevent it. If Satan was bold enough to start conflict in heaven, given the chance, he will trash your church in a moment. Your best defense is to prepare your church with a peace plan.

There is no immunization vaccine for pastors and churches against the onslaught and ravages of conflict, destructive conflict. The approach against conflict offered in this book is perhaps your best chance. Satan uses conflict to divide and conquer; it is perhaps his most effective strategy against the work of God. Jesus warns against conflict when He said that a house or family or kingdom divided against itself cannot stand (Matt.12:24-26). Jesus knows how critical the unity of the church is to the success of its mission, so the longest of His prayers on record, is one for the unity of the church. We commonly refer to it as the highly priestly prayer of Christ (John 17:1-26).

Satan attempted to use conflict to divide God's kingdom and he is so effective that he has not accepted his failure (Rev.12:7-12). Satan used conflict to divide God from his creation, including humankind (Gen.3:1-24). Satan is busy using the culture of conflict to get churches destroy themselves. Conflict is Satan's counterstrategy to the Great Commission (Matt.28:19-20). Disciple-making goes beyond soul winning. Jesus said, teach the me to observe all things that I have commanded you. Peacemaking is part of what He has commanded us.

The culture of conflict is playing havoc in spite of the proliferation of peace education in secular and Christian higher education. Available conflict resolution training is mostly at the graduate level and has not filtered down to most local churches. Second, most local churches have no peace education ministry despite the Bible setting forth peacemaking as a Christian duty (Matt.5:9). Peacemaking and peacekeeping are Christian duties, the task of the entire church. But most local churches have no intentional ministry of such to deal with conflict, so when it arises, it is left to become destructive, destroying everything in its wake. There is no institution or organization that is so quick to turn upon itself as the church. Churches are not destroyed by outsiders; they are destroyed from within. They implode, it is an inside job!

A Biblical Precedence

In previous chapters, we have looked at the biblical precedence for peacemaking in both Old and New Testaments. From Adam to the Exodus we see various ways of dealing with conflict, some very violent (murder and war) and others civilize and godly. Abraham was the first to use *the interest of others* to settle a dispute with his nephew Lot. As the senior person and the one God called, Abraham could have exercised the right to choose first and choose the best, but instead, he gave that choice to his nephew. His nobility of character in Abraham and approach to conflict settlement is forever memorialized.

In terms of corporate leadership, Moses used a singular, top-down approach to settle disputes in his congregation. His singular approach was ineffective because it was time consuming, cumbersome, and put his own health at risk for burnout. He was advised by his father-in-law, Jethro to settle conflict differently. Jethro's approach was one of delegation, multi-level delegation according to the difficulty of the cases. Honest, trustworthy and impartial men, men who hate bribery were chosen from the congregation to hear the cases of the people; the more difficult cases would go to Moses (Exod.18).

This approach was more effective for several reasons: it utilized the gifts of lay people in the congregation, it was less time consuming and cumbersome, and it gave the man of God freedom to attend to the weightier matters. God not only dwells in the ordained leadership of a congregation; He dwells in the congregation and each member is gifted to do the work of ministry. God endorsed and adopted Jethro's delegated lay leadership approach to the resolution of conflict (Deut.1:9-18).

The NT shows that Jesus had a peace theology, a preferred way of settling conflict. He communicated that preferred way to his disciples. The early church had a preferred way to settle conflict; it was the peace theology of Jesus they put to practice (Acts 6:1-7; 15: 1-35). Every believer, every local church has a duty to put into practice the peace theology of Jesus (Matt.5:9-12). So, we do have a biblical precedence for an inhouse, lay-leadership, conflict resolution ministry.

Preparing to Be a Peacemaking Church

First and foremost, Jesus was a peacemaker when He walked upon the earth; His walk was an example for our walk. It was prophesied 700 years before his birth that His name would be called, "Wonderful, Counselor, Mighty God, Everlasting Father, Prince of Peace" (Isa.9:6). The announcement of His birth to humankind was a song of peace rendered by an angelic choir. The lyrics: "Glory to God in highest heaven, and on earth peace to those on whom his favor rests" (Luke 2:13-14).

In his life and ministry Jesus refused violence; He refused to use the sword even in His own defense. He counseled his followers to put the sword away, for they that use the sword will perish by the sword (Matt.26:51-52). But most notable of all--Jesus did not give the church the power of the sword; He gave the power and authority of the keys (Matt.16:13-19). He gave the power of the sword to the ministers of the secular state (Rom.13:1-7). But even here justice must be restrained by mercy.

It is the duty of every pastor to shape the church of Jesus Christ the way Jesus wants it. Jesus wants a peace-loving church to match His character and personality. Here are a few guiding principles to help you launch your peace ministry or *Resident Counsel* at your local church. It will transform that church into the peace-loving fellowship it ought to be. They are listed as rules, but they are guiding principles.

Rule #1: Strong *Pastoral Initiative is Required to start a viable peace ministry.* I am not optimistic that any church can seriously and effectively establish a peacemaking ministry without pastoral commitment and leadership in the initial phase. Even churches with a strong governing board of capable persons, they also will need pastoral help to get this ministry off the ground. With the pastor fully on board, it is much easier to establish this ministry with a high degree of importance, support and confidence.

Furthermore, it is to the pastor's advantage to be committed to the launch of this ministry. In as much as the end goal is to have a lay-leadership peace ministry with pastoral oversight, the peace ministry begins with pastoral *commitment and leadership*. It evolves out of the pastor/teacher spiritual office. One function of this office is to equip the saints for the work of the ministry (Eph.4:8-16). There are certain works or tasks that the pastor doesn't necessarily do but he or she equips workers or lay leaders to do. Conflict management and resolution is one of them (Acts 6:1-7).

When the peace ministry is fully established and off training wheels, the pastor is no longer responsible for the day-to-day function; it is handed off to lay leaders. However, hand-off does not mean abandonment. The pastor continues to provide support and training as needed. Again, it is to the pastor's advantage to have a strong peace ministry. A peace ministry not only moves the pastor away from the hearth of conflict, it mobilizes the entire congregation to protect the ministry along with the *resident counsel (RC).* It is worth emphasizing, the RC is the inhouse security force. A security force works in the interest of the entire organization, including the pastoral leadership.

Rule #2: Have a supportive leadership coalition. Get the support of your board members, elders, officers and department heads before you announce your plans to the general congregation. The support of these lay leaders is critical to the vision of a peacemaking church. You need all hands-on deck, pulling the same direction. It is said of the early church—the people were of one heart and of one mind (Acts 2:46). The whole church is committed to this transformation.

As good a leader as Moses was, there were times that his congregation wanted to stone him; every pastor, sooner or later will come to that junction. Moses finally come to the realization that he could not do ministry alone and he complained to God. God had him put the anointing that was upon him upon seventy elders (Num.11:14-17). The elders were his leadership coalition and allies.

By reason of their position, pastors are prone to be in the hearth of conflict and they don't normally have a press secretary to go out and face the heat for them. The RC becomes pastor's allies; the RC puts out fires and advised him or her when to change course to keep the ship afloat and moving. King David was one of the best leaders of Israel, but his life was fraught with conflict. It took capable and reliable men close to him to save his life and kingship. His own son, Absalom had him on the run. In the honeymoon years of ministry, we all make the mistake that we are superman, we can do it alone. One is on a fool's errand trying to do ministry alone.

Rule #3: Familiarize yourself early with the Agents of Peace-Managers of Conflict Curriculum (for basic training). This book you are reading is the training textbook (the curriculum for instructors is sold separately as well as the Student Manuel).

The curriculum lessons are also in the Student Manual. All students taking the course will need the textbook plus the Student Manual. There are supplementary texts referred to in the curriculum. This is the basic training, Level One course (Level 1). The Intermediate Training (Level 2) and the Advanced Leadership Training (Level 3) will be released shortly.

Rule #4: Allow enough time from the first announcement to the start of training. A minimum of six weeks is suggested. When the public announcement is made, most of the planning is already done. Allow enough time because when plans are rushed, they are likely to be executed poorly and you end up with mediocre results.

Rule #5: Utilize available and capable Persons from the congregation to Help with the Training. Some people are available but not capable; others are capable but not available. Both are not the right fit. The pastor plus one or two other teachers from the congregation is suggested for leading the basic training phase.

These three will study the text and the curriculum independently, then meet as a group to discuss it in two or three sessions well in advance of the basic training date. The pastor will assign what lessons his support teaches will teach. All three teachers should be present during the training when the other is teaching to provide support to each other. One of the three can be registrar or record keeper for the training. Be sure to keep good and confidential records.

Rule #6: The cost of training. *Some churches have students share the cost.* People tend to give more value to what they receive when it costs them something. But each pastor knows his or her congregation best and will make that decision.

Some churches underwrite the entire training and provide half scholarship for those members who cannot afford the full cost. This training is a lifetime investment in their own spiritual growth and development. But it is also a corporate investment that the church is making for its own growth and flourishing.

On the other hand, the training should not be used as a fundraising event for the church, that will defeat the purpose. Make it affordable for all adult participants, even if it just paying for their own textbooks. If a member cannot pay for his or her own textbook, the church should loan one. Some member with resources can also underwrite the full cost of training or half of it for another member. But they are unlikely to do so unless the idea is suggested early or they are asked.

Rule #7: Make training fun, exciting and enjoyable but maintain focus and discipline throughout. People who successfully complete the course work by attending, doing the assignments and final evaluation will be awarded a certificate at graduation. Be sure to keep proper attendance record and record of quiz and exam scores on each student, so they can be properly evaluated and credited.

Furthermore, the scores should be kept safe and confidential long after training is completed. Again, be sure to keep accurate records. When the time for Level-II and Level-III training, you already know who to send invitations to.

Rule#8: At the end of the course of study, choose five to seven of your best qualified students to form your Resident Counsel on conflict management and resolution.

Best qualified is not limited to high score in the basic training. Other attributes should be considered, such as: experience, ability to shoulder responsibility, spiritual formation and maturity, willingness and interest toward the work of the church, the ability to work and get along with people, wisdom and problem-solving skills (Acts 6:3).

The work of the *Resident Counsel* requires much more than a good exam score. People who are nerds can always get good score, yet poor on social skills. Qualification for the counsel, therefore, goes far beyond a good score in the Level-I Basic Training. Again, the quality of the person's spiritual life and the respect the congregation holds for him or her should count for much.

Rule #9: Maintaining Counsel Size. Your vision for a peace ministry calls for wise thinking and planning with regard to training and counsel size. From the very beginning keep counsel size in mind. It will make your work in the long run much easier. To maintain counsel size, you must have a pool of trained prospective members to draw from, so make the basic training a big event with wide participation.

For example, a small to medium size church, the counsel size should be about five members. For a larger size church, seven members. But always train more than you will need on the counsel, so you have a pool from which to draw should a *council* member or two are longer available to serve. *Basic Training* is an involved investment; you will not be able to do it every year, so train enough people that you have a pool of bout 10-20 to draw from to people your counsel when there is a vacancy. If you don't have a pool, you will have repeat *Basic Training* every time you have attrition on your *Resident Counsel*. Furthermore, your *Resident Counsel* members plus those in your pool can go on to level-II *Intermediate Competency Training* and Level-III *Leadership Training* when it is offered.

The issue of term limit for your *Resident Counsel* has not been discussed before. But less say, you have a large pool of trained, qualified persons; you could set term limits of three years to serve on the counsel. So, if your counsel has six members (one serves as director or chairperson), each year one-third (two members) go off the counsel and two from the pool go on the counsel. Those that go off the counsel return to the pool to serve again when called upon.

Rule #10: How to finance the local church peace ministry. The Pastor and officers of the church should ensure that the peacemaking ministry is considered in the church budget on a separate line or included in the Christian education budget of the church.

The counsel can also sponsor a couple events each year to help finance its work. But counsel should never become preoccupied with fundraising because that will be self-defeating to its mission and work.

The Work of the Resident Counsel

Note again that for the purposes of this book, the word *council and counsel* are used interchangeably. The author prefers the word counsel, its use is deliberate and not a mistake.

First, *the Resident Counsel* (RC) *and the Christian education department of the church works closely.* The RC is charged with educating the whole church in their Christian duties of peacemaking and peacekeeping from childhood to adult. Children have to learn how to deal with conflicts and that includes the bullying type. The home and the church have a role to play in conflict awareness and competency training, so that youngsters and adults can practice peaceful relations at school, on the playground, on the school bus and on the streets. The practice of peaceful relations is a learned lifestyle, just as violence and bullying are learned.

The RC works closely with the pastor and the Christian education director of the church, because the pastor is the educator in chief. It cannot be seen otherwise, if the Great Commission and the Pauline five-fold ministry are taken seriously (Matt.28:19-20; Eph. 4:7-12). Throughout the year, the RC plans education events in the area of peacemaking, conflict management and resolution, such as: workshops, seminars, dramas and special trainings. The church should have a peace month each year, focusing on the Christian as peacemakers in different settings: home and family, community and school, workplace with coworkers, church with members, and the marketplace with neighbors. The pastor can preach a sermon series on war and peace during this time.

Second, the *Resident Counsel* (RC) manages and resolves conflicted situations with church members to prevent them from becoming destructive to the church and its ministry. This includes the objective and impartial resolution of conflict between leaders and leaders and between leadership and the congregation. Again, the RC does not take on the counseling ministry of the church, except for when a situation impacts the ministry of the church to itself and the community.

Third, the RC is charged with working to preserve the unity of the church, guard the integrity of its worship, as well as the church's outward witness to the community. It educates church members on what is inappropriate from church life to post on social media or to talk about with non-members, that includes family members that are not members of the church. This is what keep some family members from coming to church and to Christ; they hear too much about church business that they should not have heard.

Fourth, the RC connects the church with private consultants in the area of conflict management and resolution or peacemaking. These consultants are a great resource for the peace ministry of the local church. They are effect in their work, but they have been too few to make a nationwide impact on the culture of conflict bedeviling local churches. Some of these consultants were associated with the now defunct Alban Institute. Others can be found with or through Peacemakers Ministries which of itself is a great resource to the local church.

Another reason consultant, though effective in their work, have not made a nationwide impact reducing the culture of conflict at the local church—is the fact that churches tend to engage them only when a situation reaches crisis proportion. The RC should reach out to them and draw upon this worthy resource. For example, they can come once or twice a year to conduct training in the local church where there is no current crisis. This training will help to enrich the members of the RC and the larger church in their peacemaking duties.

*Fifth, consider connecting the church to an arbitration body***.** This could be complex and will require critical thinking. As discussed earlier, arbitration is an impartial, independent body that both sides in a dispute agree to have their case referred to and abide by the ruling rendered. Unless you want to go to court, arbitration ruling is generally final. The by-laws of the church should have an arbitration provision, but chances are, most churches don't have it.

But bear in mind that there is internal and external arbitration. For example, if two groups in the church are at war and they are deadlock and the RC is unable to settle the conflict with them, the governing board may have to step in as the arbitration to settle the conflict (this is internal arbitration). The governing board has the authority to fire or remove unreasonable people from position of leadership, when the situation warrants it; the RC does not have such authority.

But if the whole church is at war and divided down the middle, an outside body will have to serve as arbitration, perhaps a denominational group or ministers' association group or a group of Christian businesspeople from the community. The RC cannot engage this external body to settle a churchwide dispute; it has to be done at the leadership level of *the pastor and the governing board.* The RC will have to notify the pastor and the governing board that this conflict is beyond their capability and needs to be referred to an external arbitration. For this to work well, such provision should be in the by-laws of the church, and the arbitration group always in place though not used for most of the time.

If the by-laws of your church do not have such provision, steps should be taken now to add this amendment to it. It is healthy for the church to have such an independent body to which a case can be referred should the RC reach an impasse with a case or the whole church is at war.

Again, the governing board of the church can serve as the internal arbitration if and when the RC reaches an impasse with a conflict that is not churchwide. The RC makes the referral to the governing board. When the conflict is churchwide, the pastor and the governing board use an outside arbitration body such as a denomination group or a ministers' association. Remember, the Jerusalem church where the apostles served as the arbitration body to the church at Antioch that had reached an impasse over a conflicted situation (Acts 15:1-35). Their ruling became binding not only on the church at Antioch but on all the churches.

The arbitration body for an autonomous church body like a Baptist Church, can only make ruling on the case that is referred to it; it cannot otherwise interfere in the governance of the church. Members of the arbitration body should have no personal interest in the congregation that they are arbitrating for; that would be a conflict of interest and also unethical. Neither should individual members of the church have any private contact with members of the arbitration body.

The Resident Counsel will become proficient at its work overtime; they must keep learning and growing as they practice their ministry of peacemaking and peacekeeping. They will also have the satisfaction of watching the congregation grow and develop more perfectly in the image of Jesus Christ.

APPENDIX A
A Framework for Training

Establishing a peace ministry or *Resident Counsel* at your local church is divided into three or five phases in this framework or templet: pretraining, promotion, training begins, public launch, work phase, and post-training. Begin to implement this framework at least six months before actual training begin.

Pretraining Period

At least six months before class begins, do your research. You have determined that you want to launch a peace ministry at your church. You discuss the matter with your key lay leaders and get their support; these lay leaders form a kind of support coalition for the project.

During this time, target two or three of your most capable lay leaders who will help you plan the training and teach the classes with you. Select the teaching materials: this textbook, the Agent of Peace-Managers of Conflict Curriculum (a copy for each instructor). The Student Manual contains the same lessons in the Instructors Curriculum Manual, short quizzes, final exams (but not the answers) and the evaluation forms. There are some additional minor differences in the student's version, so the instructor should refer to lesson instead of page number.

Plan to train as many people as possible, 10 to 20 more than the 5-7 you will need on your *Resident Counsel* (RC). Why so many? You need a pool from which to draw RC members as needed. Chances are, you might not be able to repeat this basic training every year to have freshly trained members, but if you have a pool to draw from, that problem is solved.

Like an architect, layout the training on paper; select start date at least three months away. Determine class day and hour, as well end date (graduation). Discuss with your team all the aspects of the training, who will be teaching what, who will do recording keeping and so on.

Promotional Phase (3 months from Class)

You inform the congregation of what's coming and the need for it. Have posters created with date and time, posted all over the building, in church bulletin, media announcement.

The pastor should plan to preach a series of sermons (about 5) on the Christian duties of peacemaking and peacekeeping, conflict settlement, forgiveness and so on. Have key leaders to emphasize to the congregation the importance of the coming training, that it is mandatory for all members to participate. Have people clear their calendar for training. People can begin to register during this promotion time.

Eight (8) weeks away from the beginning of class, start meeting with your instructors to discuss the lessons in 3 to 4 sessions. Again, determine who will be teaching what. Emphasize registration. Purchase textbooks and student manuals. Be sure to have extra books on hand that you can loan to late registrants. Four weeks before class, have registered students pickup their textbooks and student manuals, and begin the assigned reading. Emphasize how critical it is for students to read ahead.

Two (2) weeks before class—ramp up announcement and the need to register and pickup textbook and student manual. Repeat this at the one (1) week point. Emphasize reading assignment.

Training Begins (First Day):

- Start on time -welcome your class
- Briefly explain your purpose
- Introduce your team
- Have prayer
- Find out if everyone has textbook and manual
- Sign attendance Sheet
- Review Syllabus and emphasize expectations: attend class, be on time, do the assignments

- Student introduce themselves
- Teaching starts
- Closing: Evaluation, Graduation, School Records

Public Launch of Resident Counsel (Peace Ministry)

Sunday, about one week after training be ready to launch your peace ministry or Resident Counsel. *Resident Counsel* (RC) is the name this book uses for the local church peace ministry; you may use this name or any name you wish. The counsel is made up five to seven (5-7) members depending on the size of your church. On member serves as the director.

RC members are persons who have successfully completed the basic training course and meet other qualifications of leadership that your church may set. Spiritual maturity, love for the church and ability to work with people are important qualities *RC* members should possess.

If you are using term limit (strongly suggested), members are chosen to serve for a three-year term, one-third (1/3) of their number chosen annually. All members are chosen at the same time, so we have to be a little creative to get the term limit going (see example in appendix B).

- Set the chosen RC members before the congregation and publicly charged them on their work and responsible as the resident peace ministry of the church, then pray the prayer of consecration setting them apart for this crucial ministry work.

- Also charge the congregation on their duties of peacemaking and peacekeeping, that they do nothing to slander and disgrace the church of Jesus Christ. Don't post things on social media about your church without clearance.

The Work Phase (On Going)

There are several things to consider as you start your peace ministry work:

- **You will need an office:** The *Peace Ministry Office* is clearly marked**.** This is where the council meets and does its work. You a phone, mailbox, ministry logo, meet time.
- **Y**early Calendar: In the month of November put together a calendar of activities for the coming year. Be prepared to adjust your calendar dates. Think of the activities of all the other ministries so that there be no conflict. Discuss your calendar activities with the pastor and get his or her input before you print anything.
- Pastor Relations: Keep the pastor informed, no surprises.
- Ministry Visibility: Peace ministry is visible all year.

- Website: In time, the peace ministry can have its own web page.
- The counsel is involved in education events throughout the year. Have a peace month each year. Be creative.

Post-Training Phase

- **Lifelong Learning:** Counsel members in order to keep growing, should continue reading in the discipline of conflict management and resolution, negotiating and peacemaking. Attend workshops, sponsor workshops and seminars, connect with consultants to keep informed on new developments in the field.
- **Intermediate Training:** work with the pastor to do the intermediate training. Invite all persons that took the basic training to enroll for the intermediate training, this will broaden the pool of members that can serve on the *Resident Counsel.*
- **Advance Training:** Counsel members work with the pastor to conduct the advance level of training. Only people who successfully completed the intermediate training can be accepted for the advance training. Persons that complete this level of training are allowed to teach this course locally, in their church as well as other churches and can charge for a fee for their services.

APPENDIX B

TERM LIMIT FOR COUNSEL MEMBERS

A term limit of three years is suggested for council members but getting the cycle going calls for a little creativity. It is never good leadership having anyone serving indefinitely any church office. Grant it, three years might be too short for a good leader but way too long for a bad one. If the person is not good for the office, you must have at least a time when that term of service comes to any end. For that and other reasons, this book strongly recommend term limit of three or two years.

The person can be re-appointed after being out of office for at least one year, if you are short of qualified people to serve. This is why you need a pool of trained people to draw from, so have many students to do the first *Basic Training* course as possible; they constitute the pool.

When you first launch your peace ministry, all council members are chosen at the same time to serve a two or three-year term. But that is a problem, because they are all new members starting at the same time; their term of office will end at the same time. Your new people will have no experience to do the job. So, we have to set-up as system in which only one-third (1/3) leave office at a time, so the counsel does not consistently have all new people coming on all at once.

Here is the system: Let say, your counsel has six members, all chosen at the same time (one is the director). Two members (1/3) leave office at the ending of three years and two new ones come on the counsel. The next year (4th year) two more (1/3) go off the counsel and two new members come on. The next year (5th year) the last original two go off the counsel and two new members come on the counsel. The cycle is now established; from here onward one-third goes off annually and one-third comes on. Members who go off the counsel return to the pool. They should be off at the counsel at least for one year before re-appointed to serve again. This is the ideal scenario, real world situation at your church might be different. These are guidelines not the Ten Commandments.

So, in actuality a few RC members from among the first appointees will serve longer than the intended term but just to get the cycle going. Again, new RC members will always be drawn from the pool; those going off the counsel go back to the pool and can be re-appointed to the counsel providing they were off a least one year.

REFERENCES

Introduction

Dana, Daniel. *Conflict Resolution: Mediation Tools for Everyday Worklife.* New York: McGraw-Hill, 2001.

Fisher, Roger. Ury, William. Patton, Bruce. *Getting to Yes: Negotiating Agreement without Giving In.* Revised Edition. New York: Penguin Books, 2011.

Chapter 2

Arguello, Jean-Paul. *"Dummy Police Cars Are Not So Dumb." Lafourche, LA Daily Comet* (July 30, 2012), dailycomet.com/20130730. Accessed March 11, 2015.

Dudley, Carl. Zingery, Theresa. Breeden, David, "Insight into Congregational Conflict," Faith Community Today Publication, 1-8.

Leeman, Jonathan. *Church Membership: How the World Knows Who Represents Jesus.* Wheaton, Illinois: Crossway Publishers, 2012.

Chapter 3

Fromm, Eric. *The Art of Loving*. New York: Open Road Media, 2013.

Gilligan, Stephen. *The Courage to Love: Principles and Practices of Self-relations Psychotherapy.* New York: W.W. Norton and Company, 1997.

Halverstadt, Hugh F. *Managing Church Conflict*. Louisville, KY: Westminster John Knox Press, 1991.

Hull, Bill. *The Disciple Making Pastor.* Grand Rapids, MI: Baker Books, 2007.

MacArthur, John. *Worship the Ultimate Priority*. Chicago: Moody Publishers, 2012.

MacArthur, John. *Strange Fire: The Danger of Offending the Holy Spirit with Counterfeit Worship.* Nashville: Thomas Nelson Publishers, 2013.

McIntosh, Gary L. *Growing God's Church: How People Are Actually Coming to Faith Today*. Grand Rapid, Michigan: Baker Books, 2016.

Chapter 4

Carter, James E. "A Christian Approach to Handling Conflict in Church" in *The Theological Educator.* 45 (Spring): 79-88.

Halverstadt, Hugh F. *Managing Church Conflict*. Louisville, KY: Westminster John Knox Press, 1991

Jenkins, Michael, "Great Expectations, Sobering Realities: Finding on Clergy Burnout," *Congregation.* 28, no.3 (2010).

Kartz, Arnold. "The Pastor as Conflict Manager," Andrew University Seminary Studies, 20, no.2. Summer 1982: 111-126.

Leas, Speed B. "The Basis of Conflict in Congregations" in *Conflict Management in Congregations. David B. Lott, ed.* Bethesda, MD: Alban Institute, 2001.

Warren, Rick. *Forward* in Erwin Ralph McManus.' *An Unstoppable Force.* Orange, CA: Yates & Yates, 2001.

Chapter 5

Dworkin, Ronald Myles. *Freedom's Law: The Moral Reading of the American Constitution.* Boston: Harvard University Press, 1997.

May, Max. "Jewish Criminal Law and Legal Procedures," *Journal of Criminal Law and Criminology.* 31. 4. Nov/Dec. 1940. Scholarlycommons.law.Northwestern.edu/cgi.

Scott, Jack L. *Shalom: The Content of a Peaceable City.* Nashville, TN: Abingdon Press, 1973.

Willis, John. "Old Testament Foundations of Social Justice." *Restoration Quarterly.* 18, no 2 (1975).

Chapter 6

Avis, Paul D.L. "Wrestling with the Diaconate," *Ecclesiology.* 5. no.1 (2006).

Leas, Speed B. "When Conflict Erupts in your Church" in *Conflict Management in Congregations.* Editor David B. Lott. Bethesda, MD: Alban Institute, 2001.

Waltke, Bruce F. *An Old Testament Theology: An Exegetical, Canonical, and Thematic Approach.* Grand Rapids, MI: Zondervan, 2011.

Chapter 7

Dewar, Michael W. *The Book of Life & The Books of Wrath.* Maitland, FL: Xulon Press, 2013.

Himes, Kenneth R. *Christianity and the Political Order: Conflict, Cooptation, and Cooperation.* Maryknoll, New York: Orbis Books, 2013.

Holcomb, Justin S. *Knowing the Creeds and the Councils.* Grand Rapids, MI: Zondervan, 2014.

Yoder, John Howard. *Christian Attitudes to War, Peace and Revolution.* Grand Rapids, MI: Brazos Books, 2009.

Chapter 8

Pneuman, Roy W. "Nine Common Sources of Conflicts in Congregations" in *Conflict Management in Congregations*, Editor David B. Lott. Bethesda, MD: Alban Institute, 2001.

Kotter, John. *Leading Change*. Boston, MA: Harvard University Press, 1996.

Haugk, Kenneth C. *Antagonist in the Church: How to Identify and Deal with Destructive Conflict.* Minneapolis: Augsburg Press, 1988.

Shelley, Marshall. *Well-Intentioned Dragons: Ministering to Problem People in the Church.* Minneapolis: Bethany Publishers, *1985.*

Rediger, G. Lloyd. *Clergy Killers: Guidance for Pastors and Congregations under Attack.* Louisville, KY: Westminster/John Knox Press, 1997.

Greenfield, Guy. *The Wounded Minister: Healing from and Preventing Personal Attacks.* Grand Rapids, MI: Baker Books, 2001.

Chapter 9

Becker, Garvin De. *The Gift of Fear: Survival Signals That Protect Us from Violence.* New York: Dell Publishing, 1997.

Sande, Ken. *The Peacemaker: A Biblical Guide to Resolving Personal Conflict. Third Edition.* Grand Rapids, MI: Bakers Books, 2004.

Shell, G. Richard. *Bargaining for Advantage: Negotiating Strategies for Reasonable People.* New York: Penguin Books, 2006

Ursiny, Tim. *The Coward's Guide to Conflict: Empowering Solutions for Those Who Would Rather Run Than Fight.* Naperville, IL: Sourcebooks, 2003.

Chapter 10

Ante-Nicean Fathers: https://en.wikiversity.org/wiki/Ante-Nicene_Fathers.

Becker, Garvin De. *The Gift of Fear: Survival Signals That Protect Us from Violence.* New York: Dell Publishing, 1997.

Dana, Daniel. *Conflict Resolution: Mediation Tools for Everyday Worklife.* New York: McGraw-Hill, 2001.

Haugk, Kenneth C. *Antagonists in the Church: How to Identify and Deal with Destructive Conflict.* Minneapolis: Augsburg Publishing House,1988.

Rediger, G. Lloyd. *Clergy Killers: Guidance for Pastors and Congregations Under Attack.* Louisville: Westminster John Knox Press, 1997.

Sande, Ken. *The Peacemaker: A Biblical Guide to Resolving Personal Conflict. Third Edition.* Grand Rapids, MI: Bakers Books, 2004.

Shell, G. Richard. *Bargaining for Advantage: Negotiating Strategies for Reasonable People.* New York: Penguin Books, 2006

Ursiny, Tim. *The Coward's Guide to Conflict: Empowering Solutions for Those Who Would Rather Run Than Fight.* Naperville, IL: Sourcebooks, 2003.

Weeks, Dudley. *The Eight Essential Steps to Conflict Resolution.* New York, NY: Jeremy P. Tarcher/Penguin Group, *1994.*

Chapter 11

Birch, Ken. Managing Conflict: A Practical on Reconciliation. Nairobi, Kenya: Evangel Publishing House, 2008.

Haugk, Kenneth C. *Antagonists in the Church: How to Identify and Deal with Destructive Conflict.* Minneapolis: Augsburg Publishing House,1988.

Poirier, Alfred. The Peacemaking Pastor: A Biblical Guide to Resolving Church Conflict. Grand Rapids, MI: Baker Books, 2006.

Rediger, G. Lloyd. *Clergy Killers: Guidance for Pastors and Congregations Under Attack.* Louisville: Westminster John Knox Press, 1997.

Sande, Ken. *The Peacemaker: A Biblical Guide to Resolving Personal Conflict. Third Edition.* Grand Rapids, MI: Bakers Books, 2004.

Shelley, Marshall. *Well-Intentioned Dragons: Ministering to Problem People in the Church.* Minneapolis: Bethany Publishers, *1985.*

Tutu, Desmond and Tutu, MPHO. *The Book of Forgiveness: The Four Paths for Healing Ourselves and the World.* New York: HarperCollins Publishers, 2014.

Tutu, Desmond. *No Future without Forgiveness*. New York: Doubleday, 1999

White, Andrew. *Father, Forgive: Reflection on Peacemaking.* Grand Rapids, MI: Monarch Books, 2013.

Chapter 12

Rainer, Thomas S. *Autopsy of a Deceased Church.* Nashville, TN: B & H Publishing, 2014.

About the Author

REVEREND DR. MICHAEL W. DEWAR, SR. is pastor, Bible teacher and mentor in the spiritual life for more than thirty-five years. He is a specialist in conflict management and resolution who provides counsel and consulting to pastors and ministry leaders in leading a peacemaking church and ministry.

Rev. Dewar earned the *Master of Divinity* from Eastern Theological Seminary (now Palmer Theological Seminary of Eastern University), the *Master of Social Work* from Wurzweiler School of Social Work, Yeshiva University, and the *Doctor of Ministry* from Regent University, School of Divinity.

Pastor Dewar has written several books on the spiritual life. He is founder and pastor of the New York Congregational Baptist Church in Brooklyn. He lives here in New York City with his family.

OTHER BOOKS BY THIS AUTHOR

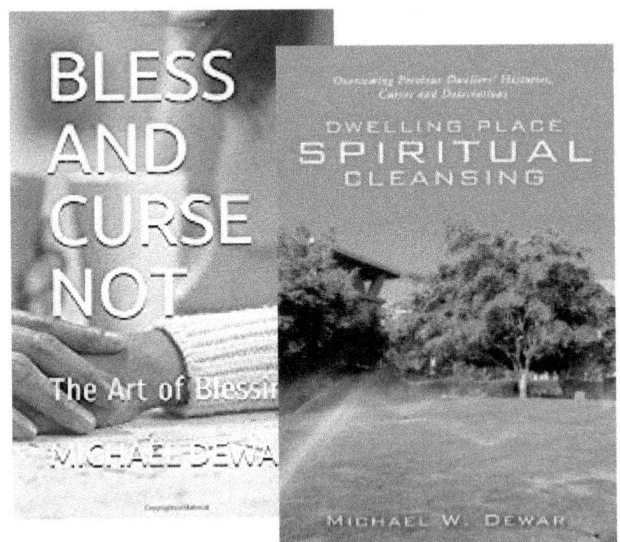

All available on Amazon.com

CHURCH AND FAMILY CONFLICT

- Destructive conflict is a pastor's worst nightmare; it is perhaps, Satan's most effective weapon against churches. Sooner or later, every pastor will face a major conflict crisis. The peace plan in place prior to that conflict, will determine how well the pastor and church survive the conflict assault.
- If no peace plan is in place, the fire of conflict will destroy everything in its wake, downside the congregation, threatens pastor's health and even send him or her packing.
- Learn how to prevent this catastrophe, by establishing a lay leaders' peacemaking ministry. It takes the pastor out of the hearth of conflict, preserves congregation's unity, extends pastoral tenure, and preserves ministry legacy.
- Churches are destroyed from within; they implode. It happens when good people turn upon each other and against leadership. A peace plan prepares you for the big conflict crisis coming.

www.ingramcontent.com/pod-product-compliance
Lightning Source LLC
LaVergne TN
LVHW020523100826
845148LV00010B/1326

* 9 7 8 1 7 3 3 4 3 7 7 9 0 *